W9-DAS-667

Black Enterprise

AGAINST ALL ODDS

Black Enterprise Books provide useful information on a broad spectrum of business and general-interest topics, including entrepreneurship, personal and business finance, and career development. They are designed to meet the needs of the vital and growing African-American business market and to provide the information and resources that will help African Americans achieve their goals. The books are written by and about African-American professionals and entrepreneurs, and they have been developed with the assistance of the staff of *Black Enterprise*, the premier African-American business magazine.

The series currently includes the following books:

Titans of the B.E. 100s: Black CEOs Who Redefined and Conquered American Business
by Derek T. Dingle

Black Enterprise Guide to Starting Your Own Business
by Wendy Beech

The Millionaires' Club: How to Start and Run Your Own Investment Club—and Make Your Money Grow!
by Carolyn M. Brown

The Black Enterprise Guide to Investing
by James A. Anderson

Against All Odds: Ten Entrepreneurs Who Followed Their Hearts and Found Success
by Wendy Harris

The following book is forthcoming:

Take A Lesson: Today's Black Achievers on How They Made It and What They Learned Along the Way
by Caroline V. Clarke

Black Enterprise

AGAINST ALL ODDS

❖

Ten Entrepreneurs Who Followed Their Hearts and Found Success

Wendy Harris

John Wiley & Sons, Inc.

New York • Chichester • Weinheim • Brisbane • Singapore • Toronto

Library of Congress Cataloging-in-Publication Data:

Harris, Wendy Beech.
    Against all odds : ten entrepreneurs who followed their hearts and found success / by Wendy Beech Harris.
        p. cm. — (Black enterprise books)
    Includes index.
    ISBN 0-471-37472-5 (cloth : alk. paper)
        1. Businesspeople—Biography. 2. Entrepreneurship—Biography. 3. Black business enterprises. I. Title. II. Series.

HC29.H37 2001
338'.04'092396073—dc21
[B]
                                                00-043584

Printed in the United States of America.

10 9 8 7 6 5 4 3 2

To my husband Jonathan, for his pep talks during the rough times and encouragement to always focus on the Lord to bring me through. You are my heart. I love you.

CONTENTS

ACKNOWLEDGMENTS

To my Lord and Savior Jesus Christ, words cannot express my thanks for the talent you have blessed me with to complete such a project. I thank you for the gift of writing, for moving around circumstances in my life and putting certain people in my path to use as instruments for giving me the opportunity to author this book. First and foremost, I give all glory and honor to You.

To the entrepreneurs profiled throughout these pages, I give heartfelt thanks to all of you for spending days talking with me and for allowing me to tag along all over town, to your meetings and events, so that I could capture the true essence of your operations. The experience was instructional, enlightening, motivating, and just plain fun. My thanks and prayers go out to Sylvia and Herbert Woods, Vivian Gibson, Effie Booker and Dr. Jean Morency, Lorraine Carter, Alonzo Washington, Frank Mercado-Valdes, Roscoe Allen, Vera Moore, Renée Warren and Kirsten Poe, and Albert and Odetta Murray.

To my family for encouraging me to press on, every day, even when I didn't feel like it. Thanks to my husband Jonathan, my mother and father Wallace and Ernestine Beech, my brother Kevin, and my sister Cathy.

To my *Black Enterprise* family, who continue to have confidence in my ability and desire to chronicle the achievements of small black businesses, I appreciate your support, guidance, and patience.

To Caroline Clarke, editor of BE Books, I extend a special thanks for remembering my interest in wanting to participate in such a phenomenal project months after I had already left a full-time position with *Black Enterprise* magazine, and then giving me the chance to do so.

Ruth Mills, my former senior editor at John Wiley & Sons and an original player in the development of the BE Books, I enjoyed working with you and I thank you for your editorial expertise and for the suggestions that made this and my first book in the series worthy reads.

Airié Dekidjiev, my new editor at John Wiley & Sons, I am grateful for your keen eye and direction.

And last but not least, to every editor, copyeditor, typesetter, and proofreader under the direction of John Wiley & Sons, Inc., who spent hours poring over this manuscript, I say thank you for seasoning my words and making them better.

If I have forgotten anyone who has made this book possible, please charge it to my head and not my heart, for I appreciate each and every one of you.

Until next time, God Bless.

W.H.

INTRODUCTION

How many times have you said to yourself, on January 1, "This is the year that I will start my new business"? But by the next December 31, like every armchair entrepreneur, you've talked and talked and *talked* and TALKED about your idea so much that you have talked yourself right out of getting started. If you fit this description, don't worry: You're not alone. Thousands of great ideas never get off the ground—for one simple reason: fear of failure.

Starting your own business is risky and, for some people, terrifying. Why give up a steady paycheck and good benefits, and take on the challenges of being your own boss when you know the perks will not be quite as perky—at least not at first? You mull over this question and you let it echo through your head until you've convinced yourself, once again, that the time is not right. Well, when *is* the right time? When the challenges of becoming an entrepreneur dissipate?

Don't hold your breath.

Small business owners are challenged every day. They're challenged to compete with the big boys of their industries; to secure the capital that can take their companies to great heights; to find employees who can embrace their vision and help them grow their operations to the next level. There's little that *doesn't* test the endurance, the determination, and the wherewithal of these entrepreneurs.

For the black small business owner, the obstacles can be even greater. The entrepreneurial environment now contains a shrinking contract supplier pool and increased competition from mega mergers, past and present. Still, that's no reason to count yourself out. The number of black entrepreneurs continues to rise each day—and not because of government handouts or a stroke of good luck. These African-American business owners have the drive, passion, creative genius, and stick-to-it-iveness to pursue and achieve the American Dream.

According to the U.S. Small Business Administration Office of Advocacy, the number of black business owners is higher than it has ever been. Nearly 900,000 (881,646, to be exact) black-owned firms are scattered throughout the country. These companies have produced $59.3 billion in revenues and employ 580,000 workers (according to the latest available reports). Service businesses are the fastest growing segment among minority-owned firms. But these companies are also finding their riches in the areas of finance, insurance, real estate, manufacturing, and technology. Wouldn't you like to be among them?

This book tells the stories of ten individuals who yearned to be counted in these growing statistics. The small entrepreneurs described here threw caution to the wind, followed their hearts, and overcame great odds to transform hobbies, lifelong interests, and other novel ideas into unique and highly profitable enterprises.

In the racially divided 1960s, one entrepreneur turned a tiny Harlem luncheonette into one of New York's best-known tourist attractions and created a multimillion-dollar food empire that is revered around the world. Another took the simple service of a car wash and converted it into more than just a place to get bubbles and a bevy of hot wax by offering a mini trip to the Caribbean Islands. A third decided to revive classic black films such as *Shaft, Carmen Jones,* and *Lady Sings the Blues* by creating the largest and fastest growing black-owned syndication company in the nation. And a fourth tested society's commitment to present positive black images in the media by creating an independent comic book company that exclusively features African-American characters.

Like so many others, these entrepreneurs had to face unsympathetic bankers, copycat competitors, shady partners, and social injustices, but they didn't give up. Instead, they combined their talents with hard work, vision, optimism, and faith, and did what others only think and talk about. Dubbing themselves "tomorrow's titans," these movers and shakers realize that they are the future of black business. In fact, each business owner profiled in this book has set a goal to make *Black Enterprise* magazine's B.E. 100s, an annual listing of the largest black-owned companies in the nation. Their ambition and self-confidence make it clear that they are here to stay.

From beginning to end, their stories will give you clear instruction on equipping yourself for the journey called entrepreneurship. Their tips, rules, proven strategies, and lessons learned will help you to start and stay in business. More importantly, their tales will inspire and motivate you to stop being an armchair entrepreneur and to become an active participant in the growth of the black business community. If a penniless college student, former factory worker, full-time bank executive, and high school dropout can cast fear and doubt aside, swim in the unsure waters of ownership, and surface as successful shopkeepers, *you can too.* So stop putting off until tomorrow what you should have done yesterday, and get started now. The business world awaits you.

Black Enterprise

AGAINST ALL ODDS

SYLVIA AND HERBERT WOODS
SYLVIA'S RESTAURANT

The Queen and King of Soul Food

I don't stay still long enough to relax. Even when I'm in bed, I'm thinking.

It had only been 30 minutes since the doors to the world-famous Sylvia's Restaurant opened, but, as usual, the place was already packed. Scores of family, friends, fans, and some of the biggest names in Harlem had come to help Sylvia Woods celebrate the release of her second cookbook, *Sylvia's Family Soul Food Cookbook.* Under slightly dimmed lights, flashbulbs flickered, camcorders rolled, and nearly 400 guests shared "Remember when . . ." stories. The bluesy sounds of a live jazz band filtered through the quaint and cozy quarters of this Harlem-based restaurant that has become a historic landmark and a revered tourist attraction.

Not one person was without a plate. Some diners had piled-high portions of smothered pork chops, fried catfish, crisp collard greens, golden-brown macaroni and cheese, and sugary candied yams. Others were working their way through barbecued ribs, southern fried chicken, potato salad, black-eyed peas, and fluffy squares of cornbread. These are just a few of the soul food favorites for which the down-home restaurant has become known over the past three decades. (The recipes are in the cookbooks.) Then there is the "Queen of Soul Food" herself: Sylvia. She is just as popular as the home-style Southern cuisine she serves.

Dressed in an understated yet classic black dress, and greeting her diners with a motherly smile, Sylvia effortlessly made her way from table to table, exchanging hugs and kisses, posing for pictures, signing autographs, and chatting with guests. She even picked up some empty plates and cups along the way and deposited them in the kitchen. There is nothing pretentious about this 74-year-old restaurateur whose fame and fortune entitle her to a diva's demeanor. Sylvia is just plain Sylvia, a simple and sagacious woman who has gone from picking beans in the fields of a small rural town in South Carolina to owning Manhattan's oldest—and world-respected—soul food restaurant.

Sylvia's Restaurant is a family-owned and operated business in which two younger generations now work. But, on most days, Sylvia strolls around the restaurant in a white laboratory coat that makes her look more like a professor than the Queen of Soul Food. If she's not checking on the chef or going over menus and other day-to-day tasks, she's greeting and talking with her customers.

I don't stay still long enough to relax. Even when I'm in bed, I'm thinking.

Never too far from her side is her husband of 56 years Herbert. A soft-spoken man with a round, gentle face and piercing eyes, he helped turn the once small mom-and-pop outfit into a palace of Southern dining located just around the corner from the legendary Apollo Theater. He has contributed his specialties to the menu: Rise-and-Shine Salmon and Bacon with Grits, Honey-Grilled Yellow Squash, and "Hot As You Like It" Fried Corn. If Sylvia is the queen of soul food, Herbert is definitely the king. Both come from a community of great cooks, which explains their passion and penchant for getting behind the grill. But it took a lot more than culinary genius to make Sylvia's a success.

Starting the restaurant was not easy for this couple. Neither came from affluence. They recall being raised where few families had indoor plumbing and electricity, and a kitchen wasn't necessarily a room in most houses. Drawing on a family nest egg was out of the question; the nest egg didn't exist. But, together, Sylvia and Herbert worked, scrimped, and saved to buy every table and chair, every knife and fork needed in their establishment. They weathered turbulent economies, devastating riots, and the competition. They maintained and grew their restaurant, which today generates around $3.5 million in annual revenue and feeds millions of people around the globe every year.

In any part of the United States, people who know good food have either heard about or eaten at Sylvia's. The mere mention of the name conjures up mouthwatering descriptions of its succulent salmon croquettes, flaky butter-filled biscuits, and creamy mashed potatoes. But Sylvia's soul food lovers are not confined to the United States. They can also be found throughout Europe (even Finland!) and Japan. Several international tourist groups have made Sylvia's a "must see" on their New York itineraries. Celebrities, political figures, and some royalty have ventured uptown—Bentleys, chauffered limousines, and all—to 126th Street and Lenox Avenue for the experience of old-fashioned Southern hospitality. The walls of the four-room restaurant pronounce its popularity within the entertainment world and among the political and social elite. There hang photographs of media mogul Quincy Jones, Oscar winner Denzel Washington, the late songstress Phyllis Hyman, former South Africa first lady Winnie Mandela, and former Republican vice presidential candidate Jack Kemp. But this collage barely scrapes the surface concerning the number of stars who have experienced soul food—Sylvia's style. Diana Ross asked for seconds of the sassy rice when she stopped by. Muhammad Ali used to fetch his own biscuits at the steam tables. Then there is Russell Simmons, Sidney Poitier, Richard Gere, Susan Sarandon, Don King, Barry White, Michael J. Fox, Stevie Wonder, Janet Jackson, Liza Minelli, Teddy Pendergrass—the list goes on and on. Over the years, longtime Harlemite and businessman Percy Sutton held meetings here with Robert F. Kennedy and the Reverend Jesse Jackson. Noted actor and director Spike Lee shot a scene from his 1991 film *Jungle Fever* in a corner of the restaurant, which is now memorialized with a large autographed poster from the blockbuster movie.

The Sylvia's name is far reaching, and the menu is the main draw. But the food, which offers some baked and grilled dishes for the calorie-conscious, is not the only thing that keeps people coming back for more. The feelings of family, togetherness, love, and comfort are also important. Where else could you find

Secretary of State Madeline Albright and her Secret Service guardians dining just tables away from a working-class family of four, ten yuppies from midtown Manhattan, and a group of young urban males? There's nothing stuffy about Sylvia's. One does not have to tilt his or her head in embarrassment if a piece of silverware accidentally ends up on the floor. Behind the counter, Mama Mae serves up the special of the day. Regular customers come in and hug their waiters and waitresses, many of whom have worked at the restaurant for 10 to 15 years. And more often than not, Sylvia sweeps through, stopping at tables to talk and to tease. If a person is not eating the food, she wants to know why. And don't give her that old excuse, "Well, I'm not hungry." With a tough-love look that only a mother could give, she still gets diners to clean their plates.

> *When you're in the restaurant business, you have got to make people feel like they're at home and feel like you appreciate them. That's what we do here and I think that's part of the reason for our success.*

In 1992, Sylvia and Herbert launched a canned soul-food line which has now birthed 33 items, including Sylvia's Specially Cut Yams, Kicking Hot Sauce, Original Barbecue Sauce, and Specially Seasoned Mustard Greens, all of which are available nationwide in such supermarkets as Pathmark, Bi-Lo, and Stop, Shop and Save. Five years later, the Woods family embarked on an expansion plan to place clones of the famed restaurant in various cities across the map. In 1997, they opened their first branch with much fanfare—and, admittedly, a little disappointment—in Atlanta, Georgia. Today, their total food empire generates nearly $13 million in yearly revenue, deservedly putting the Woods at the top of the food chain. But, to understand how long and hard the climb has been, one need only read the story of their rise.

Rule 1: Save, Save, Save

Theirs is truly a rags-to-riches, boy-meets-girl, happily-ever-after story.

Sylvia Woods was born in 1926 in the small Southern town of Hemingway, South Carolina. The only child, she was raised on a farm by her mother, Julia Pressley, and her grandmother. They were the town's only midwives. Her father, Van, died just three days after she was born. Her grandfather had been lynched some 20 years earlier, so the women ran the house and the family farm. They grew everything they ate. They bartered skills with their male neighbors—a typical practice at that time. The women would do matronly tasks, such as washing, mending, and cooking. In exchange, the men would handle the heavy-duty chores such as plowing and barn raising. Sylvia learned early to respect and embrace hard work. She also learned how to save money, an "easier said than done" practice that, years later, would give her the opportunity to start, run, and expand her restaurant.

When I was three years old, mama left me with my grandmother in Hemingway and went to New York to work as a laundress. She wanted to build a house next to my grandmother's, and she knew that there were more opportunities to earn more money up North. So there in New York she scrimped and saved every penny that she earned and placed the money in a homemade satchel attached to a waistband that she wore under her dress at all times. That was her bank. No matter how much money she made, she always changed the singles into large bills and those large bills were for saving money. So if she made eight dollars, a five-dollar bill was folded into her money belt and the singles and quarters and other change were for spending on rent, food, and other necessities. After a few fives accumulated, those were changed into tens and twenties and eventually into fifties. My mother had a good technique for saving money and it's a technique that I observed throughout my entire childhood. I adopted her technique when I became an adult and was glad that I did because it enabled me to save money to help start the restaurant without having to get a bank loan. Of course I had no idea at the time that I would one day have my own business, but her lessons about saving money taught me discipline so when the opportunity presented itself for me to have my own restaurant, I was able to bring something to the table.

By 1933, Sylvia's mother had returned to Hemingway. Julia purchased the property next to her mother's house and, within two years, had her own little four-room home built through bartering. Now old enough to work in the fields, little Sylvia picked cotton, tobacco, and string beans. The chore, which belonged to every child in the community, was completed every day after school. One afternoon in 1937, in the thick of the bean fields, Sylvia met her future husband. Herbert was only 12 years old at the time, but she knew that this was the little man she would one day marry.

> *It was more than 60 years ago, but I remember seeing Herbert for the first time just like it was yesterday. I saw this little boy in that bean field and I remember his knees stuck out of his pants and that he was barefoot just like me. But I swear I couldn't take my eyes off that little brown-skinned man to save my life.*

Nor could he take his eyes off her. After 56 years of marriage, he still can't. When Herbert talks about the day he met his future bride, he focuses on her face and cracks a tender smile as if he is seeing her again for the very first time. "You were so beautiful with your dark chocolate skin and big soulful eyes. You didn't have your hair braided like most kids in the fields, which was unusual." Sylvia interjects to ask seductively, "How was it?" Almost blushing, he replies, "It was curled like an adult's. You were a cute little thing out there in the fields, and I was smitten with you before we ever spoke."

Herbert, 75, was born in Richmond, Virginia, but his family moved to South Carolina when he was only four months old. His father worked as an itinerant pastor so wherever he got a job preaching, the family followed. After his father died (of pneumonia), his mother, a teacher, moved to Friendship, South Carolina, to work at a school there. It was ten miles from where Sylvia lived, but she and Herbert talked and passed notes in school. Neither of them had telephones. When Sylvia was 14, her mother allowed Herbert to court her twice a week. Their puppy love began to blossom, and the two just knew they would stay together forever. But in 1941, before Sylvia could finish the tenth grade, her mother sent her to New York to study cosmetology.

Meanwhile, Herbert devised a plan to see his sweetheart. He joined the Navy. Herbert thought that, as a sailor, his ship might sail to Brooklyn, where Sylvia was staying with relatives. He only got as far as Norfolk, Virginia, but Sylvia managed to travel there occasionally to visit her beau. By 1943, Sylvia, who was pregnant with their first child Van DeWard, was back in Hemingway and running a beauty parlor she had built on her mother's 40-acre farm. The two married a year later. Soon afterward, in the midst of World War II, Herbert was serving as a cook and making biscuits for officers on light cruisers and transports.

They were separated again.

Sylvia continued to work; more importantly, she saved. Every nickel she earned washing and curling hair for $1.50 per person was put into the satchel she wore around her waist, just as her mother had done years before. By the time Herbert was discharged from the service in 1945, Sylvia had saved over $1,000 and the two moved to Harlem, in New York City, where the opportunity for jobs seemed to be better. Herbert worked in a dye factory before doing a second tour of duty in the navy. Sylvia went back to Hemingway for a while before joining him in California, where he was stationed. But by 1950, the two were back in the big city to stay. Herbert drove a New York City cab, and Sylvia took hair appointments in their apartment. Later, she worked as a domestic and then in a hat factory. While shopping one day on 126th Street, Sylvia walked right into her future. It was waiting for her at Johnson's Luncheonette. Sylvia's cousin worked there as a waitress, but she was about to leave her job and return to school. She suggested that Sylvia ask the owner, Johnson, who owned two other restaurants, for her position. Always concerned about saving money, Sylvia thought working in the luncheonette would be a good way to stash away even more cash. No longer would she have to spend money on carfare to get to her factory job. The restaurant was only a five-minute walk from her uptown apartment. She could also save money on buying new clothes: She would have to don a uniform at the restaurant. So Sylvia took her cousin's advice and applied for the job.

Despite her lack of experience, she was hired. For the next eight years, Sylvia worked behind the counter, waiting on customers. She saved her wages and her tips. Then, in 1962, she realized what all of the saving had been for. Johnson, a young black Southern entrepreneur who had overextended himself financially in trying to build a resort for blacks in upstate New York, made her a business proposition to help raise money for his project.

> *He said to me, "Sylvia, you want to buy a restaurant?" I laughed because I thought it was a joke. I knew that I had saved a lot of money but I didn't have that kind of money socked away to buy Johnson's Luncheonette.*

Nevertheless, she had *some* cash. Johnson, a fellow South Carolinian who had also been raised on a farm, suggested that Sylvia ask her mother to mortgage the family acres to help raise the $20,000 down payment. She did, and on August 1, 1962, Sylvia started operating what would become one of the most respected and historic sites in New York City.

Rule 2: Start Small But Don't Expect to Stay Small

The restaurant wasn't renamed right away. About six months after she purchased it, Sylvia substituted her name for Johnson's on the awning that hung over the entrance. The luncheonette was nothing fancy. It was basically a small mom-and-pop operation with a stove, deep fryer, grill, one long counter that accommodated about eight stools, and a couple of booths against the wall. The staff was extremely small at first: a short order cook who doubled as a waitress, one or two additional servers, and Sylvia. When the restaurant first opened, Sylvia and Herbert, who worked 12- to 15-hour days, did practically all of the cooking.

> *People often ask me what makes our soul food so great and I've realized that it's because I come from a long line of great cooks. In fact, I come from a whole community of great cooks. Hemingway, South Carolina, probably has*

more great cooks per square inch than you would find in most cooking schools. Growing up, we didn't go to school to learn how to cook. We learned from our mothers, grand-mothers, aunts, uncles, cousins, and neighbors. We shared recipes in the fields, across the back fence, and at special events. Wherever there was food there were cooks talking about how they prepared it, so we were always swapping ideas and sharing new techniques. So naturally, throughout generations of sharing these exchanges, we found ways of making the food we ate taste and look even better than before.

Sylvia's menu started off with the typical hamburger and cheeseburger platters. But it also included neckbones, pig's tails, pig's feet, fried chicken, hominy grits, pork chops, rice, black-eyed peas, collard greens, and a few other Southern breakfast and dinner dishes she and Herbert had grown up eating and still put on their dinner table at home. The community loved it, and the tiny restaurant quickly earned a reputation as a warm and friendly place to get a good down-home delicious meal at a reasonable price.

For the first five years, Sylvia's fared well. The neighboring restaurants that generally competed with one another for the same type of diner were no match for this unique establishment that offered stick-to-your ribs Southern cuisine. But in 1968, after the Harlem riots following the assassination of Dr. Martin Luther King Jr., the health of every business throughout the city was threatened. Herbert remembers the chaos well.

We were living in the Bronx at the time. I used to come down at four o'clock in the morning to go to the market and then I would cook. Well, on this particular morning, there was news on all of the television and radio stations about the riots, but I didn't expect the fires. But when I got into Harlem, my heart jumped into my mouth. Everything was just smoke.

Sylvia's did not suffer a single broken window. Even back then, Harlemites saw it as their home. The riots caused irrevocable damage to many small businesses in Harlem, but they presented an opportunity for Sylvia's to grow. That year, Sylvia and Herbert, who by this time had four children, moved the restaurant to its current location on Lenox Avenue and 126th Street. They rented a portion of the double building for a year before purchasing the entire property. They transformed a burned-out hardware store into a slightly larger, much brighter, and more modern place to break cornbread. They added to their staff by recruiting family and friends, and they upgraded the menu. By this time, McDonald's had made its debut in Harlem and knocked out the hamburger and french fries portion of luncheonettes' menus. Sylvia simply expanded her choices of Southern cuisine. Instead of serving only fried chicken, she added smothered chicken. And rather than dishing out only fried pork chops, she pushed smothered pork chops, smothered beef, and barbecued ribs.

News of Sylvia's hearty soul food continued to travel fast, and the restaurant's name started to gain greater popularity, not just among blacks and not just among people who lived uptown. In 1979, a restaurant critic from *New York* magazine ventured to Harlem to sample the cuisine. Shortly after her visit, she wrote a highly complimentary review about Sylvia's. The article exposed Harlem's best-kept soul-food secret to the entire city and beyond. Although at first the article seemed to be the worst thing that could have happened to Sylvia's, it actually turned out to be the best. The organizer of a tour company called Harlem Spirituals approached Sylvia about bringing one of his sightseeing groups to her place. Sylvia reserved tables for 12 people. But their reservation coincided with publication of the issue of *New York* magazine that described Sylvia's. For the first time since she had opened, Sylvia had more customers than she could handle.

> *Back then we only had one side, the counter side, and just four booths along the wall. The booths took up the space I had reserved for the 12 people from this tourist group, but I still had all these people, black and white, who had read the article coming in from downtown and there was no place for them to sit. I was so scared and embarrassed because we only had this dainty little restaurant with mismatched dishes and china and little room to sit down. I wasn't ready for the rush of people that we got behind this article. So a lot*

of them just came in, looked around, waited a while, and then left.

Prior to the restaurant review, business was good. After its publication, customers started coming in droves. It was as if someone had turned on a light, directing the rest of the world where to get great soul food. Sylvia knew then that she could no longer remain a small operation. To accommodate the influx of new patrons, she had no choice but to expand, so she did. Using money she had saved under her mattress and in her bank account, Sylvia and Herbert opened their first dining room in 1982. They owned the building in which the restaurant operated, so they used the other half of the facility—previously occupied by another tenant—to fulfill their space needs. The new dining room had seating for 50 people, but the restaurant soon outgrew this space. In 1986, the restaurateurs purchased an adjacent store and used it to open a second dining room, with seating for another 100 customers. Three years later, a third dining room was added. Sylvia's started to garner international appeal because of the increasing number of tourist groups that visited Harlem, and it made the "It" list among the stars—all without a single paid advertisement. People who had never been to Harlem were driving and taxiing there just to get a taste of black culture and to meet the woman and man who started it all.

Rule 3: Give Customers What They Want

In the early 1990s, it seemed as though soul food junkies couldn't get enough of Sylvia's. Many customers came at least three times a week. Others came more often—if not for her chicken and dumplings, candied sweet potatoes, or fiery greens, then most definitely for her homemade barbecue sauce. One night, a group of off-duty firefighters came into the restaurant with a gallon jug and asked Sylvia if she would fill it with her sauce.

They weren't the only ones.

During the Thanksgiving and Christmas holidays, customer after customer would line up with a jug or other container to buy the sauce. They talked with each other, and with employees at Sylvia's, about how the restaurant should bottle some of its products for retail sales. It wasn't enough for patrons to get just a taste during their lunch break or at a Friday night dinner outing. They wanted to take a piece of Sylvia's home with them. By this time, Van DeWard, the eldest son, was extremely focused on growing the family business. He quickly recognized the increasing demand to package some of the restaurant's products.

> *A lot of people started making the remark, "Oh, this is good; you should bottle this." The more and more I thought about it, I realized that it could and should be done, for two reasons. Number one: because we wanted to give our customers what they were asking for. The demand was real. And number two: because the supermarket shelves were full of products targeted toward other ethnic groups, but there were none for African Americans. We saw packaging our products as an opportunity to fill a niche that had been ignored.*

Doing so would take lots of money. Sylvia had continued to put away $5s, $10s, and $20s in her money belt and other unconventional savings accounts, including beneath her mattress, but the restaurant was not doing well enough for Sylvia and her family to launch such a costly project all by themselves. They were able to contribute about $500,000 to jump-start the canned food line, but would need hundreds of thousands more to develop it. Van DeWard, the architect of the Queen of Soul Food line, decided to seek outside investors as well as consultation about how to manufacture, package, and distribute food products.

> *One of the biggest challenges of putting the food line together was learning the process of manufacturing, distribution, and sales. Once I learned about the UPC coding, design, and other aspects of producing the line, then I had to be concerned with distribution and how I was going to get the products onto the shelf. Then once they were on the shelf, I had to worry about how I was going to get them off the shelves and into the hands of paying customers. When I started out, I didn't have a clue how to do any of these things, so I started doing some research and started looking around for people who could help me get it done both mechanically and financially. I wanted to keep this project all black because of the horror stories I had*

heard concerning Famous Amos and his cookie business. So I knocked on every door you could think of, to keep this thing in the community, but it didn't happen. I met a young lady who was not from the community—and when I say "not from the community" I mean that she was not black—but she had worked for General Foods for about five years, had an MBA from Columbia University, and very useful contacts. She came on board as a consultant, and then I got J.P. Morgan to invest some money in the food products.

The Woods called the new venture Sylvia Woods Enterprises LLC, a company separate from the Harlem restaurant that was legally formed Sylvia Woods Inc. The reinvestment division of J.P. Morgan assumed an equity stake of 20 percent in the new company. When they were ready to select which soul food favorites they would package, they started with the barbecue sauce. But so as not to get lost on the shelf with only one product, they decided to launch several others at the same time: a bottled hot sauce and salad dressing, and a series of canned vegetables such as black-eyed peas and collard greens. A smiling picture of Sylvia dressed in a chef's uniform was on the front of every package.

Putting on his salesman's hat, Van DeWard then approached grocers about carrying the products. By this time, Sylvia's had extremely impressive brand-name recognition, so it seemed that a hard sell would not be needed. There was some resistance from nonminorities; not all store owners saw a market or a need for canned soul food. Still, the majority of buyers he approached had a positive response and asked, "What took ya'll so long to come to the table?"

In 1992, the food products appeared in Bloomingdale's and in several gourmet shops throughout New York. The buzz behind the line was great. But Van DeWard found that the canned food line was not making any money.

The gourmet stores would only order maybe $1,000 worth of product here and $1,500 worth of product there, which made us no profit. I realized that in order to do the kind of volume that I wanted—and knew that the products could generate—I had to take the line to the supermarkets.

So he got his pitch ready. But before he could utter a word, BI-LO, one of the largest supermarket chains in the nation, contacted him. Buyers at the market had heard about Sylvia's latest venture and were looking to do business with more minority-owned companies. Sylvia's was just as good as any, if not better. In 1993, the canned products reached the shelves of BI-LO stores across the country, blazing the trail for other supermarkets to follow.

And they did.

A year later, Pathmark began carrying the line. Before long, A&P/Food Emporium, Stop, Shop and Save, and other major chains cleared shelf space for the items as well. Meanwhile, Van DeWard continued to expand the line by adding yams, pinto beans, kidney beans, turnip greens, and a host of seasonings, including the now popular "No Salt Secret Seasoning" to cater to customers with hypertension. Today, the $7 million line, now with 33 items and growing, is available in most major supermarkets nationwide.

Coming soon to a store near you: Cornbread Cookies.

How's that for innovation!

Rule 4: When Expanding Your Brand, Be Open to Change and Learn from Your Mistakes

With the success of the canned food line and her first cookbook—*Sylvia's Soul Food*, introduced in 1992—Sylvia was ready to expand the brand further. This time, she planned to open branches of the famed restaurant in various cities across the country. As with the soul food products, customers had been inquiring about when Sylvia would set up her soul food kitchen in their neck of the woods.

> *For years, we had been asked to open restaurants in Brooklyn, Baltimore, Chicago, Detroit, Los Angeles, Philadelphia, Washington, DC, and various other cities. People were coming out of the woodwork about us opening up other sites.*

At the suggestion of a group of developers, Sylvia chose downtown Atlanta—across from City Hall and minutes from the

Underground Entertainment Complex—as her proving ground for the restaurant's first clone. To finance the $1.6 million expansion, she teamed up with investors from the J.P. Morgan Community Development Corporation, and the plan was put into action in the latter part of 1995. Some critics wondered if the beloved restaurant could even be duplicated. Sure, they could replicate the menu and fill it with all of Sylvia's signature soul food dishes. But so much more was unique to the 33-year-old establishment: the heartfelt signatures of stars scribbled across photographs that hung on the unofficial "diners' wall of fame"; the smoky barbecue perfume that had taken over the kitchen after decades of grilling and frying; the down-home feelings that customers would get when Sylvia would sit at their table and chat while they ate. Some people feared that the restaurant's identity might get lost in an expansion. But Sylvia put the best people in place to ensure that the essence of her establishment would remain intact. She hired Regynald Washington, an Atlanta-based entrepreneur who had worked for more than a decade in the restaurant business, and made him the project's president and chief operating officer. When choosing a chef, she recruited Tim Patridge, the former food and beverage director for the Atlanta Committee of the 1996 Olympic Games. And she assigned her oldest daughter, Bedelia, to interview prospective employees who could evoke the type of Southern hospitality and family feeling that the original restaurant had become famous for. Some of the top consultants and experts in the food industry served on the team to help get the Atlanta restaurant up and running. Still, problems occurred. According to Sylvia's youngest son, Kenneth, it all began once the Harlem location was automated, and it continued once the doors to the new site were opened.

> When we decided that we were going to open the Atlanta branch, I hired a consultant to come in and help us systematize our operation. Now when you are trying to systematize an operation that has been operating a certain way for 30 years, it can be a very difficult thing to do, but it had to be done. The Atlanta branch was designed to be more contemporary and more modern, so in order to open it the developers needed some type of model to work from—which meant

that the Harlem restaurant's infrastructure had to be solid-ified and updated first. So that's when we computerized the original site. We did all of our recipes, exact food costs, theoreticals, average check covers, and other aspects of running the restaurant on the computer. For us, that was a learning experience because we had not been operating in the status quo of the hospitality industry. We didn't go to the top-notch restaurant schools or get the right degrees. For the most part, we learned on the job so we had to be open to change in order to satisfy our desire to expand the business, and we were. But as a result of that change, the project was delayed.

They had planned to open in June 1996, in time for the Summer Olympics, which were held in Atlanta that year. But another six months passed before the ribbon could be cut. On January 31, 1997, the grand opening of the 200-seat clone, with its high ceilings and art deco mezzanine, was held. The festivities were grand and the turnout was huge. But Kenneth says the food was awful.

We had worked for weeks with the staff and managers of the new restaurant . . . trying to get our recipes together. I was flying back and forth to Atlanta to make sure every-thing was in place. But when we went down for the Friday night grand opening, we found out that they had not done a trial run of the restaurant. The gas had not been turned on well in advance and the kitchen had not been operated, so the recipes had not been tested like they should have been. As a result, we had taste problems.

The Atlanta staff then closed the restaurant for the weekend to regroup, work out the kinks, and open to the general public the following Monday. When it did, the lines were around the corner. To an outsider looking in, it seemed as if everything was OK. But to Kenneth, who was called back to the restaurant in a panic just a day after returning home, it was not.

When you open a new restaurant, you should have a "soft opening," which means that you just open the restaurant to a

few people—or even the employees—to try out your equip-
ment, recipes, and things of that nature. That's what the
professional places do but we did not. When we reopened
the restaurant the Monday after the grand opening, we had
it operating at full blast and our systems were still not in
place—at least not well enough to handle the crowds of peo-
ple that came. We got clobbered. My mother called me and
said, "Kenneth, get your butt back down here and bring
Mike and Evelyn [employees at the Harlem location]" be-
cause she was throwing food out left and right. We had poor
quality food and poor service. And it hurt us because there
was this big major demand to come and see what Sylvia's
was all about, and we really weren't ready.

Over the next couple of years, the Woods family dealt with difficult management and production issues at the Atlanta site. They
hired and fired several chefs, as well as other employees who
could not perform well enough to uphold Sylvia's standards. They
experienced problems with getting the managers to use the same
meats, brand of ingredients, and equipment—all of which make a
difference in taste—that were used at the Harlem location. And although the menu at Sylvia's Atlanta started off being identical to
that at Sylvia's Harlem, over time, Kenneth, who travels to the
restaurant about every other month, found that it had to be
changed slightly to cater more to the appetites of the customers.

For example, short ribs of beef are one of our biggest items
here in New York, but that had to come off the menu in At-
lanta because people down there didn't seem to like it.

Admittedly, the family continues to experience some growing
pains in operating the baby branch. But things are beginning to
gel, and it shows in the revenue: $2.3 million in 1999. As for the
plan to open other Sylvia's satellites:

We do want to put other restaurants in other areas. In fact,
we would love to have one in Brooklyn and the other New
York boroughs. But right now we want to focus on making
sure that Atlanta stands strong so that we can continue to
successfully move forward.

Rule 5: Prepare for Tomorrow Today

Sylvia and Herbert have been preparing to pass down their legacy to their children almost from the very beginning. In fact, each of their four kids grew up working in the restaurant. If they weren't washing dishes or clearing tables, they were sweeping floors or wiping off the counter. As a high school student, Bedelia earned her spending money by working behind the counter. Today, she is the director of Sylvia's Catering, yet another arm of the multimillion-dollar food empire. Van DeWard is the president of Sylvia Woods Enterprises. Kenneth is director of operations. And their youngest daughter, Crizette, is the restaurant's financial officer. Each family member fully devotes his or her time and expertise to overseeing the various aspects of the family enterprise. Their warmth and personality contribute to making Sylvia's a success. And to think that not one of them had immediate plans to join the family firm!

Like many kids who are raised in a family business, once they became old enough to choose their own careers, they wanted to test their talents elsewhere. After college, Van DeWard headed for the Peace Corps in Africa. Kenneth accepted a management position at a shoe store near the university that he attended. Crizette worked for a short period of time at the former John Wanamaker department store. And Bedelia donned an apron at Chock Full o' Nuts, a local eatery—and a *competitor.* Sylvia recalls:

> *All of the kids went outside of the business at first. Of course we wanted them to continue working in the restaurant so that they could carry on the family tradition and pass it down to their own children. But Herbert and I never pushed them to come back home. We just told them that the door was always open and left it up to them to decide.*

Now many of the 16 grandchildren are working in the restaurant as well, contributing new and fresh ideas to carry Sylvia's through the new century and beyond. On the drawing board is a concept to create a small take-out unit, called Sylvia's Express, for major shopping malls. And some day, a delivery service may bring Sylvia's succulent soul food straight to your door.

Sometimes I look back and I wonder how we did it because when we started we were just a small mom-and-pop restaurant. We didn't even have an electric dishwasher. But now we have an entire food empire and people of all races come from all over the world just to taste my cooking. It's a wonderful feeling.

EFFIE BOOKER
CABANA CAR WASH
The Queen of Car Washes

Whatever business I pursue, I don't just want to be in it. I want to be at the top of it.

Don't tell Effie Booker she can't scale the ladder of success. When she sees a position that she wants, she claims it, visualizes the title behind her name, then gets the job without question or hesitation. Director. Senior Vice President. CEO. Owner. No matter what the designation, Booker is quick to earn the coveted post.

Is it luck?

No.

A case of being in the right place at the right time?

Hardly.

Like a championship chess player, Booker makes methodical and calculated moves. When it comes to her career, she leaves nothing to chance—and does everything according to a well-thought-out plan. Perhaps that would explain why she is able to juggle operating a $1.3 million business and another full-time job. Booker is the owner of Cabana Car Wash, a six-year-old company with more than 80 employees spread out over not one, not two, not three, but four locations, and a fifth is on the way. She is also the senior vice president of community development for Wells Fargo Bank in Houston, Texas. Sound impossible to manage both? Booker doesn't think so. It simply requires an ability to shift your thinking. At least that's how this 41-year-old dynamo explains how she handles the task.

21

Month after month, Booker pulls double duty, splitting her 12- to 15-hour workdays between her plush corporate office at Wells Fargo Plaza and the more modest quarters at Cabana Car Wash. But she doesn't guzzle pots of coffee or pop packs of antiacid tablets to help maintain her breakneck pace. Booker keeps a cellular phone, a pager, and a daily planner at arm's length so she can conduct business almost anywhere she goes. She creates a "To Do" list filled with action items to complete by day's end, and then tackles each one as if yesterday was the deadline. As for the influx of mail, between her two offices, Booker could fill up a small postal truck. But this entrepreneur/executive, who clearly has all the trimmings of a corporate honcho, doesn't assign the time-consuming task to her secretary. She opens and reads each piece herself.

Booker takes every aspect of her work seriously and wastes no time at either job. She doesn't like lunch meetings because they eat up too much of her time. Often, she dines at her desk. She even refuses to break for brief midday telephone chats with friends. Her personal calls during office hours last barely five minutes and usually involve her scheduling an after-hours meeting with companions. Booker makes every minute of the day count; she entertains no thoughts of procrastinating. But don't assign her to the category of *workaholic*. She does allow time to play. Every Tuesday night is movie night with her parents, and the parties she often throws at her home range from the most elegant champagne-filled soirées to a good ol'-fashioned fish fry. Booker's plate is rarely empty. But despite all the structure that seems to define her daily regimen, she can't describe her typical day.

> *A typical day? I don't even know what that is. I just get up and prepare myself for whatever comes my way. One day I may have to go to the bank to deal with somebody who is picketing or protesting outside one of the branches because of something that we did or didn't do for their community. The next day, I could find myself trying to save an irate customer who claims we scratched their car at the car wash. So throw the word* typical *right out the window because I don't know what to expect on any given day.*

On this particular Wednesday morning in August, Booker is in bank mode . . . at least for the moment. Wells Fargo's 100-plus branches throughout the Houston area and beyond have yet to open for the day, but Booker, dressed in a red linen pantsuit, is already conducting business from the driver's seat of her silver Mercedes-Benz. On Airport Boulevard, headed downtown in rush-hour traffic, she sandwiches her cell phone between her left ear and shoulder as she talks with a city resident about the bank's commitments to the community. Booker, a liaison between Wells Fargo and the towns that it serves, is responsible for developing and monitoring the bank's community development programs. Essentially, she identifies lending opportunities throughout various neighborhoods, particularly those that are underserved, for economic development, affordable housing, product advertising, charitable contributions, volunteerism, and small and minority business development. She handles over 50 phone calls per day in which she discusses the bank's goals and objectives. By the time she reaches her sixth-floor office at Wells Fargo Plaza, she has made at least five.

Inside, Booker settles into a black leather swivel chair in her 900-square-foot office. She hits the speakerphone, begins to check her messages, and immediately returns the phone calls. The immaculate room is every bit a part of the corporate clubhouse. Everything from the doors to the desks is drenched in mahogany. Every book, plaque, picture, and piece of equipment finds its place among the trim surroundings. Booker prides herself on being organized. She has instituted a rule that helps to keep her financial house in order.

I touch a piece of paper one time.

She does no shuffling, stacking, or moving of letters from one corner of her desk or office to another with the intention of postponing action until tomorrow. Booker meticulously reviews each memo, letter, card, and piece of literature that crosses her desk, and she reacts immediately. That also goes for the 30 to 50 E-mails she typically receives each day.

By noon, Booker has dialed another 20 numbers and put a small dent in the mountainous stack of mail that sits squarely on her desk. After a light lunch, she breaks from playing banker, shifts into a car-wash mode, and heads for a 3:00 P.M. meeting at McGuff Associates Architects to discuss the construction of her fourth car wash, a more upscale version of the other Cabana sites. Stretching the blueprints across the conference room table, Booker reviews the logistics of the expansion with her architect, electrician, and partner for this planned location. For two hours, the foursome outlines every aspect of the facility, from its miter curtains (the cloths that mechanically swoosh across the car as it moves through the tunnel) to an espresso machine for customers' use.

By 6:30 P.M., Booker is back at her first Cabana location to conduct a mandatory staff meeting. Forget the fact that her workday is about to stretch into its tenth hour. A svelte woman, standing 5 feet, 5½ inches tall in walking shoes, her makeup is flawless and her hair is styled to near perfection. Booker's vigor has yet to fizzle, so she rallies the troops and begins to discuss the meeting's agenda. Virtually all of her employees at this location are Spanish-speaking, so Booker's manager, who is bilingual, translates. Then Booker, playing the customer from hell, pulls her car onto the lot. She wants to reevaluate her employees' sales and service techniques. Booker has learned the hard way that running a successful car wash requires using certain procedures for just about everything. For the next two and a half hours, she reviews, among other things, the proper way to dust a dashboard, vacuum seats, and towel-dry a car. Midway in the mock run, Dr. Jean Morency, a dentist and Booker's equal partner on the first three Cabana locations, pulls up. Known simply as "Doc" to everyone, he begins to watch Booker's demonstrations. But soon Doc huddles with two employees and begins to generate his own lighthearted discussion. Booker, never afraid of confrontation, brings them back into the fold.

> *Doc. I'm trying to have a meeting. Could you please stop talking.*

The three quiet themselves and revert their attention to the drill. When the meeting adjourns, each employee grabs a slice of pizza, compliments of the boss, and heads home. But not Booker. She meets briefly with Dr. Morency in her office overlooking the lobby. Then the two dash off to dinner at a nearby restaurant, where they talk shop over seafood. At 11:00 P.M., Booker takes the wheel again and heads home.

The next day, she starts all over but still leaves just a little time for Effie. She jumpstarts this day at the car wash.

It's a lot of work handling both jobs. I've tried all the strategies for juggling a dual career and I'm always revamping and reorganizing, but basically I stay on track by setting goals that represent the things that I want to get accomplished for that particular day. Now, somewhere in my schedule is always something for me that I will do before the day is over. I don't care what it is. If it's just washing my hair, working out at the gym, getting my nails done, or buying a half-dozen glazed donuts from Shipley's, I find something that I can do for me that I enjoy and incorporate it into my day. It helps to balance things out.

Her schedule, at the car wash and the bank, makes Booker's time extremely tight. Yet not once has she ever considered sacrificing one career for the other. Instead, she passionately toils her way through both, always striving to be the best.

Whatever business I pursue. I don't just want to be in it. I want to be at the top of it.

Few would argue that she still has far to go in either field. The community has already dubbed her "the car wash banker." And her colleagues at Wells Fargo accept, applaud, and encourage her desire to fill both roles. They always have.

When I first interviewed for the position at the bank, I had to disclose any kind of outside activity that I was involved in. But the bank didn't see my owning a business as an issue because of the duties required of the senior vice president of community development. In fact, they saw my being an entrepreneur as a complement to the position and felt that it would allow me to stand out even more in the community and relate to the people, groups, and organizations that the bank served. So there has never been a conflict of interest between Cabana Car Wash and Wells Fargo. Of course, the flexibility that I have—being able to come into the bank for a few hours, take off in the middle of the day to handle business at the car wash, and then go back to the bank to finish up my work—did not come without me proving myself. But as committed as I am to my business to make sure that it's the best and I'm the best at it, I am that committed to my job.

I never sacrifice one for the other. If I compromise certain hours that I could have spent at the bank to oversee operations at the car wash, or vice versa, I simply make up the time during the evenings or on weekends.

Booker has worked in the banking industry for over ten years. She cut her teeth in the area of real estate and finance during the heyday of Savings & Loans. With each job that followed, she became director of this and vice president of that, and earned impressive kudos along the way. But unlike her meteoric rise up the corporate ladder, her road to entrepreneurship was not smooth. It was stormy, questionable, and filled with some very hard lessons about ownership. She endured ridicule from car wash counterparts and was challenged by copycat competitors, backstabbing partners, thieving employees, and wishy-washy investors. Booker also suffered huge profit losses at the hands of an inexperienced manager. Having endured such pain and hardship as new entrepreneurs, lesser men and women may have bailed out of the business. Not Booker. Her Christian faith would not allow her to give up.

I see my business as a ministry, and I use it to witness to other people who have dreams and aspirations of wanting to own their own businesses. By sharing my experiences, it allows other people to use them as examples of how to overcome adversity and sustain themselves through all the ups and downs of being an entrepreneur. Starting this business was far from smooth sailing. In fact, there were some days that we probably should have just closed our doors, but Cabana has been prayed up so much that I wasn't worried that we would make it. And we're still here.

Rule 1: Don't Reinvent the Wheel to Create Your Business; Carve Out a Niche

Cabana Car Wash is a full-service car wash with a fully loaded detailing center and lube facility. But unlike most car washes, which typically offer just bubbles and a bevy of hot wax, Cabana sports a Caribbean theme. When you drive your car onto the one-acre lot, you find palm trees on either side, floral patio seating beneath huge umbrellas, and attendants dressed in tropical uniforms, usually Bermuda shorts and floral-print T-shirts. Even the names of the services that are provided symbolize the tropics. A wash and wax is called Tropical Breeze, and "the works" is dubbed Coral Reef. If you are fortunate enough to pay a visit to Cabana on the right day, you may even discover a Caribbean still band playing on the grounds. If not, you can always enjoy the Caribbean music that filters through the lobby as you wait for attendants to finish giving your car the royal Caribbean treatment.

Who says you have to reinvent the wheel when starting a business?

When Booker decided to take on the challenges of entrepreneurship in 1992, she didn't try to become a Madame C.J. Walker, Garrett A. Morgan, or Benjamin Franklin. She simply took an everyday service that people craved and added her own personal touch.

Back then, Booker was working as a liquidator for the Federal Deposit Insurance Corporation (FDIC). The FDIC was expanding its Houston operation to take over liquidating all the assets of failed banks, so Booker found herself spending a lot of time in her car, driving back and forth to various institutions. Always a well-organized individual, she wanted everything in shipshape, including her car. But every time she wanted to get her car washed, she had to travel 15 to 20 minutes out of her way—for her, a huge inconvenience. But easier access was not Booker's only reason for opening her own car wash. The facility she had used for so many years was deteriorating. She wanted to give people something better.

When it first opened, it was clean and neat and the staff was pleasant. But the last time I visited the car wash, it was just horrible. When I pulled up, the sales attendant was wearing jeans and a regular shirt. There was nothing about him that could identify him with the car wash. His sales technique, which was basically a hustle, was poor. The lobby floor looked like it hadn't been mopped in months. The cashier was unkempt, not in uniform, and chewing gum. And the bathrooms . . . I am very picky about restrooms because they tell a lot about the business and the care of the business. In fact, my pet peeve is not having any toilet paper or paper towels in the bathrooms, and if one or the other is not there, somebody is fixing to go home. I'm very serious about that. You can eat off the floors in the restrooms at Cabana, but not in this particular car wash that I visited. The price was fine and they did a decent job washing the car, but the decorum was terrible. Still, people were coming there to get their cars washed because there was no other place in town. The customers deserved something better, and I felt that I could give it to them. I said to myself, "I can do this. I'm going to take this on." I thought, "How hard could it be? A car comes in dirty, the customer takes his or her little ticket, I load up the car on the conveyor, dry it off, and send the customer on his way. Piece of cake."

Driving off the lot that day, Booker cruised down West Bellfort Avenue, the road on which the original Cabana Car Wash now stands. She hadn't yet thought of creating a theme for her facility. However, she was secure in the notion that she could at least duplicate what others had done, but in a more professional manner. Then it hit her.

I thought that I didn't know anything about operating a car wash, so I'm driving out of the parking lot, looking back at the building, saying to myself, "It looks about so many feet long and wide." I had no idea what went on behind the scenes, so I started thinking about all the types of equipment that I thought I might need to become fully operational and began to wonder where I could get everything. Before I got to the first traffic light after leaving the car wash, I remember looking up and seeing this abandoned miniature golf course. There was a "For Sale" sign tacked on the grounds. I said to myself, "Well, this looks wide enough and deep enough" because that's all I knew about car washes at that time. I knew that the facility had to be long and wide.

Everything about the car wash business was foreign to Booker. She knew nothing about miter curtains or the system that programs the length of the car the moment it is loaded onto the conveyor, and signals the curtains to turn on and off. She was not privy to the reclaim pit used by car washes to store recycled water. The amount of labor required to run such an outfit? That too was a mystery. But Booker was willing and anxious to learn. By the time she reached the traffic light, she had made three phone calls inquiring about prices for three pieces of vacant land, including the miniature golf course. She was not quick to reveal her business idea; she feared that someone would pilfer it from her. But when she made her last inquiry, she felt inclined to open up. Good thing. The landowner referred Booker to a friend whose company supported new car washes. Booker gave the friend a call. It looked as though getting started would be easier than she thought.

It wasn't.

What soon followed was a series of humiliating meetings with a bunch of arrogant and chauvinistic owners who thought the car wash business was not the right industry for Booker.

I went to one meeting and when I went into the office, the owners started cracking up. I guess I was a big joke to them because they were just so tickled to see a 30-something female, dressed in a business suit, enter their office to talk about starting a car wash. One owner looked at me and made comments about me being prissy and about my neatly manicured fingernails. He said, "This is not an industry for you. Why don't you go get a franchise or why don't you open up a fried chicken place?" Now, I don't know if he was trying to be racist or stereotypical by making that last comment. I do know, however, that he thought I was kidding about becoming a car wash owner. So I let him talk. Before I had this meeting, I did a little research on my own. I asked other car wash owners about the cost of building a car wash, the challenges of operating this type of business, the types of equipment used, typical car counts [average number of cars washed in a certain period of time], *pricing, and potential profits. So when I was talking to this guy, I was able to speak some of the lingo, but he was still not impressed or convinced that I could actually do it. He brought out all of his multifinancial paperwork and labor reports. He just gave me everything because he thought that I didn't know anything; so he figured, why not show me just how much I didn't know, because the business wasn't going to happen anyway. When I realized what he was doing, I used that to my advantage and let him feel like I was this poor little helpless person who didn't have a clue and I played up to his ego.*

It worked.

Booker got the information she needed, and then moved on to the next car wash owner to gather more details about the industry. Fortunately, her next encounter was with someone who cared about helping her achieve her goal. His name was Bill Lawrence. At the time, he owned about eight car washes in Houston, so he was able to give her the good, the bad, and the ugly about the industry. And he did. Booker even volunteered on weekends at one of his sites to get a feel for every facet of the car wash business.

While making her marketing research rounds, Booker also met a guy who suggested that she add a lube to her facility. This, he thought, would make her car wash a one-stop shop for car care needs. With the lube, customers could have their oil changed, radiator flushed, and transmission serviced in addition to getting their car washed. It was not a part of Booker's original plan, but she liked the idea. Her contact put her in touch with a friend at Texaco who worked out an agreement in which Booker would sell Texaco products in exchange for advertising dollars.

Lube or no lube, Booker knew that, given the level of competition in and around the Houston area, she would need to offer more than just tidy washrooms and oil filter replacements if she hoped to attract and keep customers. She needed a hook. Reflecting on a piece of advice that Lawrence had shared with her ("Identify a niche"), she decided to develop a Caribbean theme. Her facility would offer customers the sights and sounds of the islands. Booker had traveled throughout the Caribbean and always enjoyed its vibrant culture. She thought, "Why not bring a piece of that to the city?" It was something that had not been done before, at least not in Houston. Maybe, just maybe, customers would welcome the refreshing concept.

They did.

When we first opened and people would hear the Caribbean music playing in the lobby, what is the first thing you think that they did? Dance. I don't care what was going on in their lives, when they heard that music, they started to move and feel good. When customers come onto my lot, I want them to feel good about the service that they are getting, but I also want them to feel good about themselves and have a good time.

Booker dubbed her business Cabana Car Wash after toying with a few tropical-sounding names, and she continued her search for the perfect location. She finally decided to go for the miniature golf course. If nothing else, it was long enough and wide enough. She began developing a comprehensive business plan that laid out all the logistics of her start-up company, including the all-important financials, and started searching for investors to help fund her venture. Booker would need nearly $1 million to get her business off the ground. The land alone cost $245,000. She had $50,000 in personal savings to infuse into the start-up, but planned to obtain a partner to add more capital to her coffers. Then the two would finance the rest of the costs through an outside lender(s). It sounded simple enough. But as you might expect, when she tried to get the cash, the real problems in starting Cabana Car Wash began.

Rule 2: Knock on Every Door Until You Get the Funds You Need

Finding potential investors can be one of the most difficult aspects of starting a new business. It's hard enough when you have no money, no collateral, and no contacts. But Booker, who worked in finance and real estate and who had bought, renovated, and sold small houses on her own in the past, had a few dollars socked away. Plus, she had the names of some very rich, very enterprising, and very influential people in her Rolodex. Still, her initial search for seed money came up empty.

Before I partnered with Doc, I initially went to five other people about becoming a partner and investing in the business. Three of them were ex-football players, who each could have written a check. But none of them did. Then I went to another guy and his wife. They were both surgeons. Between *the two of them, they took home $70,000 a month. He could have written a check and never batted an eye. He knew me very well, knew that my back was up against the wall, and that I had worked very hard on developing this business idea, so he asked me to come by. I did. My spirit was as low as it could get at this point, because I couldn't get anybody to help me prior to our meeting. So I went to him carrying my little business plan. Basically, I was asking him for $50,000 and giving him 50 percent ownership in a business that I knew would fly. I thought to myself that he didn't even have to be a part owner if he didn't want to. If he wanted to just invest in the business, that would have been fine with me also. Well, he kept me at his house for more than four hours showing me practically everything that he owned. He showed me his four Ferraris that he had stacked up on a ramp in his three-car garage. He told me about the guy he had come by and wash the cars even when they weren't dirty. He knew why I was there and he just skirted around the issue by bragging about his money, his house, his wife's business, and anything and everything else. Then after the tour was done, I sat down with him and tried to go through my business plan, but he very arrogantly looked at it and said, "Well, I've given some thought to this and I don't think it's something that I really want to do at this time." I thought to myself, "He could have told me that some four and a half hours ago." I left, got into my car, and just cried. I realized that all he really wanted to do was just show me all the things he had acquired, as if to say that I would never have them. It was just a humiliating experience.*

Despite these stumbling blocks, Booker didn't give up. She continued to knock on every door possible, to get the cash that she needed. She used a business broker to identify a potential funding source, and was referred to Allied Capital, a Washington, DC-based venture capital firm and a preferred lender of the Small Business Administration (SBA). Meanwhile, Booker entered preliminary talks with the landowners to make the buy. But she still needed a partner. After weeks of searching, she found someone she thought would make a decent match. He owned his own business and was financially secure. She presented to him the business plan she had worked on for over a year, and the two began preparing their financial package to submit to Allied Capital. Then trouble brewed again. The partner—who, despite past differences today remains one of Booker's very good friends—did not agree with how the deal would be structured. He wanted to forgo taking the SBA route and find another funding source. Booker didn't agree.

Needless to say, we had a very unpleasant discussion about what to do with the business. I remember him telling me one day that if I ended the deal with him, the deal would not get done at all. Then he said, "If I have to, I will get the thing done my damn self. I'll take it and I'll get my bank to do it." Now keep in mind that he hadn't done any of the work, but I had prepared one hell of a business plan. I can't tell you the hours that I put into that business plan. He had a copy of the plan, and he said that he was going to take it, and the lender package, to someone else. I said, "Over my dead body." I told him, "You may do it and build a car wash, but you're not going to build it at the location I picked out." He said, "Oh, yes I am. I will call the owners of the land and I'll just buy the land myself." At that point I knew I could not partner with him.

Beating him to the punch was not going to be easy. He was more financially stable than Booker. In fact, he planned to put up an additional $100,000 to help clinch the deal. Booker knew she had to do something. The question was: What?

At that point, I had a good relationship with the three guys who owned the land. I had been keeping them up-to-date with everything that I was doing with regard to the business, so they were as much a part of it as I was. I didn't have to explain any of the specifics to them—after all, they just owned the land so they could really care less about what I did with it—but I kept them in the loop. I would call them to bounce ideas off of them. They became mentors to me and began to give me direction on certain things, so when I had this falling out with my partner, I contacted the leader of the group and explained the situation. When I was finished talking, I just burst into tears. He told me to meet him later that day. When I met with the guys, they said, "We have been where you are right now. We have had partners try to screw us before. So he can't come at us with a better offer because we don't need the money. It ain't about the money. It's about the principle of the matter. So let him call. Let him do whatever he wants to do, but don't worry because this is your deal and it's a done deal."

For three and a half hours, the landowners talked with Booker about partnerships and how to choose the right cohort. But they also restructured the deal. The asking price was still $245,000. But the owners were willing to take $145,000 at closing. They would loan Booker the other $100,000 to cover operating costs for the first six months. There was still the question of where she would get the rest of the cash, not only for the purchase of the land, but also to settle the expenses of building and furnishing the car wash.

Enter Doc, a tall brawny man with a successful private dental practice.

Booker had known him since 1991, but she never thought about the possibility of his becoming a partner. She would talk to him about her intended venture from time to time during her regular checkups, but that was it. Then one Friday, during a routine visit, Dr. Morency simply volunteered.

This was right after I had just gone through this horrible bout with my partner. Doc asked me how the business was shaping up and I said, "The business is dead," because I knew that I didn't have enough money to at least purchase the land. He asked me about the kind of investment he would have to make and if I had a copy of a business plan, so I gave it to him. He said that he would take a look at it with his attorney and accountant over the weekend and get back to me Monday. In my mind, I was saying, "Yeah right. How many times have I heard that." So I just blew it off. Well, that night, he called me and told me that he was in. Originally, I asked him for a $50,000 investment. I didn't even ask him to be a partner because he had a successful dental practice and I thought that he wouldn't want to shoulder the liability *involved with owning a car wash. But he said, "If I'm going to be in it, I'm going to put my butt on the line with you."*

In 1993, Dr. Morency, now 50, became an equal partner in the business venture. However, the combined $100,000 personal investment he and Booker made, plus the $100,000 loan from the landowners, was not enough. The partners still needed to borrow $733,000 to seal a deal with costs that added up to $933,000. The newly formed duo submitted their financing package to Allied Capital through the SBA's 7(a) Guaranteed Loan Program. The loan was approved, and Booker and Dr. Morency moved to the closing procedures. For four and a half hours, the two sat behind closed doors and signed documents for a deal that they thought was done. Then Booker got a call from a SBA official. It was a call that she won't soon forget.

It was from Bill Love, with the SBA. I've never met him, but I will never forget that name. He called at 4:30 on a Friday afternoon to say that the SBA was withdrawing its guarantee of the loan and that the deal was dead. I lost it. I cried uncontrollably. I got mad. I was in disbelief.

At that point, Booker felt as if there was nothing else that she could do, so she drove home. There she came across a business card belonging to the person who would save the deal. Two weeks prior to the closing, Booker, who worked at Wells Fargo at the time, met Milton Wilson, then the deputy director of the SBA. She didn't know him well, but she gave him a call anyway. It was 5:30 P.M. when Booker picked up the phone, so she thought that there was little chance that he would still be in the office, but he was. Fighting back the tears, Booker reintroduced herself to him and began to explain her situation. Fifteen minutes after hanging up with Wilson, she got a call from Love, who explained his concerns regarding the land deal she and her partner had with the property owners.

He said that the SBA wanted to make sure that the guys who were selling us the land didn't come in and put a real high stipulation on the $100,000 that they were going to let us use as equity. As the deal read originally, the SBA thought that it *might have put too much debt on the business on the front end, so Mr. Love said that he would sit down with his staff on Monday to take a look at it more closely. . . . Milton turned that deal around.*

The following week, the SBA, Booker, Dr. Morency, and the landowners entered a second closing and finally sealed the deal. Construction, which took a year to complete, began shortly after. In 1994, Cabana Car Wash opened its doors and serviced about 50 customers the first day.

Rule 3: Be Open to Change, and Learn from It

Booker's ability to weather the toughest of entrepreneurial storms—financial or otherwise—comes as no surprise. She has been resilient during her entire life. Growing up as the daughter of a "po' Baptist itinerant preacher," change was virtually the only constant in her life. Wherever her father would acquire pastoral positions, the family would follow. By the time Booker graduated from high school in 1977, she had lived in just about every community throughout Houston. Still, she remained centered and focused on the future.

After getting her diploma, Booker started working for Project Aid, a government agency and social service program that helped Vietnamese and Cambodian refugees adjust to life in the United States. Her parents never pushed her to go to college. They were the products of an era in which young girls got married, had kids, and took care of the house. But Booker didn't want to don an apron just yet. She wanted to further her education, so she enrolled at a small local college. During her studies, she met her future husband, a counselor for Project Aid, and, by June 1980, the two were married. Booker worked at a day job and went to school at night. After getting her associate degree, she enrolled at the University of Houston to study real estate. In 1982, she, her husband, and their 16-month-old daughter moved to Dallas before she could nab her second degree. He wanted to attend seminary school at Southern Methodist University (SMU). A dutiful and God-fearing wife, Booker was not going to deny his calling.

The young couple lived in merit housing on the campus of SMU. Her husband was a full-time student, so Booker was the sole breadwinner for the family of three. Working as a legal assistant for a law professor at SMU, she made a measly $13,765 a year. Still, she managed to pay tuition at SMU, which was $26,000 a year, buy groceries and clothes, pay the bills, and subsidize night school for herself. It would be another decade before she would start Cabana Car Wash, but she was already learning bootstrapper techniques as a way of getting things done.

I lived off of credit cards. But more importantly, I planned and created a budget for what little money I did have. There would be days that I would have only $32 left to last us until my next paycheck, which came every two weeks, so I would stretch those dollars. For example, I made sure that I only used the car to go to and from work, since I didn't have enough money to buy gas to go running around the entire neighborhood. I bought groceries on sale and just used other cost-cutting measures like that to carry us through.

Admittedly, it wasn't easy, but Booker knew her circumstances would soon change. She was studying to become a broker and had entered an accelerated program to obtain her broker's license. She also left her job at SMU and accepted one as a loan processor/closer at Western Savings & Loan in 1984. There she learned how to structure and negotiate real estate deals. But, bothered by the excessively social atmosphere, she left Western Savings & Loan after only 11 months. Fortunately, by this time, she had received her broker's license and graduated from night school with a degree in real estate/finance. With her newfound credentials, she courageously branched out on her own and worked, on a straight commission basis, as a tenant representative who negotiated new leases for renters.

I didn't make one dime. In fact, we almost starved to death, but I believe the experience prepared me for my life now and being able to deal with some of the adverse situations I've faced in running my business. When you are having problems as an entrepreneur, I think that it will help if you can look back on some of the scariest points in your life and pull something from that that will help you overcome whatever obstacles you are facing.

Booker's husband soon graduated from seminary school and headed back to Houston to be a pastor at a church. But she stayed in Dallas to continue building her career. First she landed a job as the director of property leasing for Republic Bank, where she worked for two and a half years. Then, in 1987, an opportunity to head up a receivership in Houston took her back to her hometown and her husband. Unfortunately, Booker's marriage, already strained from the distance, got worse. She eventually divorced. But her work ethic remained the same. Booker continued to climb the financial ladder of success. By 1990, she claimed a post with the FDIC. Two years later, she joined Wells Fargo Bank and began laying the foundation for building Cabana Car Wash.

> *Looking back on my life in Dallas, at that time I thought that it was the most miserable time in my life. But it ended up being the best blessing that I have ever had because I learned so much and it helped me determine my mission in life. Had I stayed in Houston after getting married, and not taken that chance and not stepped out on faith, I'm not sure where I would be right now. But I tell you that I wouldn't be sitting here as a car wash owner and senior vice president of a major lending institution. I definitely wouldn't be here because I would not have had the exposure, the experiences, and the training that I have now. All of the hardship and readjustment that I had to do before becoming a business owner helped to develop, shape, and mold me, and bring me to this point in my life. It certainly prepared me for the challenges I would experience that first year of operating Cabana Car Wash.*

Rule 4: Control Your Customers; Don't Let Them Control You

Year One of a new business is often the most exciting because it's fresh and full of promise. But getting past the grand opening can also be the most frustrating time of entrepreneurship, especially if you are inexperienced in dealing with any aspect of what makes your operation tick. Although Booker had thoroughly researched the car wash business, obtained a firm grasp on how it worked, and survived the roller coaster ride to gaining financial support, she was still challenged by a variety of issues. She had problems with training and employee theft. Then there were the stresses of how to deal with copycat competitors. A very similar type of car wash, called Caribbean Car Wash, opened up right after Cabana and used the same color schemes and tropical uniforms. But none of these problems seemed to be greater than those she encountered when it came to dealing with customers.

At first, Booker tried to satisfy every complaint, whether it was justified or not. In fact, during her first year in operation, she spent about $13,000 paying for damages that were not even caused by the car wash—just to save customers. But the dissatisfied patrons seemed to come from everywhere, and each performed a different little production of "Customer on a Rampage." Some threw tantrums over something as trivial as an attendant's putting the wrong air freshener in their car, or a bit of dust that was mistakenly left on the rims. Others came through in a drunken stupor and threatened to *drive* through the automatic car wash. Still others bellowed over nicks and scratches they claimed were caused by Cabana. With these types of incidents happening on a regular basis, Booker knew that she would eventually have to hold her ground if she wanted to stay in business.

I've had numerous customers who have charged us with damaging their car. But there was one that I distinctly remember who said that we scratched the front of his hood. I said that that was impossible because our car wash uses miter cloths, not brushes. Still, to satisfy him, I offered to put some compound over the scratch and put some wax on it at no charge. But it wasn't enough. This man performed like nothing I have ever seen in my life. He was screaming and spitting all over my face. His veins were popping out of his head. The customers in the lobby were looking at him as if he was crazy, but I just stood there and listened. He wanted me to scream back and get ignorant with him, but I have found that when customers perform the way he did, silence kills them. I think the best way to handle an irate customer is to just stand there, listen, and let them finish. Then calmly resolve the situation. So I let him scream and scream, and when he was done, I turned to his wife to let her know that we would handle the problem. All the while, this guy is standing off to the side cursing at me. But I just continued to focus on his wife and maintained control of the situation. I find myself battling with customers like this even to this day. But I hold my ground and don't give in the way that I used to.

Rule 5: Hire Employees by Using Your Head, Not Your Heart

As though dealing with customers was not enough of a headache for Booker, she also struggled to figure out how to deal with staffing during that first year. Her first mistake was hiring too many workers. Then she put an inept manager in charge.

I think we had 38 people in the beginning. That was way too many. This is a labor-intensive business and it will make or break you, so you need to learn how to manage your labor. Unfortunately, we hired a manager who didn't know how to do that. This particular manager was running at 60 percent in labor every day, which meant that, for every dollar that I made, $.60 went to cover payroll, which left me $.40 to cover my expenses and everything else. That doesn't work. In fact, it's upside down. That's way too much in labor costs. He had too many people on payroll and brought everybody in full time, all working 40 hours per week, just so he could satisfy everyone.

Despite the glaring and costly mistakes, Booker kept the manager for an entire year. She thought that she couldn't possibly let him go. Here was a guy who loved the business to death. He had watched the birth of Cabana from the time the first bit of concrete was poured. He helped put up shelving and purchase inventory. There were even times, before the business opened, when she would drive by and see him sweeping the floor or wiping the windows.

I couldn't have asked for a person to love the business more than myself and my partner, so we thought that that was enough to run the company. But it wasn't. We had to soon learn to quit making emotional decisions based on whether we liked the person, and make more objective choices that were best for our bottom line, so we had to let him go. We also had two lube guys that first year. Both were managers. One was Mr. Personality Plus. He had a million-dollar smile and the customers loved him. He was friendly and pleasant and knew his job well. But he never wanted to train the new guys. He couldn't see the bigger picture. Plus, there was always an issue where there was a lot of playing going on in the lube area. He would get out there and laugh and joke, and I would have to tell him to work. I had to let him go. It broke my heart because he also loved the business unconditionally and loved me and Doc, but he was costing me money.

Booker suffered $150,000 in losses her first year in operation, because of bad hiring choices that she had made. Admittedly, she was inexperienced in a lot of areas of running a car wash, and she had to learn through trial and error. But the fact that she was an absentee owner, placing the business into the hands of those she felt shared the same passion and vision for the company, also had a great impact.

You have an idea or vision of what you want your business to look like and to feel like, so you try to convey that message to your managers and the staff. But unless you are there on a regular basis to go back and check to see if things are being done properly, it doesn't happen. You have to take a hands-on approach to running your business if you want to be successful. But you also have to identify the right people who can help you achieve your goals. You try your best to hire employees who get the bigger picture, who don't see the job as just a job, and who are committed to the business, but finding those types of people, especially in this business, is not always easy. You don't always choose the right people, and that's OK. The key to saving your business if you have made the wrong choice is to acknowledge the mistake early enough in the process and make an adjustment. Don't walk around and hope that things are going to improve if you just ride it out, because [they] won't. When hiring people for your business, make sure they have the type of experience you need and a strong work ethic. When you realize that you have someone on board who does not measure up, cut your losses quickly, and move on to find those people who can help you grow.

Rule 6: Carefully Consider Your Opportunities to Expand

American actress Mary Pickford (1893–1979) once said, "If you have made mistakes, there is always another chance for you . . . you may have a fresh start any moment you choose, for this thing we call 'failure' is not the falling down, but the staying down."

By the first-year anniversary of Cabana, Booker was worn out and feeling as though she had bitten off entirely more than she could chew. Although positive experiences did occur, the bad seemed to outweigh the good, and made her question her reason for continuing. She lost customers, went through six inept managers, hired and fired dozens of employees, and took a bath in unprojected losses. She wanted out. Even if Doc wanted to stay on, Booker was ready to bail. She called her longtime friend Lawrence to discuss the possibility of selling her interest in the business. But after weighing the pros and cons of the situation, she found far too many reasons *not* to sell. Cabana Car Wash was still standing. She still had customers and a devoted partner at her side. And, perhaps more importantly, she had enough operating income to carry her through the rough times.

It is very important to be able to properly allocate enough cash flow going into your business so that whether or not you make a dime that first year, you can keep your doors open. Undercapitalization is what hurts most businesses. They will open one day and if they are not making some money that same day, they go under. You need to have at least six months' operating income when starting out. If it costs you $50,000 to get started, have six times that amount sitting in the bank somewhere, so that you know, whether you generate a profit or not, you can keep your business going. The only thing that sustained us was having enough *cash flow to carry us through the hard times because that first year we just made losses.*

But things got better. By 1996, business was booming. The car wash grossed $875,000 in revenue. A year later, earnings topped $1 million and Cabana Car Wash became one of ten finalists competing for the Pinnacle Award, an honor bestowed on the top African American-owned businesses in Houston. It would be another year before the winners would be announced, but Booker already received an offer to duplicate Cabana Car Wash. The City of Houston heard about Cabana's status as an award finalist and approached Booker about entering into a barter exchange agreement to put a replica of the site at the Theatre District Parking Garage, where 5,000 people parked on a daily basis. As part of the agreement, the city would provide a secured area for the cars to be washed. Booker would shore up the manpower, equipment, signage, and a small shed to house her lube area. It seemed to be a win–win situation for everyone because the city would get an amenity that it could offer to existing customers and use as a carrot to attract more. And Booker would receive more publicity and more profits as a result of the expansion.

I have to admit that before they approached me I wasn't even thinking about having multiple locations. I was perfectly happy with just one Cabana Car Wash. I thought, from the experiences that I had with the first one, that I just wanted to survive with that. But when they did call me about the opportunity, I went for it (after carefully reviewing the benefits) because it just seemed like a good business move to make.

In 1998, Booker opened her second location—a hand wash rather than an automatic site—with just $7,000. That year, she also won the Pinnacle Award and became the subject of a *Houston Chronicle* article that opened the floodgates to tons of additional offers to bring Cabana to other parts of the city. She accepted one from Ampco Express.

Ampco Express, a company that owns most of the parking facilities surrounding the major airports in Houston, wanted her to set up a shop at Houston's Intercontinental Airport, a 40-minute drive from Cabana's original location. Similar to the deal with the City of Houston, Ampco would provide the facility, Booker would bring her car wash expertise. For Booker, the deal meant an opportunity to obtain a captive audience, and a chance to spread the word about Cabana Car Wash to virtually any place in the world. Using $15,000 in start-up money, she opened her third site in 1999.

The Ampco location is very upscale. It has a huge covered parking area with washing bays already installed. There is a ticket counter and a valet service. When airline passengers pull their cars into the garage, they check their bags right there, get their seat assignments, and leave the cars to be serviced by Cabana employees. Customers do not have to park their cars. They simply step out and leave the keys in the ignition. A Cabana valet then takes the car to another area of the garage to be hand washed and/or serviced in the lube. A shuttle bus, which displays Cabana Car Wash signs, takes customers to their terminal. On the return trip, the shuttle bus carries customers back to the parking garage where their cars are prepped and ready to go.

Booker also has a deal to wash Ampco's shuttle buses.

> *In addition to doing the customer vehicles throughout the day, at night I have a separate crew that goes over and washes all of Ampco's shuttle buses and company vehicles. It's still Cabana, but it's a whole other business deal. Ampco also has us locked into putting Cabana at their new parking garage at the William B. Hobby Airport.*

Booker has certainly received her share of plum offers to expand. But she does not jump at just any prospect. As always, she does her homework and painstakingly plans her course of action. In 2000, she opened up yet another location—this time, just a five-minute drive from her home in Pearland, an affluent suburb just 15 miles outside of Houston. A year earlier, Booker noticed that her community was becoming one of the fastest growing areas outside of the city. Developers were putting up shopping centers, supermarkets, posh housing developments, and office buildings, but no car washes. Booker then thought: What better place to expand and get a jump on the competition? So she did.

> *It's very important to know what's happening in your area because there may be opportunities for you to expand there. I*

was anticipating growth in Pearland, so I met with the Pearland Economic Development Division and major corporations and commercial entities to talk about what they planned to bring into the area. By doing this, I found that there was a good chance for me to bring Cabana to my community.

Booker started planning the $1.3 million project in 1999, but this time she had a different business partner. Dr. Morency did not participate in this expansion; he had enough responsibilities with his practice and helping to operate the first three locations. Booker and her new cohort secured financial support from First Community Bank, a bank in Pearland, and began meeting with architects, electricians, and other parties to start the ball rolling. Unlike the other Cabana locations, this site would have to be entirely different aesthetically.

Pearland is an area that is very traditional, very conservative, and very rich. It's a community where espresso replaces just plain old coffee, and Jaguar and Mercedes are the cars of choice. The homes, in a price range from $200,000 to $750,000, have two-story foyers, double doors, and three-car garages. Most of the residents are doctors, lawyers, professors, business owners, and corporate executives. When planning the facility, Booker knew that, for her car wash to generate customers, it would have to cater to this clientele. The design of the building would have to be compatible with those surrounding it. That meant brick instead of stucco. But she would also have to develop a theme that would appeal to this particular demography.

I had to come up with something that attracted an elite group of people. I couldn't do the palm trees, . . . the Caribbean music, or tropical uniforms that I used at all of the other locations. I had to develop a look that was more upscale.

Using the name Auto Spa, Booker developed an all-brick car wash complete with a pitched roof, skylight tunnel, and landscaping that would make some Beverly Hills homeowners stand at attention. She filled the lobby with an espresso bar, bar stools, and fax machines, plus an indoor play area filled with tables, books, and toys for the kids.

So what's next for the car wash queen?

I have another one that I am going to put down the street from the first Cabana Car Wash. That's going to be the fifth location. But I think in terms of our long-term goals, I'm not that concerned about becoming bigger. I'm concerned about becoming better. I am conscious about not taking on too much to the point where I will compromise quality or have a series of mishaps. I want to be set aside for the quality of work that we do. If that ultimately results in other locations that are profitable, we'll do them. I will take them as they come. But the truth of the matter is, if I only had one car wash with a good reputation, good employees, good location, and a good environment, I could live with that.

3

VIVIAN GIBSON
THE MILLCREEK
COMPANY, INC.

The Hot Sauce Specialist

Getting into business all boils down to building relationships. Without them you will have difficulties.

While many small business owners spend their typical workweek sitting behind a desk, Vivian Gibson logs most of her time behind the wheel of her 1991 Volvo. Part taxi, she uses it to chauffeur her son Ross to tutoring classes and T-ball. Part business-mobile, she races it from one end of Missouri to the other to promote and sell her sizzling line of hot sauces.

On this drizzly Friday morning, Gibson is in the business-mobile. With the gas-gauge needle pointing to "Full," she leaves her Richmond Heights home and cruises westward on Highway 40 toward Chesterfield. It's 8:30 A.M. and Gibson has a 9 A.M. meeting with her food broker to discuss putting her newest product, Vib's Bar-B-Q Today, on supermarket shelves. It's not a hot sauce, but it has just as much fire as her previous products. With a seasoning blend made from paprika and other spices, Vib's Bar-B-Q Today gives a keen kick to steak, pork chops, chicken, and fish. Gibson developed the tasty concoction last year. Now she is ready to put it in supermarkets alongside her other successful condiments, Vib's Caribbean Heat and Vib's Southern Heat.

Riding the slick roadways, Gibson doesn't rehearse the pitch she will make to her broker. Instead, she slides a tape into her tape

47

deck. In seconds, hip-hop artist Lauryn Hill's voice begins to filter through the front speakers. It seems an unlikely choice of music for this 50-year-old mother of two, but Gibson is not your typical baby boomer. She has had four businesses—including her current venture—in the past 22 years. She has reignited interest in a fallen and forgotten community through an exhibit that chronicles her childhood. And she has come through two marriages, a brutal revolution, and a near-fatal cerebral aneurysm to achieve it all. So how hard could it be to convince a supermarket, which already stocks two of her products, to now carry a third?

Gibson doesn't look worried. She's been down this road before. Finding the parking lot entrance, she whips the car into a space close to the building. Opening up the back door, she reaches for her attaché case and a plain cardboard box filled with 12 plastic bottles. The mist of the rain is not enough to squelch the scent of the seasoning salt. So although the morning has just begun, Gibson can't help but think about what she will have for lunch.

In the conference room, seated opposite her broker, Gibson exchanges greetings. Then she slides the box across the table. Grabbing hold of the container, the broker folds back the flaps, removes one bottle, unscrews the top, and sniffs. Then, with a calculating smile and lift of his eyebrows, he murmurs: "Mmmmmmm." Two months later, Vib's Bar-B-Q Today hits the shelves of Schnucks, a supermarket chain located in the Midwest.

Only six years have passed since Gibson started The MillCreek Company, Inc., a hot sauce and seasoning business named for the community in which she grew up. But in that time she has developed four products (including a relative of the original Vib's Caribbean Heat, only three times hotter) and a loyal following of hot sauce enthusiasts, self-proclaimed cooking connoisseurs, and just plain ol' folks who love to chow down.

Like her customers, Gibson loves to eat. But even more, she loves to cook. She started playing chef when she was barely tall enough to use a stove. Back then, Gibson made pancakes, cornbread, beans and neckbones, and fried corn and onions. Today, she stirs up some of the same dishes but adds to most of them her not-so-secret ingredient: hot sauce. And not just any hot sauce. Gibson's hot sauces are made from the two hottest peppers on the planet (Habañero and Scotch Bonnet), and she shakes a dash on everything from pizza to potato salad. Now thousands of households throughout the "Show-Me State" and beyond are cooking with the condiments.

Gibson's products are sold in over 100 supermarkets and grocery stores throughout Missouri and Illinois, as well as Paradies (souvenir) shops at Lambert–St. Louis International Airport. They are also available through her Web site (www.vibshotsauce.com). But when you pick up one of her products, you get more than just a mixture of spices. You get a warm feeling of being home with good food, good friends, and family. Gibson helps to evoke those tender moments by telling short stories of her own on the back of each bottle. The label on Vib's Southern Heat talks about how her grandmother grew peppers in her garden and strung them up to dry on her back porch before using them for winter meals. Vib's Bar-B-Q Today illustrates a wooden picket fence that represents the one that surrounded her childhood home. Every Saturday, Gibson's father would tack on the fence a sign that read "Bar-B-Q Today." Then he would fire up the grill and make savory meats for church fundraisers in the MillCreek community. Because Gibson's products have a hometown appeal and great taste, they are finding their way into many top-name stores inside and outside her community. But she is not satisfied. Gibson wants her hot sauce to become synonymous with St. Louis.

> *I remember when I lived in New York . . . people used to talk about the blueberry muffins in Jordan-Marsh* [a department store]. *If you were planning a trip to Boston, people would immediately say, "Make sure you go to Jordan-Marsh to get some blueberry muffins." I want to have that kind of mystique, and that's what I'm pushing for. I want to saturate the St. Louis market. But I also want to encourage people to tell their out-of-state friends about my products so when they are doing business or vacationing here, they will immediately think of my sauce.*

It's a lofty goal for this native of St. Louis, who started mixing sauce by hand in the rear of a bowling alley. But Gibson has the drive, ingenuity, and enthusiasm to make it happen. Always energetic, she rarely slows down, so leave those special-occasion shoes at home if you plan to tag along. Each day, she rises before the sun, then zips through her "To Do" list before lunchtime even gets underway. Gibson has always been a morning person who gets more done before 11 A.M. than most people do all day. And that's no small task. She wears many hats for her roles as developer, administrator, accountant, market researcher, salesperson, and, until recently, manufacturer.

When Gibson started the company in 1994, she was the single driving force behind it. She operated without a staff, or standard manufacturing equipment, or delivery trucks. Still, she managed to supply hundreds of gallons of sauce to supermarkets across her region. For this financially strapped businesswoman, that proved to be a challenge. Like most new business owners, Gibson found it difficult to secure start-up capital. Refusing to borrow (even from her husband), she launched the business using money she earned while a full-time employee of the St. Louis Public Schools system.

The biggest and greatest challenge in starting a business is getting the money that you need. That sounds trite and so much like a cliché, but it's true. I believe that you can only get money if you have money, and if you don't have enough collateral to cover a loan, then the bank is not going to give you a loan. When I started The MillCreek Company, I didn't even approach the banks because I knew that I did not have any collateral that I was capable of putting up to secure the loan. I was married and I had a house, but I didn't get my husband involved because I didn't want to argue with him about putting up our home or other valuables for my dream. If the business failed, I didn't want it to be an issue in my marriage. If I made a poor decision—on, let's say, the Internet and threw $3,000 down the hole to build a Web site—I wanted to be able to say that it was my $3,000, so since I had a job and a little money of my own in the bank, I used that to get started. There were days . . . when my paycheck came, I used it to buy bottles or to pay my rent. If there was something that I needed but could not afford to buy, I would improvise. For example, when I could not afford to purchase a $600 labeling machine, I made my own out of the eight-pound crates that my peppers were shipped in. And when I couldn't afford shipping costs, I simply delivered orders from the trunk of my car. These are the types of things I did to stay in business.

Being resourceful is part of what makes a business owner successful. It's a trait that Gibson has had from day one. Growing up in a St. Louis slum, she often had to be inventive. Her father never made more than $10,000 a year, so luxuries did not exist in her childhood home. But neither did some very basic things. Gibson had to make her own toys.

I made dollhouses and doll furniture out of matchboxes. For example, if I would make bedroom furniture, I would use the matchboxes to make little drawers and then I would put little handles on them. One of my favorite things to make, however, was paper dolls. My mother got McCall's *magazine and in it there was a paper doll series called Betsy McCall. Well, I waited for this magazine to come, and when it did, I would flip through the pages to find Betsy McCall and maybe two or three of her little outfits that came with the paper doll. I'd cut her out, along with the outfits, but I'd make 100 outfits and I would do this every month. I would sit down for hours drawing paper doll clothes and making all these new little designs. I had shoeboxes full of them. My fondest memories of my childhood are when I was playing in a very creative way. I think it really shaped my ability to be resourceful, to create, and to understand the dignity of manual labor and hard work that is required in running your own business.*

Gibson spent $40,000 in personal savings to start The Mill-Creek Company. Essentially, she paid for equipment and supplies as needed; stacks of cash were never readily available. But getting capital was not the only obstacle she encountered. When trying to purchase bottles, labels, and other materials to help run her operation, Gibson's product volume often fell short of the requirements set by most manufacturers. Some bottling companies that Gibson approached set a minimum order of 500 cases. But Gibson had not secured any customers when ordering her initial inventory. At the most, she wanted to buy 100 cases for the business she intended to get. But, with no guarantee that she would receive any invoices, supply stores were not about to bend or break their rules for one entrepreneur's good intentions.

As a new kid on the condiments block, Gibson also endured criticism from consumers—mainly die-hard Tabasco fans who adamantly claimed that her hot sauce was not really hot. Buyers were just as judgmental. Many questioned the marketability of her first product, a greenish-yellow *jus*. They wondered whether it could even be considered a "real" hot sauce, and some suggested that she add red food coloring to it—after all, isn't hot sauce supposed to be red? Always quick to answer her critics, Gibson would simply respond, "What color is *hot?*"

Company revenues of more than $500,000 a year would suggest that it's not always red.

Rule 1: Do What You Love

Gibson has been cooking ever since she was six years old. But it was not her mom who taught little Vivian how to prepare meals. Gibson learned her way around the kitchen from her godmother, a third-grade-educated domestic worker who cooked and cleaned in the homes of rich white families. Gibson spent every other weekend at her godmother's house, and she learned how to fry, bake, broil, stir, simmer, sauté, mix, marinate, slice, and dice. When it was time to cook at home, she, more often than not, would don an apron, stand before a potbelly stove, and go to work cooking everything virtually from scratch.

> *My mother was from a very well-to-do family in Alabama. Her father owned the town store and lots of property. She was college-educated and very smart, but she didn't know how to cook. Every day, when my brothers, sisters, and I would come home from school, my mother had a burnt pot soaking in the sink. My mother was like the Campbell's soup queen. The company used to have this whole series of recipes that you could make with Campbell's soup, where you would just pour it over food. My mother poured Campbell's mushroom soup over everything imaginable because she just could not cook. So I did, instead. Whatever food my daddy brought home, I would fix. Sometimes he would come home with a 100-pound sack of potatoes, so I made potatoes and onions, hash browns, baked potatoes, potato pudding, potato soup, and every kind of potato you could imagine, until all of the potatoes were gone. Then the next week maybe he would come home with a 100-pound sack of onions*

and we would have fried onions, onion soup, and anything you could make from onions. That's how we cooked and that's how I learned to be diverse in my cooking.

By the seventh grade, Gibson was cooking better than her Home Economics teacher. All indications were that she would become a culinary genius. But despite her flair for creating mouthwatering cuisine, she had no desire to don a chef's hat. She wanted to become a fashion designer. For this fifth girl in hand-me-downs, it seemed to be a logical career choice. She made all of her clothes from the time she was ten years old. Now she wanted to dress the masses. So when Gibson got to high school, she, like the other students, selected a trade. The tailor-to-be chose industrial sewing, a skill she would later use to start her first business. After graduating in 1968, she attended Tarkio College in Tarkio, Missouri; two years later, she moved to New York to attend the Fashion Institute of Technology. Like most college students, Gibson worked her way through school. During the day, she was a receptionist at an exclusive beauty salon in midtown Manhattan. At night, she attended classes. Despite a rushed schedule and the lure of New York's trendy cafés, she still cooked.

I didn't know what else to do because I've always loved cooking. Back home, my parents and I cooked on Saturday night for Sunday, because we were in church all day. So when I moved to New York, I did the same thing. When Saturday night rolled around, I was in my little room cooking ham hocks and collard greens on my little hot plate.

Gibson worked at the beauty salon for two years. Afterward, she began working at a management consulting firm on Park Avenue. She moved from switchboard operator and relief receptionist to head of personnel in just four years. In 1976, she earned an associate degree in fashion design and started her first venture, a millinery business. Operating the company part-time, Gibson designed women's hats and sold them to congregations at black churches, sometimes making $2,000 on a Sunday afternoon. It was a great business, and one she had planned to expand to include clothing, but it turned out to be short-lived. Her research about the status of black women in the fashion industry revealed that next to none worked as actual designers. In fact, at the time, most were in the sewing rooms, stitching together garments that others had created. Not wanting to become a backroom seamstress, she ditched her plans to become the next Vera Wang and continued to work at the management consulting firm.

By 1979, Gibson, who had married two years earlier, was living in Liberia with her husband Walter and six-month-old daughter Elizabeth. Walter, an executive at Chemical Bank in New York, was transferred to the West African country to help set up the Bank of Liberia. Meanwhile, Gibson operated a clothing import business from her oceanfront home.

Every three months, my husband would have to travel back to New York for business, so I would go with him. When I did, I would hit the wholesale garment district and load up on inventory. I would bring in jeans, T-shirts, and other kinds of clothing and costume jewelry, and sell them to local stores and interested buyers in Liberia. I had a market because many Africans were trying to be as American as possible, so they wanted to know what kinds of clothes we wore and what types of music we listened to. They loved the stuff I brought back and they would buy it up like crazy.

Gibson's second trip down the road to entrepreneurship was just as successful as her first. But when Liberia's Liberation Revolution (a violent coup that ousted the country's democratic party) began, she was, once again, out of business. Chaos was all around, and Gibson could not leave her home. The president was killed and his body was dragged through the streets, and bank officers and other wealthy citizens were lined up on the beach and shot dead. With the airports closed, there seemed to be no way out. Gibson lived in fear. But after a week, the government opened the runways and she and her daughter fled the country. Her husband was forced to stay behind to sort out problems with the bank. By 1980, all three were back in America. Shortly after, Gibson divorced and moved back to her hometown of St. Louis. There she began working for the St. Louis Public Schools system where she recruited volunteers to work in a reading program for K–3 students. She also started taking a few cooking courses: one in quantity cooking; another in baking; still another about sanitation. Eventually, she took so many culinary courses that she earned enough credits to serve an apprenticeship under a chef. But even after exploring other ventures that failed to pan out, she still did not want to devote her career to the kitchen. She continued to work in the school system and took night classes as a break from her daily grind. Not until she completed an assignment in a creative writing course did she finally realize that by simply doing what she loved, she would be able to build a successful business.

In this class, I had to write a story that talked about an event that happened in my life that depicted who I was and what my culture was about. The first thing that came to my mind was how I made mud pies as a kid. It might sound strange but back then I didn't make them like most kids did. I had an entire process to how I would go about preparing them. First of all, I would get the dirt and sift it through a screen that I got from an old door. I would do this to get all of the rocks and the glass out of it. Then I would add water to the dirt to form the mud pies, but I wouldn't just shape and pat them with my hand. I would roll them out with a soda bottle. That was my rolling pin. Then I would cut them out in the size of biscuits or pies, using mason jar tops. Once they were cut, I would slice them and put them on an imaginary brick oven and bake them in the sun. I was very serious about making mud pies because I loved the idea of cooking. So I entitled my story "Serious Mud Pies." And it was then that I realized that I could and should do something professional with my cooking. I never thought about starting a business using my cooking before, because it wasn't something that I felt I could turn into a business. It was just something that I did. It was instinctive. But after writing the story, I recognized the potential success of going into the food business.

Grabbing her frying pan and spatula, Gibson formed a partnership with a night school classmate and started Moveable Feast, a catering business, in 1990. Working out of an upstairs rear area of a bowling alley, the duo catered office parties, picnics, breakfast meetings, and luncheons for many corporate clients. But the business soon outgrew their level of entrepreneurial experience and, without a responsible staff to help carry the load, they could not sustain the company. They sold the business to a larger catering company three years later. Wanting to figure out where she went wrong, Gibson, who by this time was married for a second time and had two children, enrolled in Fontbonne College to take a series of business-related courses.

> *I'd had three businesses up to that point. And each one I ran by the seat of my pants saying, "OK, this is logical, this makes sense." So I went to business school to see what I did right and what I did wrong.*

Gibson would not start The MillCreek Company for another year, but through these classes she laid the foundation to launch her line of hot sauces.

> *I took a course in business plan writing. And one of our assignments was to write a business plan for a company that we wanted to start. I knew that I wanted my business to be about food after having the catering business, so I came up with this idea to produce a yellow hot sauce. I didn't want to do barbecue sauces and salad dressings because everybody was doing that. I thought I would try this hot sauce. I knew producing a yellow hot sauce would require that I educate the consumer, but I knew that it could work, so I wrote my business plan around this product. So The MillCreek Company was pretty much designed in this course.*

Gibson developed a name for her hot sauce—Vib's Caribbean Heat. It was short, clever, and easy to remember. But before she would get started, she would experience yet another obstacle. After 22 weeks of rigorous training, Gibson graduated from Fontbonne College in May 1994 with a B.S. degree in business administration. Four months later, she suffered a cerebral aneurysm that left her partially paralyzed and unable to speak. For several weeks, she lay in bed recuperating. But not even this near-fatal scare could keep her still. Gibson finalized her business plan for The MillCreek Company, a name she chose to help preserve the fond memories she experienced while living in the small town which is now commemorated by an exhibit at the Missouri Historical Society, and to educate others about a special place in St. Louis history. After much therapy she regained full mobility and was able to speak again. Then she started her fourth and final business.

Rule 2: Use Your Creative Wiles to Develop and Test a Market for Your Product

The first steps to starting The MillCreek Company were really taken in Gibson's own kitchen, trying to give her Caribbean-style hot sauce the viscosity that she wanted and that the public would accept. When she lived in New York, a boyfriend from Trinidad had taught her how to make traditional Caribbean hot sauce, which consists of big chunks of Scotch Bonnet peppers (the source of the yellow color), cauliflower, carrots, papaya, and mango. She incorporated it in just about everything she cooked, and she had used it as a secret ingredient in her catering business. But Gibson knew that most customers attracted to her newest venture had grown accustomed to a red Louisiana-style hot sauce that they didn't have to spoon out of a bottle. She would have to develop a more consumer-friendly consistency. Rather than spend thousands of dollars (which she did not have) working with a chemist to develop the right formula, she solicited free help from the Food Science Department at the University of Missouri.

I spent a lot of time at home blending it and putting things in it to thin it out and keep it from separating. I would make up all kinds of batches and then send it to the university. They would taste it and give me suggestions on what to do differently. They also tested it for the pH balance, and to tell me whether I needed to put preservatives in it. So I kind of worked with this department over the phone for maybe three or four months. Once I found the right formula, I sent batches to the FDA to determine its shelf stability and to make sure that it was safe.

Then she tested her market. Like most new business owners who are strapped for cash, Gibson used the least expensive method to poll potential customers.

I created a little questionnaire and sent it along with some of the sauce to my neighbors to try. The questionnaire asked what they liked and did not like about the hot sauce. I used this method because it's all I could afford. It's not like I had $60,000 to just pull from, to do the market research or to pay for anything else in starting my company. Virtually everything that went into launching The MillCreek Company I paid for out of my own pocket and had to pay for up-front, in cash. In starting this business, I learned that you have to have money from the beginning. That's just the reality. I realized that nobody was going to sell me a refrigerator or stove on time, or grant me a loan for office space or anything else, when I was talking about making a hot sauce that I did not even have one customer for yet. So I had to be resourceful and come up with creative ways to get the job done, and that's what I did.

Getting neighbors and friends to try the hot sauce was a good way for Gibson to get some initial feedback. But she knew that, to fully gauge how well her product would fare in the marketplace, she would have to use a bigger barometer. That meant doing far more extensive research—and, of course, spending lots more money.

The cost?

The forever-resourceful Gibson managed to get thousands of dollars' worth of market research done for free.

I approached a marketing professor at the Washington University School of Business and asked him if he would take on my company as a class project for his marketing students and have them do the research for me. To my amazement, he jumped at the opportunity and assigned me four graduate students. Essentially, I became their class project. Over the course of the semester, they produced this wonderful full-scale marketing plan that had a lot of statistical research, focus group information, and surveys. It had all the kinds of data that I could not afford to gather on my own.

Getting the graduate students to assist her was not only a financial blessing. Gibson found that it also brought up other issues that she could immediately deal with before mass distribution of her product.

I sat behind a one-way mirror during some of the focus groups listening to the participants talk about everything concerning the product, including the taste, suggested price point, and color. What came out of the focus group was that the color was a serious barrier. More than once, they said, "It tastes good and it's interesting, but the color is weird."

To answer potential critics, Gibson developed a creative and thought-provoking advertising slogan: "What Color is Hot? It's Not Always Red." She designed an eye-catching label for her product (with the help of some computer graphics), pleaded with bottlers and other suppliers to sell her amounts far below the minimum volume requirements, and secured space to begin production. Gibson had yet to attract one customer, but when the orders started to roll in, she wanted to be ready.

Rule 3: Work Your Connections to Help Build Your Business

Finding the right location to house your business can be one of the most challenging parts of starting your operation. For Gibson, it was easy. She simply went back to the same space she had used for her catering business—the Brentwood Bowling Alley.

The space was cramped but it had a kitchen and everything that I needed and that the health department required for me to make my hot sauce. It had a stove, an oven, an exhaust system, a walk-in refrigerator, and a three-compartment sink. And the rent was only $125 per month. Just imagine how much it would have cost if I had to purchase all of this equipment myself, plus rent space. I wouldn't have been able to get started.

There was one drawback, however. Gibson, who needed to order 55-gallon drums of vinegar to make her hot sauce, operated on the second floor of the bowling alley. There was no loading dock and no elevator. Always the improviser, she just worked around it.

> *I simply purchased the vinegar in one-gallon containers and then dragged all of the containers up the stairs one at a time. That was a workout.*

By the spring of 1995, Gibson was ready to introduce Vib's Caribbean Heat to the public. Like any aspiring food manufacturer, she wanted the eye-level shelf in the center section of the condiment aisle in every major supermarket. But she knew that, to get there, she would need an inside track. Many supermarkets charge slotting fees up to $20,000 to place products on their shelves. Not having that kind of cash, Gibson would have to work her connections.

She did.

Her first stop was *not* the supermarket. Instead, she supplied ten cases (120 bottles) of Vib's Caribbean Heat to the Paradies shops at Lambert–St. Louis International Airport. Paradies, a national company based in Atlanta, operates stores and souvenir shops across the country through partnerships formed with local business owners. One of Gibson's friends, who held a financial interest in the airport shops, helped her gain an entry. From there, Gibson went on to land her first major account—Schnucks, a Midwest supermarket chain consisting of 85 stores. Again, she had good contacts. But Gibson's refusal to take No for an answer also helped her to seal the deal.

> *I saw one of my former catering customers months after my illness. He had a very high position at Monsanto, which is a chemical company, and was responsible for many of the customers that I was getting. Anyway, he asked how I was doing and I told him that I was making this hot sauce. He then told me that he could introduce me to somebody at Schnucks and asked if I would bring him a sample of the sauce for him to look at. Well, I did. He said, "You know I talk to a lot of people with lots of ideas, but I've never had anybody come into a meeting with an actual hot sauce in a bottle with a label. I think we can get this on the shelf." He called this person at Schnucks, told him about me, and told*

me that the guy from Schnucks wanted a sample too. So I sent him a bottle and a letter that said I would follow up with a call. But when I called he was out of town. The next time I called, he had just left the room. Then I was told he would get back to me. Well, I wasn't about to give up. I never do. I was blown off for about two weeks. Then one day I was in my office at 5 o'clock in the morning. When I first started out, I would go in early to get a couple hours of work done, then go to my job at the school. Well, 7 A.M. rolled around and I decided to try calling again. I dialed the number and he picked up the phone. His secretary wasn't there this time. He said, "Scott Schnuck." I said, "Vivian Gibson. I gotcha." He said, "You sure did." We chatted on the phone about my product and then he gave me the name of the vice president of marketing. He told me to call him the next day. I did. We set up a meeting to talk. Initially, they asked if I would take a booth at the Black Expo to sell my sauce. Schnucks was hosting the food court at the Expo that year, and they thought it would be a good idea if I was there. But I said I could not exhibit if people could not leave the Expo and go straight into a store to purchase my product, so I got an order from Schnucks for 200 cases, plus a slot at the Black Expo, and all in less than three months after making the initial contact. Getting into business all boils down to building relationships. People ask me every day how to get started. I always tell them that it helps to know somebody because you can have the best product in the world, but without strong relationships you will have difficulties.

Gibson got the kind of order she had been waiting for. But she still had to fill it. And she had only ten days in which to do it. She worked day and night, enlisting the help of children, cousins, sisters, nieces, nephews, brothers, and anyone else she could coerce into hand-pouring sauce into five-ounce bottles.

I had never made more than ten cases at a time and now I had to produce 200 cases. There are 12 bottles in a case, so that's 2,400 bottles. I didn't have a mixer or a bottling machine. I was mixing this sauce by hand in a big stainless steel bowl. My daughter would line up the bottles and I would come behind her with a pitcher of hot sauce and a funnel and pour it in. I had virtually every relative in my family picking peppers and bottling sauce. It was incredible. We had hot sauce on the walls, on the stairs, on the tables, everywhere. It was a marathon, but we delivered on time.

Although Gibson had acquired a major supermarket chain, sales were mediocre during her first year in business. As with any new product, it took time for the public to catch on to Vib's Caribbean Heat. With no budget for advertising, she sold her hot sauce through word-of-mouth, taste tests, festivals, and events such as the Black Expo and the Best of Missouri Market at the Missouri Botanical Garden. When she was signing up for a booth at the Best of Missouri Market, in the fall of 1995, Gibson was approached by a writer for the *St. Louis Post-Dispatch*. As part of the promotion for the festival, the newspaper wanted to run an article about some of the people who would participate. The article ran a week before the market opened. It described Gibson's business, but it also talked about her growing up in a small town called MillCreek, living in Africa, and surviving serious illness. The paper printed some of Gibson's recipes and a picture of her holding a Scotch Bonnet pepper plant (the main ingredient in Vib's Caribbean Heat) that she had grown in her backyard. The article touched the hearts—and the stomachs—of people throughout St. Louis.

The first day of the market, people were lined up outside the tent waiting for me, because of this article. There were people who were hot sauce collectors and pepper gurus and groupies. I sold out everything. Everything that I brought to sell for the two-day festival I sold by noon. I had to come back to my office after the first day and make some more sauce for the second day. It was crazy. I was not prepared for the onslaught of people, but it was great. After the article and the festival, my business just took off. It was the first time I really saw a jump in my sales.

The popularity of Gibson's hot sauce shot up faster than the mercury on a hot summer day. Shortly after, Dierbergs, an upscale supermarket chain with 22 stores and in-store cooking schools, contacted Gibson about carrying her sauce.

Gibson was finally on her way.

But with sales increasing and more and more orders coming in, she needed more space to work. The bowling alley was no longer functional for her growing business so, following the advice of a friend, she moved into the St. Louis Enterprise Center. Today, as one of about 30 companies in the business incubator, The MillCreek Company is highly recognizable. Visitors can't walk 20 feet beyond the offices' gray double doors without the aroma of spicy hot sauce tickling their nostrils. When they step inside, they find out why. Gibson's headquarters contains more than just a PC, paper, and a few pencils. It's 480 square feet of space that serves as part office, kitchen, laboratory, warehouse, and showroom. Everywhere visitors turn, there's the sparkle of stainless steel equipment and the smell of seasoning. A small spice rack opposite Gibson's desk displays her hot sauces and seasoning blend. The floor is covered with pallets of bottled sauce packed in boxes for shipment. The walls are covered with recipes and newspaper articles that chronicle how Gibson has managed to keep her business hot all these years.

Setting up shop in a business incubator was a smart move for Gibson. She saved money on some needed amenities that the facility provided to its tenants: fax machines, copiers, secretarial assistance, computer and word processing equipment, and delivery services. But it too had its shortcomings. Unlike the kitchen in the bowling alley, which came furnished with most of the production equipment she needed, the incubator was simply four walls, a floor, and a ceiling. When she moved in, Gibson had to purchase major pieces of equipment—a refrigerator, a sink, and a bottling machine—as well as supplies to maintain her operation. She even had to lay the proper plumbing and gas lines for her stove and three-compartment sink. Realizing that she could not bear the financial burden alone, she approached another contact—a banker friend—to secure a $10,000 loan. She admitted that she had no idea how much to borrow and was too afraid to ask for more. But by stretching every dollar, she managed to get the necessary machinery. She used her space to produce, package, and store her products. She also started making a small supply of her XXX Hot Traditional Recipe of Vib's Caribbean Heat (which she sells through mail orders, festivals, fairs, and gift boxes) to silence those who still insisted that her hot sauce was no more lethal than traditional Tabasco. To help run the production line for Vib's Caribbean Heat, Gibson brought in temporary staff from a nearby agency. But never one to totally relinquish any of the work, she joined the assembly line right alongside her temps. And once production was complete, she put on her salesperson's hat and hit the pavement to find new customers.

Rule 4: Use Every Tool Within Reach to Promote and Sell Your Product

Initially, Gibson managed to spread the word about Vib's Caribbean Heat virtually all by herself, but, before long, she decided to solicit a food broker for making a pitch to other large supermarket chains that were not yet carrying her products. She developed a relationship with O'Brien & Associates Brokerage Company. But it was not an easy find.

> *When I met with Schnucks and they saw that I was legitimate, they gave me a list of brokers to go to. But what I found was that they really weren't interested in me because I was too small. I wasn't selling enough hot sauce for them to make any money so they didn't pay any attention to me. Brokers work off of a percentage of the net cost of the products you sell. If you aren't selling a huge volume, they aren't interested.*

At first, Gibson's requests to work with a broker were denied repeatedly. But a trip to a local food show finally gave her the access she needed. There she met a representative from Glory Foods, a Columbus, Ohio-based business that manufactures a line of precooked canned soul food. Gibson talked with the rep about her struggles with securing a broker, and he recommended her to the broker that his company was using. By working with O'Brien & Associates, Gibson has been able to get Vib's Caribbean Heat into all 85 Schnucks locations without having to pay a single slotting fee. And, to work with the firm, Gibson pays only 5 percent of the net cost of her products sold. In exchange, the company's sales staff solicits potential buyers, creates presentations, and makes the pitch. But her broker also travels to individual stores to comb the aisles and make sure that her products actually get on the shelf, are placed in the right section, and are priced correctly.

With the brokerage firm playing the role of food police with her first product, Gibson took on yet another role of her own: writer. In 1996, she began penning a cooking column for the *St. Louis American*, the largest black weekly newspaper in St. Louis. Admittedly, Gibson is not a confident writer. She wakes at 4:00 A.M., often on the eve of her deadline, and spends several hours writing a column that typically runs less than 20 inches. Her push to get in print had nothing to do with a desire to win a Pulitzer Prize. She simply wanted to use every tool at her disposal to generate exposure for her business.

I have a friend who is the publisher of the St. Louis American *newspaper. He was talking to me about adding some new departments in the paper. I was talking to him about advertising in the paper: how I could not afford it, and what could be done about that. Well, he and I began to brainstorm. I thought that it would be interesting for me to write a food column for the paper that would incorporate my own product line into the column. I felt doing that would give the paper a food section that it did not have previously and would give me free advertisement about my product. So we agreed. Now, once a month, I write an article about cooking. I talk about the history of some foods. I talk about the difference between barbecuing and grilling. I try to give useful information about cooking, but I also incorporate personal stories about my experiences in the kitchen as well as recipes, of which 50 percent involve using my product. And in addition to running the column, whenever there is some extra space available, the publisher puts in an ad for me for free. It's a relationship that works for both of us.*

While writing the column, Gibson also began to teach cooking classes at Dierbergs. This was yet another attempt to gain free publicity for her product.

She was successful.

They have a regular schedule of classes that comes out maybe three or four times a year. They have daytime and nighttime classes in just about anything you want, such as gourmet cooking, baking bread, making pizza, children's menus, barbecuing—you name it. So I called to find out what the criteria were to teach at one of their cooking schools. They said that you had to be a chef or a professional cook and that you had to send in a resume and some recipe ideas. Well, I thought, "I'm a professional cook. I had a catering company. I've had professional training," so I sent them all of my information. I gave them recipe ideas and I talked about how I would promote my product and give away bottles of my sauce as part of my promotion. They soon called me back and said that they would love to have me, so I started teaching. The course was called Vib's Caribbean Style Recipes.

Gibson had 22 paying students in each of the nine classes she taught during two seasons. She traveled to different Dierberg locations to share her expertise and spread the word about her fledgling business. In 1997, she stopped teaching the course.

It was very strenuous because I had to plan out every single step of the recipe. . . . I was teaching people to cook it and then giving them the recipes to take home. So it was a lot of work and as my business began to grow and I started to develop additional products, I just didn't have the time. But it was worth the time that I put into it because, through it, more and more people became aware of The MillCreek Company.

Rule 5: Find Alliances to Relieve the Pressures of Growth, But Stay Close

By 1998, Gibson's premier product was doing very well in the marketplace. However, many prospective customers still asked for a *red* hot sauce. Gibson answered with Vib's Southern Heat, a fiery mixture of cayenne and Habañero peppers, vinegar, salt, garlic, and xanthan gum.

My heart wasn't in it, but I made it because you still have to give customers what they want. I thought that if people wanted a red hot sauce, let me give them a red hot sauce; and those people who have the red, maybe they will try the yellow sauce, and vice versa. I think it was a good move on my part because it gave me two facings [slots] on supermarket shelves. Now Southern Heat is outselling Caribbean Heat.

By introducing a second sauce, Gibson was beginning to develop a much-needed and anticipated product line. But with more products came more work. Prior to developing Southern Heat, she made all of the sauce herself. It was cheaper to do the work in-house, so she imported the Scotch Bonnet peppers needed to create Caribbean Heat, cleaned them, and prepared all the ingredients for blending. Now Gibson had a new hot sauce to deal with and no permanent staff to help her.

I started contracting out the Caribbean Heat when I started making the Southern Heat because it was just too much for me to do both. Both require slightly different procedures and ingredients. So, to have to set up and break down a totally different production for each was just too difficult to do on my own. I was able to get my formula for Caribbean Heat to a point where a bottling company could make it for me, so I handed it over. It increased my costs because I definitely could have made the product cheaper myself using a staff, but the headaches of managing a staff in a full-fledged manufacturing facility is not something that I wanted to deal with. I had employees before, with the catering business, and found that it just took up too much of my time. I didn't want to spend my time, my money, or my efforts managing people who may or may not have come to work. I felt as though my time would be better spent finding customers. Today, I contract out the manufacturing of Caribbean Heat, Southern Heat, and Vib's Bar-B-Q Today. When my sales are high enough and my volume is high enough, it will make sense for me to bring manufacturing back in-house with employees. But right now I think my time is better spent finding buyers than mixing sauce myself.

Turning over the production of her chief product was not easy for Gibson, physically or psychologically. She had grown accustomed to having total control over every aspect of her operation. Now she was putting a piece of it into the hands of strangers.

The very first time that the bottling agency actually made some product and put it in the bottle was probably the scariest point of my whole adventure in this business. I was so nervous about what I was going to actually get because once

I identified the bottling agency, it took six months before they were actually ready to make it. Some of the products they used were slightly different than mine and it didn't always work. I would make five gallons at a time, but they were making 75 gallons at a time, so the whole process of blending it, mixing it, how fast they blended it, and the size of the mixer all made a big difference in the appearance and texture of the sauce. So it took six months of them trying it, showing me, me rejecting it, and us just trying to figure out what was best. I had a slow mixer with a wire kind of beater that stirred it. They had this powerful thing that whipped it and gave it a totally different appearance. It made the pulp of the cayenne and Habañero peppers too fine. The sauce was just too homogenized and it looked almost like mayonnaise. So we had to work all of that out. It was a slow process.

Once the formula was finished, Gibson had to find a buyer. But even though she already had a product on store shelves, getting space for Southern Heat was not automatic. In fact, Gibson still had to make her pitch.

For a while, Schnucks was operating no stores in the black community. So when I heard that they were opening one in North St. Louis, a predominantly black area, I grabbed my new product and headed for the opening reception. I told them about my new pepper sauce and had it on hand for them to try. The next couple of days, I had two facings of Southern Heat on their shelves. When launching a new product, you have to seize the opportunity to sell it when that opportunity presents itself. You can't wait for someone else to make the pitch for you. Then you have to follow-up. There have been many occasions where I would go into other Schnucks locations to check and see if they had my hot sauce on the shelf. If they didn't, I would say, "Where is her red sauce? I heard she has a red sauce. I saw her on TV and I hear it's at the warehouse." People would look around and say, "How do you know it's at the warehouse?" They didn't know it was me and it got the job done because, after playing the role of a concerned customer, my hot sauce would be in there in two days.

Gibson's hot sauces and seasoning have yet to spread nationwide, but they are blazing up the shelves in many Midwestern stores. Vib's Bar-B-Q Today is available in Schnucks; it retails for $2.39. Vib's Caribbean Heat and Vib's Southern Heat, which are carried in Schnucks, in Dierbergs, and in Straub's, sell for $2.69 and $1.99, respectively. The triple-X Vib's Caribbean Heat, available via her Web site and through mail order, is priced at $5.00 per bottle.

Gibson's sauces and seasoning are definitely high-end products. They sit next to hot sauces that cost $0.69 a bottle and 3 for $1.00. But she is not worried about the competition.

The price was a major issue initially because the consumer was used to paying much less for hot sauce, so I had to do some educating about why my product was more expensive. I let people taste it at the Black Expo, at street fairs, and at every place I could. Plus, I talked to people about how I developed the sauces and seasoning because that is what it took for people to buy them. Now my products have gained recognition through word-of-mouth and people telling others that it is a different kind of hot sauce, a better hot sauce than what they had been using. So I don't worry about cheaper priced sauces because I have regular customers and I know that those who want it will buy it.

Gibson looks forward to growing her business to the next level, which will include developing future products such as a prepackaged blend for stews and soups, a seasoning for sweet potato pie, and maybe a salad dressing. But she doesn't plan to go it alone.

For me to expand, to be able to advertise as I should, and to go into other products requires a lot of money. To sometimes get the money you need involves bringing in other people, so I'm looking very seriously at attracting investors right now.

Investors or not, you can bet that Gibson won't slow down. After all, old habits do die hard.

4

LORRAINE CARTER
CAPTION REPORTERS, INC.

A Woman of Her Word

When you start a business, you have to do your homework
first. I just jumped right out there not knowing a thing,
and . . . I paid the price.

In 1993, when Lorraine Carter entered the studio at WUSA,
Channel 9, in Washington, DC, she had mixed feelings. On one
hand, she was elated. A sole proprietor, Carter's home-based
business, Caption Reporters, Inc., had outbid the National
Captioning Institute (NCI), the world's leader in closed-caption
television, in securing a one-year contract to provide closed
captioning for the station's six o'clock evening news. And, unlike some entrepreneurs, Carter didn't pull any strings to net
the $170,000 agreement. Nor did she send an agent, attorney,
marketing representative, or extroverted partner to work the
deal for her. Carter made the pitch herself, emphasizing her
training and previous work experience as a court reporter.
Never mind the fact that she had never once written captions on
the air. Wielding her down-to-earth attitude, confident disposi-
tion, and, of course, modest bid, she convinced the station that
she was the best person for the job.

But on the other hand, Carter was scared stiff. Ironically,
NCI, a major competitor, was the same company that had refused her a job within its ivory towers just five years before she
launched her business. Carter was certain that her rival would
be watching with a critical eye, so she was determined to prove
her ability to caption.

Captioning, a process that creates written transcription of the audio content of live broadcasts, is an exacting skill that requires speed, precision, and consistency. NCI claimed that it was a level of expertise that she would never master. Carter remembers the rejection well.

It was 1988. NCI was offering a ten-month paid training program to teach captioning. Those who completed the course and passed a series of accuracy tests were hired by the company to work as caption reporters and were sent to television stations all over the nation. It was a totally different terrain for Carter, who, by this time, had logged four years as a court reporter for the District of Columbia (D.C.) Superior Court System. But it promised a welcome change from documenting the gory details that often unfolded at the courthouse, so she enrolled in the course. But when she finished and took the tests, she failed. NCI, unwilling to review her exam, help her work through her problem areas, or give her an opportunity to take the test a second time, simply dismissed her and said that she was not good enough to work in the industry.

> So you can imagine how shocked NCI was when I, this little old black girl, got this contract with this major television station, because they were the ones who told me that I couldn't do it. So when I got ready to go on the air, I was extremely nervous because I knew that they were watching and waiting for me to make a mistake so they could feel like they were right all along. When the theme music stopped playing and the anchor said, "Good evening. I'm Doug Hill . . . ," I just sat there. The people in the control room said, "Go, Lorraine." But for a few moments I couldn't type one word because I was paralyzed with fear. I eventually typed, but because I put so much pressure on myself to prove that I could do it, I made all kinds of mistakes. For example, Doug Hill, the news anchor, came out Dog Hill one time. It was tough. I remember going off the air and crying because I made so many errors. But the people at the station were very supportive and assured me that I would get better.

Those on the outside weren't as encouraging. In fact, after the newscast was over, Carter received several complaints—many from the same colleagues who initially slapped her on the back and congratulated her when she got the job. Determined not to let the negative feedback get her down, she worked tirelessly to hone her skills. She arrived at the television station five hours before airtime to practice writing captions on tapes of old newscasts. To help boost her confidence, she also surrounded herself with nothing but positive people. In fact, unless someone had something encouraging to say to Carter, she didn't want to hear it. There were times when she could not escape the barrage of negative comments, but Carter responded by simply practicing and practicing, and then practicing some more. Perhaps more importantly, she never wavered from her belief that she could do it.

> *I'm a woman of my word. So when I say that I'm going to do something, I mean it. When I bid on the Channel 9 contract, I didn't do it just for fun. I honestly believed that I could handle the work, and I was determined to prove to the naysayers that I could.*

Two weeks after making her debut, Carter was writing with ease. She had silenced her caption counterparts, developed a renewed self-confidence, and caught the eye of potential clients who would later become substantial accounts. Like all successful business owners, Carter exemplified the drive needed to make a go of a tough and humiliating situation. And she walked through it always with her head held high.

Carter launched Caption Reporters in 1993, out of her home and with just one client, Channel 9, and one employee, herself. Today, she runs a three-person operation from a 1,350-square-foot suite a stone's throw from the Potomac River in Old Town Alexandria, Virginia. A full-service real-time captioning company, Caption Reporters provides closed captioning for television stations, government agencies, corporate and private organizations, sporting events, press conferences, and conventions. Using word-of-mouth as her sole source of advertising, Carter has generated an impressive client roster that includes The National Institutes of Health (NIH), Channel 13 in Toledo, Ohio, and Gallaudet University, the country's largest and most prominent school for the deaf and hard of hearing. Until 1998, she also captioned for the Federal Communications Commission (FCC).

Carter provides both on-line and off-line captioning for her clients. With on-line captioning, she writes captions primarily while on site and at the time of the program's origination. However, she can produce them in-house and then, using a modem and phone line, feed them electronically to out-of-state TV stations. Off-line captioning is done strictly in-house and involves a process whereby captions are inserted on prerecorded programming, such as training tapes produced by corporations.

Essentially, Carter helps to serve the over 24 million deaf and hard-of-hearing people in the United States by transcribing verbatim every word that is uttered by her clients in front of an audience. And that's no easy task. The average person speaks anywhere from 230 to 250 words per minute. Using a 22-key stenography machine (which doesn't even cover all the letters of the alphabet), captioning software, and a computer, Carter helps the deaf population see what they cannot hear.

Here's how it works: Let's say Carter has to write captions for the 6 o'clock news at Channel 9. She obtains information about the District from the local chamber of commerce. For instance, she gathers details such as the names of city officials, schools, streets, and counties—any particulars that are likely to be mentioned in a typical newscast—and creates, in shorthand, a dictionary of terms that are specific to the locale and, ultimately, to the broadcast itself. Carter also gets information from the television station, including the names of newscasters and the phrases that are frequently used during the program. A steno machine has only 22 keys so she types in shorthand, not one alphabet letter at a time as with a typewriter or computer. On a steno machine, one stroke can be equivalent to a word or an entire phrase (which allows her to write at a speed of 230 words per minute). When Carter begins captioning, she can hit just one key to write several words simultaneously. When she builds her dictionary, she programs words or phrases using a single letter or combination of letters and stores the list on her computer. For example, if the newscaster says, "Good morning" during every broadcast, Carter may program the letters G and M into her computer to spell out the phrase "Good morning" when she strikes the keys on her steno machine. When the newscast is ready to roll, she pulls up her dictionary, which is linked to her steno machine, and writes using that reference. Carter also uses a permanent dictionary of over 130,000 everyday words programmed in shorthand, such as "school," "water," and "snow." As she writes captions, the shorthand transmissions are encoded, merged with the television signal, sent to the television station's distribution network, and presto! the captions, after being decoded by a device built into viewers' TV sets, appear on home screens—and all in a matter of seconds.

Sounds like a process that only a bespectacled, pocket protector-wearing techie could handle. A tall, round-faced woman who wears smart business suits and spends her spare time playing racquetball, Carter is hardly the type. But she knows the captioning business well. Admittedly, acquiring the necessary knowledge didn't come easy. In fact, much of her learning process has been through trial and error.

> *When I first started captioning for Channel 9, I didn't have a lot of help. I remember when I submitted my bid for the contract I had no idea of what constituted a good bid or how to write one. I was just flying by the seat of my pants. I couldn't get any of my colleagues to tell me the ins and outs of contract bidding because captioning is a very competitive business. I basically had to figure things out on my own. Luckily, the station's chief engineer, with whom I had spoken in the past, worked with me because the first bid I sent to Channel 9 was too high. It was well beyond what captioning companies would charge for their services, so he gave me some hints on how to research rates.*

But Carter's troubles didn't stop once she landed the account.

> *When I went to purchase captioning software, I applied for credit and was turned down, so I decided to purchase it with cash, using the $30,000 advance I received from the station. Well, what should have been a smooth exchange ended up being an unnecessary chase. I called the salesman at the store and said that I was interested in buying the software because I was preparing to caption for Channel 9, but he wouldn't call me back. I left several messages, but he ignored all of my calls. Finally, I had to go to the station and ask that they call the store for me. It was only after they made the call*

that he called me back to sell me the software. But when he came to my office to set it up, he would not review important parts of the applications with me. I came to find out later that he was a good friend with all the major caption companies that bid on the contract, but lost; so he was trying to make it difficult for me to get the materials that I needed. Having to deal with situations like this were not uncommon for me because there were people who were envious of my position and who didn't want to see me make it.

This petty game would be just the beginning of the obstacles and rejection that Carter would later have to overcome to maintain her business. From that experience, she realized that working in captioning was not going to be easy. But then again, nothing in Carter's life up to that point ever was, so she braced herself for resistance. This wasn't the first time that she had hung out a shingle. Carter ran a small court reporting firm in Seattle, Washington, in the early 1980s, so she knew generally what to expect when running a business. Like so many new business owners, one of her challenges was finding the funds to operate her company. But securing capital was not her only dilemma. Recruiting and retaining experienced employees was also a problem. Carter would pluck prospective employees fresh from the graduating classes of some of the nation's most notable court reporting schools, take them under her wing, and train them in the art of captioning. But after the lessons were done and her employees had racked up a few months, or maybe a year, with her company, they'd leave for greener pastures. Carter didn't know how to keep them on board. To add insult to injury, her rivals refused to acknowledge her as any "real competition," and caption companies that bid on the same contracts would rush to undercut her offers. Then there was the constant rejection she experienced from government agencies that issued grants to caption companies to provide closed captioning for stations that could not afford to pay for the service.

I would apply for captioning grants with the same skill level, same equipment, and same experienced captioned reporters as my larger counterparts, but I was constantly turned down. I was paying out thousands of dollars for some of the best grant writers to help me write the proposals, but I would never get the funding. There was a point in which we were constantly being turned down for grants. Then I couldn't get financing from a bank because we needed to have more contracts, but I couldn't get more contracts without getting the grants, so I got really discouraged and even thought about just closing down. My accountant even suggested that I just file bankruptcy and go work for somebody else.

That suggestion fell on deaf ears. Even though Carter was feeling whipped, she persevered. She has always been a go-getter, refusing to settle for what lay before her. Carter is ambitious and just as aggressive and hardworking as her larger competitors. And it shows. Carter, 47, clocks an average of 60 hours per week servicing clients already under contract and soliciting new ones to add to her register. If she is not working in-house putting captions on corporate training tapes or political spots, she's prepping for the evening news in the control room of an area television station. Carter, who prides herself on providing personalized attention for her clients, can even be found in the ivory halls of academia, providing one-on-one captioning for deaf students attending universities that do not have special provisions for the deaf population.

I basically sit there with my laptop computer, write captions for everything the teacher says and the student watches the conversation on the computer. This service is very helpful to deaf students because it allows them to be a part of the class, ask questions, and do whatever they need to do.

This type of service is one of the things that set her apart from many of her larger counterparts, who prefer only to produce captions in-house and feed them over phone lines to their clients. Still, this one hallmark has not been nearly enough to generate the receipts of her rivals. Company revenues are a modest $200,000 annually, in an industry where her counterparts are making millions of dollars. But Carter is confident that new legislation regarding closed captioning will help to boost her bottom line.

The Americans With Disabilities Act and the Television Decoder Circuitry Act, passed in 1991 and 1993 respectively, paved the way for Carter to start her business. Later, she generated even more revenue as a result of the Telecommunications Act of 1996, which requires closed captioning of all video programming.

There are a bunch of laws coming into place that will work in our favor. With all the rejection that I have experienced, that's part of what motivates me to continue growing my business.

Rule 1: Never Box Yourself In

Starting a business was the last thing Carter ever anticipated doing in life. Like the generations that came before her in her hometown of Toledo, Ohio, she expected to graduate from high school and head straight for the assembly line at one of the area's car factories. Staying true to this visionless tradition, Carter did just that.

Nobody encouraged me to do anything outside of working at one of the factories. My mother never talked about me going to college to broaden my horizons. She never brought it up because she couldn't afford to send me to school, so college was a word that simply was not in my vocabulary—and neither was entrepreneurship. There were no business owners in my family, so the thought never even crossed my mind to start my own company. My plan after high school was to just get a job.

After earning her diploma in 1971, Carter had her first child, got married, and began working as a water inspector at American Motors—in that order. She climbed in and out of cars on the assembly line, and checked each for leaks in its structure. She earned a decent blue-collar wage, but Carter wasn't happy. It took her only two months on the job to realize that she could not and would not spend the rest of her life playing Inspector Gadget.

The money was good, but I hated that job because I realized that it boxed me in and painted an unrealistic picture of what I was capable of achieving. It limited my opportunities and had begun to damage my self-esteem. For example, I had to wear jeans all day long. I used to come home from work and dress up, just because I needed to remind myself that I was a lady. I didn't go anywhere. I just sat around in my good clothes. That was just one aspect that I didn't like about the job. Another was that I wasn't using my brain. I knew that I was smart and that I wanted to do something different. I just didn't know what. Well, one day I was reading this magazine and there was a picture of a woman getting out of a taxicab. She had on a business suit and was carrying a briefcase. She looked so professional. I thought to myself, "That's what I want to be—a businesswoman." I wanted to do something that allowed me to use my mind and be a productive member of society. So I kept that image in my head because it reminded me of what I could become.

By 1974, Carter was emotionally worn out from working at the factory. Her marriage was on the rocks, so she decided to move to Seattle, Washington, to live with an aunt. She had no idea what she would do after making the cross-country move. She just knew that she needed a fresh start, so, with her two-year-old daughter Dawn, she headed for the West Coast. For the next two months, Carter scrambled to find something that fulfilled her life. First, she enrolled in Seattle Central Community College to study nursing. Realizing that taking care of the sick was not her true calling, she ditched her nursing studies and tried her hand at becoming a police officer. But Carter failed to follow through on this endeavor as well. Before she even set foot in the academy, a very indecisive Carter moved back to Toledo. But her stay was not permanent. Six months later, she moved back to Seattle, this time for good. She resumed her search for a satisfying career. When her aunt introduced her to Robert Thomas, a black court reporter and a family friend, she finally found a promising possibility and the path that would ultimately lead her to starting Caption Reporters.

He took me out to lunch and I remember sitting there listening to him tell me what he did for a living. At first, I said, "Oh, that's nice." I had never heard of anything like it. I mean I had seen the little steno machines, but that was it. Well, this guy had his own business and was working as a court reporter, so I started asking him questions about what school he went to, and he told me. I didn't tell him that I was going to go look up the school, but the minute I got home I called the admissions department. They told me to come in for an interview, so I did. They let me play around with the equipment and I was totally hooked. I liked it because it was something that immediately drew my attention to it. So afterwards, I filled out all the necessary paperwork, applied for financial aid, and the next thing I knew I was studying to become a court reporter.

By 1975, Carter was a freshman at Awerswald University. However, the business school soon fell on hard times and closed down. Carter then transferred to Edmonds College, in Linwood, Washington, a suburb of Seattle, to finish her studies. She also began working part-time in the claims department at Allstate Insurance and attending school at night. Carter was finally realizing her potential. She was excited about school and what could become of the little black girl who grew up poor, wearing nothing but bargain basement clothing. Carter was determined to imitate the image of the briefcase-toting woman in the magazine advertisement, and no one and nothing was going to stand in her way, not even the grim statistics that revealed the number of African American court reporters.

When I was attending court reporting school, there were probably about 30 people in my class. Of that number, only five were black. By the time I transferred to Edmonds College, that number dwindled down to three, and when I graduated, I was the only black left. The dropout rate was real high back then, and to this day is still high for court reporters, black or white, because the course is so grueling. You have to be able to learn stenography, which isn't the easiest thing to do, write at speeds of 225 words per minute in order to graduate, and pass your courses in English, accounting, and other basic classes. I hung in there because I was determined to make something of myself. There was a time near the end of my schooling that I stopped working and went on welfare so I could focus on my studies. I was getting food stamps and the whole bit. But I was able to feed Dawn and finish school.

It took nearly four years, but, in 1979, Carter graduated with a certificate in court reporting from Edmonds College.

Her next stop: Thomas's office.

Rule 2: Don't Be Afraid to Go It Alone, But Make Sure You're Prepared to Fly

Carter didn't waste any time working her contacts—a skill indicative of a business owner in the making. Before the ink could dry on her business school certificate, she had lunch with Thomas.

"Guess what: I went to school and I am ready to be a court reporter," Carter said. "Get outta here. No you didn't," exclaimed Thomas.

"Yes I did," she replied.

Shocked, but impressed by the revelation, Thomas gave Carter a job in his court reporting firm, Thomas & Tamfer & Associates, in the heart of Seattle. Carter worked as a freelance associate and was assigned to take depositions for lawyers. She received a percentage of the work that came into the office, but it didn't take Carter long to figure out that her boss was going to hand over only so many assignments. Not surprisingly, he and his partner kept the bulk of the work for themselves and threw Carter a bone here and there. The money she was making was hardly enough to live on, so Carter set out to generate her own clientele. After all, she had the skills and the equipment, and since she was not a permanent employee of Thomas & Tamfer, there was no conflict of interest. Through the assignments she did receive at her job, she met an attorney who did not have her own court reporter. Carter asked for and got the open position.

The woman worked for the Attorney General's Office in Seattle, so Carter began taking depositions for all of her cases. She now had the very first client that she had found on her own. Shortly after, through word of mouth, she acquired her second. Although Carter couldn't see it at the time, she was slowly building a business all by herself. And, like any great entrepreneur, she started to generate ways to expand her customer base.

> *I started making a little bit more money because of the clients I was soliciting on my own, so I got this brilliant idea to send all the secretaries of the lawyers who worked in the Attorney*

General's Office flowers to celebrate Secretaries' Day. I wanted to impress them, and hoped that my gesture would encourage them to put in a good word about me with their bosses. I spent, like, $150 on flowers and had them delivered to this whole row of secretaries. As a result, my business picked up tenfold. Next thing I knew, as I sat at my desk at Thomas & Tamfer waiting for them to give me an assignment, I got all these calls from the Attorney General's Office, asking me to do depositions. The guys at the office would see me packing up my stuff, and they would ask me where I was going. Although I was never really considered an employee with their firm, I think they did resent me finding work outside the office. So after their answering machine started to fill up with nothing but messages requesting my services, they told me that I couldn't answer the phone anymore. One day, I missed three calls because they wouldn't let me touch the phone. I had to respect what they said because it was their company, so one day I said, "I don't know why you won't let me answer the phone. I don't think it's right because now I'm starting to build my own clientele, so what I am going to do is just move next door into my own office so I can answer my own phone." They cracked up laughing. They thought the idea of me having my own business was the funniest thing. But they didn't laugh too long.

A woman of her word, Carter picked up her supplies and moved to a small space adjacent to Thomas & Tamfer. The fact that Carter had her own business didn't seem to bother the boys next door at first. They continued to call Carter whenever they needed her to fill an assignment. But after a couple of weeks, they stopped giving her work. That didn't matter much to Carter; by this time, her phone was ringing off the hook. In 1981, she put her name on the door, officially marking the launch of Everage & Associates (Everage was Carter's last name from her first marriage). Six months after she set up shop, Thomas & Tamfer moved out of the building. Carter was unsure why they packed up, but she didn't have time to investigate or even to care. Work was coming so fast and furiously that she had to hire an employee. Finding an eager prospect was easy. Carter had formed numerous friendships with other court reporters in the area, so she simply spread the word that she needed help, and help arrived. The hard part was managing the worker.

I felt awkward because I was now responsible for someone else's livelihood, and that's scary. Also, since I was telling this person what to do, it put me in a position where I was in charge and I didn't quite know how to handle that. One of the things I found particularly challenging, in operating Everage & Associates and Caption Reporters, was figuring out how to talk to my employees. I treated them like they were friends, and I quickly found out that I couldn't do that. There were several occasions, when I operated both businesses, that my employees and I were laughing and talking, and because I gave them the impression that we were friends, when I asked them to do something that they didn't want to do, they rebelled because they didn't take me seriously. I would say, "Excuse me," and then have to jump back into the role of boss and that was uncomfortable for me. It's OK to always respect each other, but your employees must know that it is a business relationship because if they get too comfortable with you then they become misguided and that will only hurt your operation.

For Carter, as with so many new entrepreneurs, making the transition from employee to employer was a huge adjustment in many areas, but Carter was not afraid to go it alone. She worked through her problems, mainly through trial and error, and continued to build her customer base. It seemed to be the one thing she did best in operating her company. With no marketing budget to guide her, she generated clients solely through word of mouth and received the bulk of her work from the Attorney General's Office. Others heard about her business and requested her services as well. Carter earned a modest income by charging a fee per page for depositions. But things soon fell apart. Her lack of business experience started to have a profound effect on the company. Her operation appeared to be booming when it was actually taking a beating. Because she knew nothing about financial planning and management, she struggled to pay her bills.

Those she could pay were seldom paid on time because she often had to wait nearly 45 days to receive compensation from the city government offices in which her clients worked.

Things got so bad that I had my phone cut off right in the middle of a real busy period because I couldn't pay the bill. I was able to pay the one employee I had when the money would come in, but she would have to wait just like I would have to wait. When I did get the check, I would pay her first, then settle my other bills. I would advise new business owners who operate on a shoestring budget to pay their employees first because you need them to keep working.

With her business on shaky ground, Carter lost many of her clients to more established court reporting firms. Then came problems with the Internal Revenue Service (IRS). Carter knew nothing about the types of taxes she had to pay, so she just didn't pay taxes. One day after visiting her neighborhood bank to make a deposit, she realized that ignorance would hardly be enough of an excuse for cheating Uncle Sam.

I went to the bank to put some money in to cover my bills, and the lady behind the counter told me that the IRS had accessed my account to settle back taxes. The money I deposited that day also went to Uncle Sam. I was devastated, but from that experience I learned everything I needed to know about the IRS and the taxes that I had to pay as a sole proprietorship.

Down but not out, Carter borrowed $5,000 from a friend to help ride out the difficult times. It helped, but it wasn't enough to sustain her for the long haul. After two years in business, she called it quits. In 1983, Carter sold her business—ironically, to Thomas. A year later, she moved to Washington, DC, with only $3,000 in cash and her hope that she could land a position with the District's Superior Court System.

A friend of mine told me that there was an opening there for a court reporter. Since my business didn't pan out, I thought, "Why not give it a try?" I didn't want to totally scrap the idea of being a business owner because I enjoyed being my own boss. I just knew that there was a lot I needed to learn. The main lesson that I picked up from operating my first venture is that, when you start a business, you have to do your homework first. You have to know your industry, your competition, how to attract and keep clients, and how to properly manage your cash flow. I should have written a business plan to help me outline all of these points, but I didn't know how or even that I needed one until later in the game. I just jumped out there not knowing a thing, and as a result I paid the price.

Rule 3: Be Careful Not to Make the Same Mistakes Twice

With entrepreneurship on a back burner, Carter spent the next four years recording the details of some very interesting, very horrific, and very sobering trials held at the DC Superior Court System. However, by 1998, she was fed up with her job and ready to reclaim the American Dream. Carter, now married for a second time, entered the training course to learn captioning at NCI. But after a humiliating finish to the program, she went back to her old position at the courthouse. Not willing to let the new skill she had acquired go to waste, she used her spare time during the next several years to talk to television stations about providing captioning for them. One of her prospects was WUSA, Channel 9, in the District. Carter approached the station with a bid in 1991. Two years later, Channel 9 accepted her offer and Carter took another crack at ownership by starting Caption Reporters, Inc.

Excited by the feat, Carter set up shop in the basement of her home. Her main need was for an area where she could handle administrative tasks. She provided on-line captioning at the time, so the bulk of her work was done on the premises of Channel 9. Her overhead was minimal: She had no staff. Still, she needed capital to acquire captioning software and other equipment that she would soon need if she offered off-line captioning as well. The captioning software cost about $7,000, the stenography machine cost about $2,000, and the BETACAM machines (used for off-line work) ran anywhere from $7,000 to $14,000 apiece. Then there were costs for computers, VHS deck players, and a separate phone line.

Plus, there was no way I was going to start this business without having my lawyer and my accountant in place. I learned a lot from the mistakes I made in operating Everage & Associates, so I was not going to go wrong this time. So that meant an extra added expense for their fees.

Carter needed $50,000 to cover all of her start-up costs. She approached a neighborhood bank to obtain a loan. As collateral, she had to put up the $30,000 advance she received from Channel 9, her house, and her equipment.

When I look back on what I did to get this loan, I was foolish. By putting up all of these things, I gave the bank three pieces of collateral when I really should not have had to, and was paying interest on my own money. In hindsight, it was really stupid, but I did it because I had no knowledge of bank loans or how to choose a lender that was best for me. Once again, I didn't do my homework when I should have. Plus, it was the first bank that ever said Yes to me, so I thought I would just go ahead with the loan, use it as a way to build a rapport with the bank, make my payments on time, and later on go back and get some more money when I needed it.

Working the contract with Channel 9 was difficult in the beginning. It was Carter's first time captioning on the air, so it took about two weeks of writing a lot of gibberish before she was able to generate a clean copy. By the end of her first year, she was a real pro. Impressed by her work, Channel 9 renewed her contract for a second year at a slightly lower fee of $150,000. But Carter was now getting all types of phone requests from government agencies and other organizations that wanted her to provide captioning for them, so she was able to maintain a steady cash flow. Never once did she place an advertisement to promote her services; instead, she relied on word of mouth to expand her customer base. In early 1994, Carter added the FCC and some smaller groups to her client list. She wasn't beating the bush to get these other clients; her first concern was to make sure that her business was running smoothly. While she was under contract with WUSA, she started getting calls to do other assignments for both on-line and off-line work. That changed the size of her business, so Carter moved her business out of her home and into a rented office space in the District. She also brought in her first Caption Reporters, Inc. employee, a graduate of a business school in Des Moines, Iowa.

After doing more research about the captioning field, Carter found that this particular school, and others like it, churned out reporters who were caption-ready, so she contacted the administrators about interviewing graduates. Carter soon developed a recruitment strategy that involved taking prospective employees from top court reporting and business schools across the country, and then training them herself, if necessary, in the process of captioning. That approach seemed to work well, or so she thought.

My competitors would let me sit there, do all the dirty work required to train my employees, then they would swoop down and recruit them away from me. But what I have done to help retain employees today, and what I advise other new business owners to do, is to develop contracts that bind them to a certain number of years working for your business. This is particularly important if you operate a company in a specialized field like mine, where finding talented workers is not all that easy. You need to get them to sign a contract for as long as you think you might need them. However, you should have an out-clause in the contract because I truly believe that if an employee is unhappy and wants to leave, then he or she should go. There is nothing worse than having a disgruntled employee working for you. I also try to pay my employees what they are worth. Money is always an incentive to get them on board and get them to stay.

Unfortunately, this was a lesson that Carter learned *after* the competition had lured away her worker from Iowa. With an influx of work from newer clients, including Gallaudet University and Channel 16, losing her employee wasn't the best thing that could have happened to Carter. But it wasn't the worst either. Other caption reporters were waiting to be hired. Carter brought in three, plus an engineer to provide technical support. Normalcy was restored, and the business was running smoothly again.

Then, in 1996, Carter lost a major contract and was forced to restructure her entire operation.

Rule 4: Be Persistent When Going after Capital

After three and a half years, Carter lost her contract with Channel 9. A competitor had underbid her for the job.

> *They bid it so low that there was no way that I could match that, or go even lower, and keep my doors open. I was devastated initially and very scared because it was my bread-and-butter contract for the first several years of my business. I was afraid at first because I wasn't sure if I would survive. But then I realized I also had been building the company up during the time I had this contract, so even though I lost it, I still had other work that would generate income for the business.*

There *were* other clients. Still, Carter thought it best to cut her overhead expenses, to keep from bleeding too much profit from the business. She met with her accountant and started to trim the fat. The first thing to go was her swanky $2,600-a-month office suite in the District. Carter had rented such lavish digs because she erroneously thought it would make a difference with securing clients.

> *But nobody cared that I had this plush office, and since I did most of my work on-site, no one really got a chance to see it. They only cared that I could do the work and do it well. It took me a little while to realize that. I just wished I had realized that sooner because I could have saved a lot of money.*

Carter found an office in Old Town Alexandria, Virginia, that could be rented for half the cost of her previous space. It saved her a nice amount of money, but Carter needed more working capital. For additional funds, she traveled back to her neighborhood bank, but her welcome was far from warm.

> *They told me from the beginning that they were not going to give me any more money. But I also wanted to refinance my house to free up some cash to help fuel the business but the loan officer said "No." I said "Well, why not?" She said, "Well, we're just not going to do it." I said, "Well you need to*

sit down and talk to me about options." She said that neither she nor the president had the time to talk to me. I told her that I was going to sit right there in the lobby until she found somebody that did have the time, because I didn't have anything to lose but my business and my home. So she walked back into her office and let me sit on the couch from 9:30 in the morning until the bank closed at 5:00 P.M. I was furious, but determined to stand on my word. For them to not have the time or even the interest to talk to me, a patron of their bank with money in an account and good credit, was incomprehensible to me. So I sat there. I said I was not leaving and I meant it. By 2:00 o'clock I got up and went to the bathroom, but that was it. I didn't even eat. At 2:30 P.M., the loan officer came out and said, "Ms. Carter, I have been instructed to ask you to leave the bank, and if you don't leave the bank, we are going to call the police." Well, that was so humiliating to me. I told her, "You go back and do what you were instructed to do because I am going to sit right here until somebody comes out here and talks to me about my options." Now, the way the lobby was designed, the elevators opened up into the waiting area. So I'm sitting there reading the newspaper over and over again, and every time the elevator would open I would get apprehensive because I thought the police were going to step off and slap handcuffs on me. By 3:30 P.M., the president of the bank came out and said, "Ms. Carter, we thought we would give you one more opportunity to leave the bank." I said, "That's kind of you, but I will be right here until you call me." The police didn't come, but 5:00 o'clock did. At the end of the day, the receptionist got up, turned off the lights, and left me sitting there in the lobby. Finally, at about 5:10 P.M., I said to myself, "Go home, fool. Nothing is going to happen today." That was one of the lowest days of my entire life.

However, Carter wasn't about to give up. Her business depended on her persistence, so she prepared herself for round two.

The next morning, I got up and went back to the bank at 9:00 A.M. I made sure that I looked really nice because, if I was going to jail, I was going to be professional about it. This time

I took my cell phone and laptop computer. I set up shop right on their lobby table. The vice president of the bank walked in. I said, "Good morning," but he just looked at me and walked away. The waiting began. They let me sit there until about noon. Then someone came out and said, "OK, Ms. Carter, we will see you now." I snatched up my stuff, didn't say a word about what they made me go through because I didn't want to blow up in their face, filled out the paperwork to refinance my house, and went about my business.

This would not be the first time Carter would encounter overly protective and highly judgmental financiers. After downsizing her company, she stepped up her efforts to secure government grants to provide captioning for television stations and other organizations that could not afford the service. She had actually started this paper-intensive process when she launched her company in 1993. She had yet to receive one grant, but she was still attracting clients. She started captioning for the National Institutes of Health (NIH) in 1997, and did some work at a seminar in Bermuda in 1998. Still, she continued to lose scores of other potential accounts—and a few existing ones, including the one she held with the FCC—to larger and more established caption companies because she simply did not have the financial resources to service them.

There was one period where all of a sudden it got real slow, and I was looking around and asking myself, "Is the phone working?" I think part of the reason why I have lost many opportunities at securing contracts over the years is because the Department of Education and other government agencies, which give captioning companies millions of dollars in grant money to provide captioning, give the funds to the same companies over and over and over again. Therefore, when it comes time to bid on a contract, they can underbid me considerably because they can afford to. I went on the Internet one day to see exactly who was getting what in terms of grants, and I had to go home and lay down. It was just amazing to see the millions of dollars that are being handed over to the same people year after year. I just couldn't understand it. We have the same skill level, same equipment, and same experienced staff. The only difference between my company and my competitors is that they have the money to advertise and market their businesses and I don't.

Carter worked diligently to find ways to get the funds and increase her customer base. She enrolled in the Small Business Administration's 8(a) program—the nation's largest federal procurement program available to small, disadvantaged businesses. She even spent $12,000 to commission some of the best grant writers, to increase her chances of nabbing the millions many government agencies were doling out.

Still, no grants.

One time, the Department of Education turned me down because they said my office was too small to do captioning— and they hadn't even been to my office. Anyway, all I needed was a stenography machine and a computer to do the work, and, most of the time, the captioning was done on-site, so I didn't quite understand that comment. Another time, I applied for a grant to provide captioning in the Virgin Islands. I even traveled to the Islands to demonstrate the process and get a feel for its deaf and hard-of-hearing population. The television stations were very interested in having captioning, but they couldn't afford it. Once again, even after doing all of that preliminary work, I was turned down for funding after I submitted my proposal. They said that the Virgin Islands was too far away to provide captioning. My thought was that whoever was reading the grant proposal didn't really know that much about captioning because captioning doesn't have to be done on-site. It is possible to caption over a modem and phone line with the same two- to three-second delay you have when you are physically on the premises. Then they said that the deaf population was too small. So they would always use ridiculous excuses like that to deny me grant money.

Although Carter was turned down constantly, she was hardly willing to take "No" for an answer. She applied and reapplied for as many grants as possible. Her persistence paid off. In 1999, she received her first grant from the Department of Education to provide captioning for Channel 13 in Toledo, Ohio. It was for far less than the amount she had requested, but it was a start.

We applied for almost $250,000 in grant money. They gave us a three-year grant for $78,000 each year. But it's a beginning. It makes us authentic. Now we are on their Web site as one of the caption companies that have obtained a grant through them, so it opens up the door for more opportunities.

And Carter can hardly wait to take advantage of them. Although business is steady and she is pleased with her progress, she's not completely satisfied. Seven years after inception she wants and expects more.

More money.
More clients.
More respect.
And she doesn't plan on stopping until she gets it—*all* of it.

I have been a businesswoman nearly my entire life. So becoming a big-time entrepreneur is something that I want to do and plan to do, no matter what.

With that attitude, Carter is bound to make her millions yet.

5

ALONZO WASHINGTON
OMEGA 7 INC.

A King of Black Comics

I want to make money with my business, but I also want to make a difference.

Look up in the sky.

It's a bird.

It's a plane.

It's . . . Omega Man?

That's right. Move over, Superman and Batman. There's a new superhero in town. He's strong. He's black. He's socially conscious. And he's here to enlighten as well as entertain the masses. Omega Man is the last of the great warriors: a brawny, superintelligent protector from the future, from a society void of poverty, crime, drugs, racism, and violence. Moving at the speed of light, Omega Man travels back in time to track and destroy an alien spy posing as the President of the United States. Wielding archaic and prejudiced ideas, the imposter president intends to implement laws that could change the course of time. If Omega Man finds and destroys the enemy, he saves the future. If he doesn't, the perfect society from which he comes is altered forever. So up, up, and away he goes, soaring through the skies to complete his mission. After being briefly duped by an alien decoy, Omega Man resumes his search for the operative, kicks some serious alien butt, and protects the paradise to come.

93

Pretty interesting story, right? Well, there's more. Omega Man is only one of a handful of socially supraliminal comic books published by Omega 7 Inc., one of the nation's few black-owned comic book companies. Alonzo Washington, a lifelong comic book buff, launched his Kansas City, Kansas-based business in 1992 with just one title, *Original Man,* a story about a black superhero/scientist from the future who comes back to the present to fight criminal aliens. Today, Washington has five more titles, all named for individual characters he created over the years: *Dark Force, The Mighty Ace, Omega Man, Original Boy,* and *The Omega 7.* And as in the first title, all these superheroes tackle serious and sensitive themes such as political corruption, police brutality, discrimination, and sexually transmitted diseases, including HIV, the AIDS virus. Each copy of *Dark Force* is packaged with a condom, to help promote safe sex among teens. A seventh comic book title is in the making. Washington also currently produces a series of ancillary products such as T-shirts, hats, watches, and trading cards branded with his slew of caped crusaders. Then there is the Omega Man action figure. Washington added the pint-size superfighter to his team of politically correct products in 1997. His was the first black-owned comic book company to produce such a toy.

Unlike traditional comic books, Washington's titles, which have sold over 100,000 copies, have a serious edge. There are no Bart Simpson-like characters who make crank phone calls to their neighborhood bar, and no Superman clones who are cloaked in black and fighting archenemies on planet Crypton. Instead, Washington's black characters include Dark Force, a political activist who fights corrupt cops; Shadow Knight, a DEA agent and high-tech martial artist who brings down drug-dealing politicians; and The Mighty Ace, a wealthy engineer who makes weapons for the government. These heroes, and their missions, have been created to bridge the gap between the haves and have-nots in the black community, but Washington's comics still offer all the high-energy action and colorful artwork that comic book fans love to see. Essentially, his comics are a creative mix of space-age fantasy with a powerful dose of reality. Through his black superheroes who battle racism, crime, and violence, Washington's goals are to present positive black images for black youth, break the age-old stereotypes that depict blacks as being poor and uneducated, and address various social and political issues.

So far, he has been successful.

Although an independent black comic book publisher, Washington has carved a niche in a $500-million industry that was formerly dominated by such giants as Marvel Comics and DC Comics. In the process, he has earned nearly $1 million in revenue. By taking the comic genre into uncharted territory, his content has sparked the interest of politically correct readers and ignited the tempers of some staunch conservatives. By some, his comics have been labeled radical and controversial. Others have simply dubbed them foolish propaganda. When he introduced the first couple of issues, he received hate mail from many people who claimed that black superheroes had no place in society. But Washington, also a social activist, did not let what he calls "blatant racism" derail his business. If anything, the opposition that he has encountered has brought more attention to his company and his cause. He receives invitations to speak before various organizations throughout the country. Washington schedules hundreds of speaking engagements each year, to talk about the social issues that affect the black community in general and black youth in particular. In those discussions, there is always a reference to Omega 7.

My positions as a comic book publisher and social activist are intertwined. So when I talk about youth violence or some other issue in front of kids, I generally incorporate Omega 7—and what I have done with the comic books—into the discussion. It gets them interested and excited about creating change because they see, through my comic books, that they can make a change. Of course, when I travel around the country, I want to make money with my business, but I also want to make a difference.

Like his characters, Washington is strong, serious, and determined. But he's also a bit mysterious at first glance. Typically dressed in black and wearing dark sunglasses that hide even a hint of his eyes, he rambles into a room, scans the area, and then turns toward his destination. But once he's sitting, talking, and even laughing about the challenges of building his company, it becomes clear that this culturally conscious comic book wonder has nothing to hide.

Omega 7 is a business that Washington has built virtually by himself. From the moment he started his company, he has worn multiple hats as creator, developer, administrator, marketer, and salesman. The only full-time professional on hand is his accountant. His wife Dana and his mother Millie, a substitute teacher, help with the administrative tasks of operating the business. Dana also dresses up like Original Woman, one of Washington's superheroines, and travels to schools to talk to students. The rest, however, is left up to Washington.

Working from his den—which looks more like a comic book and toy store than a place to lounge—he designs all the comic book characters and writes every story line himself. A self-proclaimed master marketer, he promotes his comics without the aid of a public relations or advertising specialist. And he pitches his products to toy buyers without using a broker. Washington has almost single-handedly financed his business over the years by injecting into it nearly $200,000 in personal savings and in funds borrowed from family members. Unlike most entrepreneurs, he has never tried to get a bank loan, not even for start-up capital. It's not that he couldn't have used the money. Growing up in a single-parent household in the inner city, he had no trust fund from which to pull the cash. He just didn't want to shoulder the debt, so he saved. Now, every cent he makes goes back into the business to create and develop more products.

For Washington, raising money to fuel his business has not been especially challenging. However, getting some stores to carry his products, particularly the Omega Man action figure, has. Several large toy retailers, even those with minority supplier programs, have been reluctant to carry Omega Man. Those who have agreed to stock the toy have taken only small orders and have placed the products in select outlets in the black community. The response doesn't shock Washington, nor does it deter him from working even harder to get more exposure for his products.

Omega Man descended on independent comic book shops in 1997. Pleased but not satisfied with its placement, Washington approached major toy chains and refused to take "No" for an answer. As a result of his aggressive approach, he managed to get several Toys 'R' Us, Kaybee's, and Wal-Mart stores to carry the toy. (It is also available through mail order and the company's Web site: www.omega7.com.) The comic books, available via mail and the Web, are also sold through Diamond Comic Distributors Inc., the world's largest distributor of American comic books and a representative of over 4,000 retailers, and through United Brothers and Sisters Communications Systems Inc., also a distributor of comics. Both companies supply his titles to comic book specialty stores and cultural shops throughout the nation. There have even been Omega 7 superhero sightings abroad.

I received a letter from a guy in Switzerland who wanted me to draw something for him, sign it, and send it back because he saw one of the comic books and liked it. I don't know how my comics got over there, but I'm glad that they have.

Rule 1: When Scouting Business Ideas, Consider a Hobby and Trust in It Even When Others Don't

When Washington decided to become a business owner, he didn't have to look long and hard for an idea. Like many entrepreneurs, he simply transformed a hobby into a successful venture. For the 33-year-old father of six, that hobby began long before he was even out of elementary school.

As a pubescent kid growing up in the Sunflower State, Washington loved to play. But, unlike his peers, it wasn't sports that attracted his attention. It was comic books.

- *Spiderman.*
- *The Justice League.*
- *Archie and Jughead.*
- *Teen Titans.*

You name it. He had it. Washington began reading comic books as early as he can remember, but, like any adolescent, he had no intention of using his favorite pastime to someday build a business. Washington was busy being a kid, so at first he just read the comics and then tore them up. But, before long, he began to develop an appreciation for what he was reading and to think about how he could use comic books to create a consciousness he felt was missing in mainstream society. By age ten, he was collecting and poring over his comics with an insightful eye. Two years later, he began to recognize a disturbing trend among the black characters that appeared throughout the current comics' pages.

> *The role models in the comic books were attractive and doing the types of things that I wanted to do. They were powerful people going against violence, crime, and other wrongdoing, but the characters weren't black. Those that were black were always doing something stupid or were pictured as a criminal, streetwise thug, or just somebody that nobody wanted to be. They were never the super-heroes who came to save the day or fight the bad guys. They were the bad guys. So I started to develop my own characters and draw my own comic books using black su-perheroes that would do the same things as the white su-perheroes did. Half of the characters that I publish now I made when I was a kid. For example, back then I created a character called Super Ace, which later became Mighty Ace, and I made a superhero team called the Guardians of the Galaxy. I created black characters doing things that they didn't normally do in mainstream comic books. I had black characters that could fly spaceships and fight ghosts and monsters. I gave them the power to fly like Superman and break down walls with their bare hands. I created charac-ters that I wanted to be as a kid and that looked like me.*

But Washington didn't stop with just comic books. He also constructed his own action figures. Always the creative type, he would take biweekly trips to his neighborhood store, buy action figures that were for sale there, and press Afros, which he had made from clay, atop their heads. He would paint the faces of the figures and give them names that he liked. Washington's cre-ations were a hit among the neighborhood kids, so he began thinking that he could create a business based on his hobby. For-get the traditional lemonade stand that most youngsters experi-ence as their first taste of entrepreneurship. Washington sold his homemade comic books to friends and other children in his town for 25 cents apiece. But his artwork got an entirely different reception at school. Teachers thought Washington's work was cute. But, in their opinion, it wasn't going to get him anywhere in the "real world," so they discouraged him from even trying to pursue his dream.

There was really no outlet to be creative in school, so I would draw and write comics on my own and share them with people that I knew. My teachers would see it and say "You made and wrote all of this? That's great." But then they would turn right around and in the same breath say, "But you can't do that when you grow up. You have to get a real job." I think I always knew that I wanted to do something with my comics as I was going through school. And I think that I could have been doing it professionally as early as 17 and 18 years old if I had been told that it was something that I could achieve. But I was being taught that I couldn't do it even though I had the ability, so it was really confusing for me to figure out what I should do because what I wanted to do was not encouraged.

Washington began his education at a Catholic elementary school, but spent most of his years attending public school. A good student, he made the honor roll several times. Still, he was not very fond of the classroom. The curriculum bored him. And, unlike most students, he didn't get caught up in the cliques that seemed to define many pupils. He wasn't the jock, the outcast, or the roguish rebel. If anything, he was simply a creative talent with a passion for the arts. But Washington was also an articulate and outspoken individual who questioned and challenged the thoughts and theories of those around him. Washington was bothered by many social issues, particularly the lack of support for black students within the educational system, so he channeled his anger onto the pages of his comics by creating stories that addressed his concerns.

I had teachers who just did not care. I saw white students being pushed to be leaders, whereas black students were being shaped to just get a job. In junior high school, I was able to see teachers give speeches in which they would essentially say, "I've got mine. Now you need to get yours." I thought teachers were supposed to help you, so to hear them say that was just mind-boggling to me. But it was also an eye-opening experience and indicator of what I needed to do to help make a difference in my life and in the lives of those who were being discouraged. Ultimately, publishing my comic books became just one way of doing that.

Like the comic book heroes he grew up reading about—the ones who challenged the wrongs of society—Washington wanted to take a stand to affect change. But the harsh words of his teachers regarding his comics continued to echo through his head. Giving in to their advice, he tucked away the boxes filled with characters he had sketched over the years and even stopped adding to his personal collection, which had reached the thousands. Washington thought he would try his hand at becoming a social activist instead. In that way, he could still trumpet his cause. But Washington felt he would need a hook to get people to listen. Perhaps becoming an entertainer would give him the leverage he needed to reach people with his words. After all, who didn't listen to or look up to celebrities? He was determined to use his other creative talents—singing and dancing—to take him where he wanted to go.

After graduating from high school in 1985, Washington entered the freshman class at Kansas City Community College. After one and a half years there, he transferred to Pioneer Community College in Penn Valley, Missouri. He majored in liberal arts and formed a group called the Black National Congress to encourage young black men to avoid gang activity. But a separate school in media and communications made him realize that he could make a difference without all the lights, camera, and action. The program, called the KC Media Project, was a two-year course from which students could graduate. Washington learned about the effects that media organizations have on society and perceived how he could create his own outlet for voicing his concerns. After graduating from the program in 1989, Washington put into practice all the theory he had learned. He started producing his own community affairs television talk show, which addressed issues concerning the state of Black America. Then he began holding rallies at area community centers, schools, and churches. He talked to his peers about the importance of presenting *positive* black images in the media. It was tough talk that he had never heard beyond the four walls of his childhood home in Kansas City. Nor was it something that he had read about in school or seen on television (except during Black History Month). Washington felt it was time for a change. An abundantly confident and driven young man, he thought he was as capable as anyone else and could help to make it happen.

Before long, his activism career was in full swing and extended beyond the Kansas state line. With his focus on transforming the black community and the world's perception of it, there was never any sign that he would pick up his sketch pad again. Well . . . at least not until he came up with an appealing way to reach restless adolescents with his message of social change.

As I began to develop my career as an activist, I began to get more and more requests from people who wanted me to come and speak to kids. I thought to myself, how could I communicate my message to them in a way that they might find interesting and that would go beyond me just standing in front of them and talking. Then it hit me. I thought about creating a comic book because kids love to read them, and what we read shapes the way we think. I already knew how to write and draw comic books because I did it as a child, so I decided to try the idea again. Instead of using white characters that would save the day, I developed positive black characters that were fighting crime, racism, and other problems in society. Growing up, I saw a lack of black role models on television and in comic books. I would look at different cartoons like Fat Albert and wonder why we always had to be surrounded by junk. Then, when I would read comic books, I'd see black characters being portrayed as villains, ex-cons, or comedic sidekicks. After seeing those types of depictions, I would say to myself that we had to make black characters that were better than that. So I did. I created Original Man to break some of the stereotypes. Original Man is my first comic book as a professional entrepreneur. It was supposed to be one tool that I would use to help raise black kids' self-esteem. So I did it not really expecting it to grow into a business, but the response to it was so overwhelming that it actually turned into a successful venture—the venture that I knew all along in my heart would work.

Rule 2: Use Guerrilla Marketing Tactics to Sell, Sell, Sell

Back in the comic book business now, Washington had to find ways to finance his venture. Although he received honoraria from a few of his speaking engagements, they were hardly enough to get his publishing business off the ground. Washington needed to raise $5,000 in start-up capital to pay for printing and other production costs of his first comic book. Never wanting to seek a bank loan, he thought of alternative ways to raise the cash. Meanwhile, he looked through the Yellow Pages for a printer and continued to give talks in which he trumpeted his plan to produce a black and white comic book called *Original Man*. Everywhere he went, he promoted the idea. The feedback was so positive that people started sending him money to buy it before it was even published. He received $1,000 in advance orders—just enough for a down payment to have 3,000 copies printed. Then, in 1992, Washington took the issues to a booksigning at a cultural shop in Kansas City.

> *I really didn't want to do the signing because I didn't think anybody was going to come. But 1,000 people showed up and everybody purchased a comic book. The comic book cost $2, so I made $2,000 that day. There was also a correspondent there from* Newsweek *magazine that ran a story about me and the comic book the following week. Afterward, people from all across the country began to write in to me for copies. The response made me see that there was a thirst and interest in something that I had been doing for such a long time, so I decided to start a business doing what I have always loved to do.*

Washington took several additional orders for copies of *Original Man* at the booksigning. With the money he received, he paid off his balance at the printer and walked away with $30,000 in sales from his first issue. Washington was on his way to developing a very lucrative business. He set up shop in the den of his home and began reading books on publishing and on how to incorporate his business. He also decided on a name for his company.

Omega 7 is really just a code name I use to describe what the company is about. Since what I am trying to do is present positive black images for all of America to see, by using the word Omega, which in Greek means "the end," what I am saying is that, in the end, or after using my products, you will see a positive representation of African Americans.

Washington's fresh approach to producing comic books attracted the attention of the press and several major comic book distributors. After reading an article about Omega 7 in *Newsweek*, Diamond Comic Distributors Inc., a Minnesota-based distributor, called Washington about listing his comics in its catalog. Diamond, which supplies popular titles such as *Batman* and *Superman* to comic book stores across the country, began ordering Washington's comic books too. United Brothers and Sisters Communications Systems, another distributor, also contacted him, but major retailers declined to carry the comic books because of their political content. However, Washington didn't worry. He continued to push his product on his own. He burned up the roads attending every Black Expo, church function, school program, bookstore reading, community event, and any other location where he saw an opportunity to peddle his products. Washington also talked with law enforcement officials about ways to incorporate his products in their campaigns. As a result of that promotional effort, in 1998, the Kansas City (Missouri) Police Department began issuing trading cards featuring three Omega 7 characters to schools and circulated them throughout various neighborhoods as a part of its anticrime crusade.

How's that for guerrilla marketing?

There's less than 30 black comic book companies in the nation right now, so there's really no network or support system for black comic book publishers. Therefore, I have to think, on all levels, what I can do to inexpensively promote my products myself. As a small business owner, you often have to find creative ways to spread the word about your business because you probably won't have the money to advertise on a large scale. I'm always thinking of alternative ways that I can cheaply advertise my products, whether it's by making special appearances at some location via my activism work or setting up a booth at some cultural event. Using this approach has made a difference in my business, and I think that it is one of the keys to my success.

Rule 3: Expand Your Product Line to Stay Competitive

Although he was a newcomer to the comic book industry, Washington didn't seem to fear the competition. Lesser opponents would have become uneasy, given the growing number of independent black comic book publishers at the time. They seemed to be coming out of the woodwork—all vying for culturally conscious readers. Milestone Media Inc., then a New York-based black-owned comic book company (but now defunct), was just one of those that entered the industry in 1993 and, like the others, touted multicultural characters and themes. Also tapping into the black comic book market were Marvel Comics and DC Comics, both which continued to flirt with their own ethnic characters and topics. Washington knew that, to stay in the game, he would have to raise the stakes. And that meant expanding his product line. Having one title was simply not enough.

Using profits from the first product, in 1993 he published 10,000 copies of his new release: *Dark Force.* Dark Force is actually a character that appeared in the *Original Man* comic book. Essentially, to create many of his titles, Washington has taken single characters from the first issue and made them the main character in a separate comic book. *Dark Force,* which deals with AIDS and political corruption, is considered to be Washington's most controversial comic. The main character, an African American activist, is finally assassinated by the government. *Dark Force* also speaks to what Washington calls the "double standards of racism in society."

Dark Force is almost a carbon copy of a Dirty Harry or Batman type of character. He does all the things that they do in the exact same way, but because he is a black character doing it, he is labeled as being radical or controversial. For example, in the comic book, I have a scene where Dark Force shoots two corrupt police officers that are beating up several gay guys. Well, one day I did a Black History seminar for a school that had a mixed student population. But a lot of the white parents who came out had reservations about the comic book. They asked me, "Why did you have the character kill the cops?" It seems as though if Clint Eastwood is in a movie, says "Make my day," and then kills a cop, it's acceptable. But if a black character does the same thing, he's considered controversial or just plain wrong. I did this comic book to open up discussion about this double standard that seems to exist in our society when it comes to what black characters can do versus what white characters can do.

Always a forward thinker, Washington also used his first few characters to jump-start a line of ancillary mail-order Omega 7 products.

I try to come up with other items that will help me make more profit. The first day Original Man came out, I was also selling T-shirts with the character on them. Then, as I created other titles, I gradually added cups, watches, clocks, candy, and other items on which I could display my characters. If you are a small business owner with a product-oriented business and you have a variety of things to offer your customers, you have more of a chance of making money. In my case, some people might not read comic books, but they might want a T-shirt or a watch with a superhero on it, so I created these additional products for those types of customers. I think that the more product you have, the better your chances of selling something to someone.

Washington seems to be a master whether he is cashing in on his cultural wares or creating story lines for his comics. He's never at a loss for prose or pictures, and he is quick to pen a script or pencil a scene. He can write a story in less than a day, and illustrate an entire book in a matter of a few weeks. Although he prefers to work alone, he occasionally uses independent artists for minor portions of the artwork. For example, he may subcontract an artist to *ink* the characters—a process in which black ink is added to the penciled drawings of the comic book.

> *As I began to get into comics, I found out there are so many artists out there that cannot get jobs in the industry because it is so competitive, so I feel kind of obligated, now that I've gotten a foot in the door, to hire some of them. I've probably worked with about four different freelance artists, but that's not on a regular basis. I may use them to do a poster or a trading card if their work is pretty good. The good thing is that I don't have to solicit help. I get so many letters from artists looking for work that I can just pick and choose who I want to use.*

But, as with his first two comic books, Washington worked solo when producing those that followed. In 1995, he created *The Mighty Ace*, the story of a rich black engineer who joins forces with his sidekick Popsicle, an urban hip-hop character, to track down his nephew's killer. That same year, he released *Omega Man*. A year later, he followed up with *Original Boy*, and, in 1997, with *The Omega 7*, in which characters from the preceding issues band together to form the first all-African American crime-fighting team. Washington reinvested $36,000 of the profits made from the first two issues to finance production of his succeeding titles.

By 1997, Omega 7 comics had generated $600,000 in annual revenue and made the pages of *Black Enterprise* and *People* magazines, and *USA Today*. Washington has received coverage on the CBS Evening News, Entertainment Tonight, HBO, and National Public Radio, as well as on a number of local radio and TV stations in Kansas City.

Rule 4: Never Take "No" for an Answer, and Check Your Product Movement Regularly

Washington has never been one to rest on his laurels. It's just not his style. So, as he published his comic books and churned out his accessories, he thought about creating yet another profitable product. He called it Omega Man, a six-inch toy with African American features, including a long braid that runs down his back (a symbol of African royalty) and a multicolored bodysuit.

I created it because it furthers the mission of what I am doing with the comic books and because it was the next logical step for me as a comic book publisher. Once you have a comic book, you should go to action figures, then cartoons, and movies if possible. I want to do all of that, and this was just one step in the right direction.

With no knowledge of how to manufacture a toy, Washington began researching the process in 1996. Through contacts he made in the toy industry, he found unlimited numbers of U.S. manufacturers who could make the product from his design, but their prices were too high. He inquired about overseas factories, but was met with comparable costs plus a language barrier. Frustrated by the process, Washington designed and created his own prototype, but found little interest among buyers, so he continued to promote and sell his comic books.

Then one day, Washington received a faxed correspondence from a manufacturer in Hong Kong who had heard about his business and wanted to start producing action figures for small independent comic book companies. He immediately contacted the firm and discussed the cost. The price, including the mold, prototype, packaging, import taxes, and shipping costs, was around $350,000. It was still high, but not as high as the others that he had researched, so he moved forward with the project. He created a design, dictated how he wanted the action figure to look, and, using $15,000 of his own money, paid the factory to make the mold. From the mold, the prototype was constructed. Now it was time to market his upcoming product. Shifting into a sales mode, Washington began to tease his upcoming action figure on TV shows and in other media where his comic books received coverage. He put together lists of toy buyers and then approached them one by one.

First up—Toys 'R' Us.

I sent them my promotional materials on the company and tapes of me on television, talking about the toy. So when I met with a toy buyer at Toys 'R' Us and showed him the prototype, he said that the store wanted to work with me and that they wanted me to keep showing them the product as it went through its development stages. When the action figure was ready for retail, they said that they would take an order.

And they weren't the only ones. Diamond Comic Distributors was also interested in his newest cosmic product and preordered several thousand. Transforming the purchase order into a letter of credit—a method of bootstrap financing in which a business owner uses customer orders as security to pay for production costs—Washington paid the remainder of the expenses to have 20,000 figures made. After six months in production, Omega Man landed in 1997.

At first it was available only in independent comic book shops and through direct mail order from Omega 7. Washington had to secure liability insurance before the product could be placed on the shelves of major chain stores. But after getting the proper coverage, Omega Man entered selected Toys 'R' Us outlets in minority communities in 1998. A Toys 'R' Us store in Kansas City sold out of the action figures just two hours after they were stocked. The retailer then increased its orders nationwide.

Washington was excited by the positive initial response to his toy and the potential for more sales. Moving right along, he met with Kaybee's, another popular toy chain. But here he met some resistance. According to Washington, an assistant to a toy buyer at the store kept him from getting his product on the shelves for an entire year.

Omega Man should have been in Kaybee's the same year it went into Toys 'R' Us, but . . . the assistant to a major toy buyer there was not passing along telephone messages that I left. Initially, when I met the toy buyer, he expressed interest in wanting to carry the action figure and asked that I get back to him, but when I called I could never get through to him. When I finally did talk to him, a year later, he asked why I waited so long to get in touch. I explained to him that I was leaving messages, but he said that he never got them. I wasn't surprised because what I experienced with Kaybee's was not an isolated event. Prior to that, I met with some other toy buyers who were just completely negative, who only wanted to carry brand name toys, and who simply refused to take a chance on a new and exciting product. But with Kaybee's, I refused to take "No" for an answer and, because of my persistence, I was able to get Omega Man on the shelves.

After much prodding, Kaybee's topped Washington's list of clients in 1999. Right on the heels of that coup came Wal-Mart, albeit reluctantly.

> *Wal-Mart placed an order for 10,000 Omega Man in December 1999, but it took me two years to convince them to take the product. They lost my paperwork a thousand times and bounced me around to a thousand different departments before I was put into contact with someone who could actually help me. But I didn't let the circumstances stand in the way of my ultimate goal that was to get Omega Man into as many top name toy and retail stores as possible. As a new business owner, you have to be aggressive—and you have to keep coming back again and again and again until the customer says yes—if you want to be a success.*

Getting major retail outlets to make shelf space for Omega Man has been Washington's biggest challenge. Like many small toy makers, he has had to sell hard, place strategic calls almost daily, and set up back-to-back meetings to secure a single order. Ironically, this has been the protocol even with companies like Wal-Mart, which have minority supplier programs in place.

> *What's interesting is that the majority of these major chains that I have approached about carrying Omega Man have minority vendor programs, but none of them have taken an order except for Wal-Mart. K-Mart and Target, both of which have these programs, have not taken the toy. In fact, I have found myself wasting my time with these department stores because once you go through all the paperwork required, get certified by the National Minority Supplier Development Council, and all the other requirements to prove that you are black, the person in the program can't even order your product. That person then has to put you in contact with a buyer, who you must then try to convince to buy your product. I think minority supplier programs are crap because they always seem to have a black figurehead at the top who cannot do anything. It's just a matter of having a black face in a high place.*

Washington doesn't give much credence to minority vendor programs. Nor does he place his entire trust in the toy chains that do carry his products. He often plays the role of "toy cop" to ensure that his merchandise is well stocked for customers. History has proven the need for that role: Washington found that, after filling an order for a Toys 'R' Us store some time before, its supply of Omega Man did not meet its demand.

There were people who could not find the product in the store. They would call me and order the action figure directly from Omega 7. So I investigated the problem and, in some cases, I found out that a lot of my products were sitting in the storage room. In other cases, the warehouse didn't accurately anticipate the demand for the toy, so they simply did not order enough from the beginning. As a result, when the stores sold out of the product, that was it, because they didn't reorder. An average toy order is 20,000 pieces. The stores I distribute Omega Man to will take an order for 3,000, 5,000, or 10,000 pieces at the most. It's good money, but the numbers are nowhere near what they take from larger mainstream toy companies. I think it has to do with the stores' reluctance to order a lot of black products because they feel like they are taking some sort of financial risk. They assume that the products won't sell. My response is: If I have someone from Kansas City calling me to purchase the figure at $10 (which is what it costs through direct mail) because they can't get it at a nearby toy store, where it's sold for only $7.99, clearly the customer wants it. The stores just have to be willing to stock enough of the product and, when it sells out, reorder. If you are going to deal with major retailers, you have to be aware of how things work. You have to ask questions, track the demand for your products, and then match that against the stores' supply. When it comes to selling my products, I even go so far as to tell the store managers to educate their personnel about my toy because I've placed anonymous calls to different locations and asked about Omega Man. More often than not, the clerk knows nothing about it and puts forth little effort to find out. These are the types of things that you have to do if you expect anything to happen.

Rule 5: Never Compromise Your Beliefs to Make a Buck

Omega Man, now Washington's most commercial character and lead selling product, is available in hundreds of Toys 'R' Us, Kaybee's, and Wal-Mart stores across the country. But it has yet to achieve widespread distribution outside of the minority community. That circumstance frustrates Washington, but it has not stifled his creativity. In fact, Washington has created The Omega Force, a collection of Omega Man action figures in differently colored costumes, and he has begun work on a seventh comic book called *Shadow Knight* and a second action figure called Dark Wolf. There are also plans for a special bound edition of all Omega 7 comics.

> *If I got a production deal, a staff of writers, and other personnel who could enact my vision, it would be limitless in terms of the number of comic books and action figures that I would create.*

This king of black comics wouldn't dream of stopping with just comics and action figures. He has plans to create video games and an animated TV series and/or movie. Over the past several years, Washington has met with numerous television and film executives to discuss film projects that would take some of his characters to the silver screen. He has held talks with HBO, MTV, Paramount Pictures, 20th Century Fox, Propaganda Films, Limelight Films, Miramax Films, and a production company owned by Wesley Snipes, who starred in the movie *Blade*, a character found in Marvel Comics. But he is cautiously optimistic about the interest that has been expressed.

> *I get the calls, but what I have found is that many of the studios want me to change my characters. One company that I met with was interested in doing a movie project, but said that they wanted to spice up one of my characters a little bit by making him an ex-convict or ex-drug dealer. My company's mission is to change those . . . stereotypes, so I wasn't about to compromise my characters just to get the deal. Superman and Batman are not ex-cons. I want my characters to be*

equivalent to mainstream heroes. I also want to stay away from doing a comedy because what I do is not comedy. I think that I have a unique product, but right now studios don't want to market it the way I want to, because the characters that I project are going against the image of what society considers to be "the good guy." I think my comic books and action figures present a perspective that a lot of people just don't want to see or hear.

Still, there's a very good chance that Washington could get to Hollywood—and on his own terms. After all, controversy does sell.

6

FRANK MERCADO-VALDES
AFRICAN HERITAGE
NETWORK

He's Mad about Movies

If you simply transform what you like and have a lot of passion about into a workable plan for business and capitalism, you can do well.

In February 1997, Frank Mercado-Valdes made history.

After years of building and nurturing relationships with advertising agencies and television studios to help grow his New York-based syndication and film production company, African Heritage Network (AHN), this smooth-talking, persuasive, and innovative entrepreneur did what no other minority-owned company had ever done. Mercado-Valdes struck a deal with Universal Domestic Television (now Studios USA) to purchase the weekend syndication rights to its popular police drama, *New York Undercover*. It was the first time in the history of broadcasting that a minority-owned business had bought an off-network series for syndication. Typically, television studios maintain control of their off-network properties and use staff to sell the commercial spots. But, impressed by Mercado-Valdes's track record of soliciting TV advertisers that targeted black households—the demographic with which *New York Undercover* was most popular during its run on the Fox network—Universal sold its national barter time to the program syndicate. The price was $8.5 million, a pretty hefty sum for a company barely five years

113

old to fork over. But it was worth every penny. Mercado-Valdes is scheduled to generate over $20 million in revenue as a result of the acquisition.

Not bad for the Bronx-born CEO who spent his early days of ownership with more lint than money in his pants pockets. But Mercado-Valdes, 38, has never been one to let circumstances—especially those involving a shortage of cash—stand in the way of his goals. When he decided to start African Heritage Network in 1993, he had little more than a $350-a-month rent controlled apartment in Harlem. But he had an idea born from a lifelong passion.

To Mercado-Valdes, that's all he needed to succeed.

His passion was for old black movies. His idea was to select film classics such as *Sounder, Shaft, Lady Sings the Blues,* and *Carmen Jones,* buy the rights to them on a temporary basis, package them in a monthly movie format, and offer them to television stations across the map. Movie packaging was hardly a new concept at the time. Larger syndication companies had been doing it for decades, and doing it well. But no earlier movie package offered in syndication had focused exclusively on films featuring African American themes, actors, directors, producers, and writers. So, even though others scoffed at the idea, Mercado-Valdes believed that it would work.

He was right.

By 1995, African Heritage Network had generated $4.5 million in revenue. Its "Movie of the Month" series, hosted by film legends Ossie Davis and Ruby Dee, who discuss the film's content and cast at the beginning of each broadcast, aired in tens of television markets across the nation. It lured scores of black viewers to their tubes. And it attracted major corporate advertisers such as Procter & Gamble and AT&T to the available commercial spots. Pleased with the company's initial success and excited by the potential for more, that same year, Mercado-Valdes expanded the business by introducing the African Heritage Primetime Network. A syndicated quarterly movie package, AHN *Prime* shows contemporary black movies such as *Glory, The Shawshank Redemption,* and *Mo' Better Blues* in the highly competitive and extremely profitable prime-time market.

The additional programming proved to be a great boost to the company's bottom line. In 1997, AHN earnings reached $10 million.

The "Movie of the Month" series had begun to air in over 100 markets, and AHN *Prime* was in more than 125 markets. Two years later, revenues doubled again. Mercado-Valdes had successfully filled a niche that had been ignored by mainstream enterprise. At the same time, he proved a point that he had made long before he licensed his first reel of film: Black business owners did not have to eschew ethnic markets in order to achieve success.

Some people say my niche has enabled us to grow from a $1 million company in 1993 to a $20 million company, which is where we are now. Others tell me that this niche assures that we will someday be extinct because the niche isn't big enough, so we have to grow. I especially hear this from hip-hopreneurs who are always saying that they want to be mainstream. Well, my response is, "While you all are running around trying to be mainstream because you want to go party in the Hamptons, I'll just stay black, servicing blacks for blacks by blacks." I want to be Bob Johnson [CEO of BET Holdings II Inc., a $178-million cable television and magazine publishing company which focuses on the African American experience]. *There's no shame in that. As I got older and heard about people like Bob Johnson and Earl Graves, I realized that there was not only a moral imperative to devote the rest of my career to perpetuating the culture of African people, but that ultimately the economic rationale was there. I realized that I didn't need to be big in the white world to be big in my own world.*

Today, Mercado-Valdes's world is on the tenth floor of an office building in the Wall Street district. Inside the modest, ethnically decorated suite, African masks and sculptures are carved into the company's decor. Huge posters advertising *Nothing But a Man, Do the Right Thing, Coffy,* and other black films hang from the ivory-colored walls. Throughout the spacious headquarters, a small cadre of young, highly paid, and well-spoken employees work independently. There is no stern-faced manager to periodically rally the troops, follow behind their every move, or pay surprise visits to their offices just to make sure work is in progress. In short, handholding does not exist at AHN. A results-oriented ruler with little patience for mediocrity, Mercado-Valdes tells his staff to sell ads, produce segments, write press releases, put together press kits, and do anything and everything else that is needed to keep his well-oiled machine running smoothly. Then he leaves them alone, trusting them to do what they do best. Rarely does he micromanage. When he does, his staff knows he is bored—and that's hardly ever his state. For Mereado-Valdes, there just isn't time to become bored.

On any given day, he can be found behind closed doors, simultaneously juggling a barrage of lengthy deal-making calls, poring over Nielsen ratings, signing employees' checks, and conducting staff meetings, albeit intermittently. But despite the ongoing activity, his energy rarely seems to dim. Even after five o'clock, he is still going strong. Mercado-Valdes does not synchronize his work schedule with any corporate clock. It is not unusual for him to call a 5:30 P.M. staff meeting that doesn't ends until 9:00 P.M. And even then, he still has stuff to talk about.

Mercado-Valdes has a gift for gab. He can prattle for hours about potential business ideas; words pour out of his mouth like water from the Great Niagara. He loves to share his vision with others; when he does, he's almost political in his approach. His speech, smooth and convincing, sways skeptics to his corner. His charming "win them over every time" attitude could be attributed to the fact that he was a media director for the 1988 presidential campaign. What better place to learn the art of persuasion than in a room full of politicos? The enthusiasm he exudes when introducing new concepts is so contagious that others can't help but become infected. These attributes, which are not uncommon to successful business owners, have helped Mercado-Valdes build the largest and fastest growing black-owned syndication company in the nation.

And that has been no easy task.

Rule 1: Find Something You Are Passionate about, Then Start from There

It's a classic rags-to-riches tale.

Perhaps one of the best you've never heard.

It's about a skinny black kid with Coke-bottle eyeglasses and straight hair like the late Nat King Cole. The kid grows up in the 1960s. He plays stickball outside his South Bronx stoop while his mother sits gossiping with friends about old Cuba and old Puerto Rico. His father, a Puerto Rican, is absent, but his maternal grandparents, both Cuban, help to rear him. His grandmother works as a seamstress; his grandfather, as a gas station attendant by day and a conga-drum player by night. Neither is literate but each understands the importance of learning. When their grandson turns 11, the entire family moves to Miami, where the prospects of education are hoped to be better. There they settle in a working-class neighborhood where pickup trucks and Confederate flags are the norm. He enters junior high school, but this wiry kid from a mixed New York neighborhood now has the only brown face in a sea of crème-colored classmates. Pointing, name calling, and hitting ensue. To protect himself, he begins to fight and uses his fists virtually every day. By the ninth grade, he's a potential boxer bound for the ring. He gets there and eventually earns several Florida Golden Gloves championships while in high school. But his grades begin to suffer. It's not that he isn't intelligent. Admittedly intimidated by being around so many white students, he just doesn't try. As a result, the once gifted elementary student transforms into a below-average pupil. In 1980, he graduates at the bottom of his high school class. He had dreamed of becoming a lawyer, but now, with little chance of getting into college, he heads for the Marines. After his discharge in 1982, he attends junior college. He transfers to the University of Miami one year later. There he studies political science and begins to feel the call of the courtroom once more. But a business idea tugs at his brain. He wants to put on a beauty pageant, so he pursues the idea and even persuades a well-known entrepreneur to help him see it through. But after just three years in operation, the business begins to falter. He becomes homeless and is sleeping in a cardboard box in front of a New York City church. Meanwhile, his former business partner rides around in limousines and sports Rolex watches. With death starting to look better than failure, the idea of committing suicide crosses his mind. But he quickly remembers his passion for entrepreneurship and soon regains his focus. In 1990, the business bounces back better than ever before. The newspapers are calling him the youngest African-American executive producer in television history. And, at 28 years old, he's making a modest chunk of change. Then the winds shift again. By 1996, his first venture has faded. But he's not worried. He's already three years into his second, which is generating $8 million in revenue.

When Mercado-Valdes, who because of a common Cuban practice carries his father's last name and mother's maiden name, respectively, talks about traveling the road to entrepreneurship, he is not afraid or ashamed to discuss the rough times. There were days in which he ate nothing but Vienna sausages. There were periods when he had not one dime to his name. And there were friends who betrayed him and a business partner who cheated him. But Mercado-Valdes reflects without hesitation. A bit of a frustrated comedian, he even shares funny anecdotes, occasionally blistered with expletives, about how, despite overwhelming odds, he has made it this far. A proud family man, he credits his grandparents for instilling in him a strong work ethic and the determination to follow his dreams. But Mercado-Valdes is also quick to look to the days when he worked on developing his first business venture, The Miss Collegiate African American Pageant, to help explain his quiet, yet meteoric, rise as a program syndicator. He created the pageant—a brains-over-beauty contest that became an annual syndicated television event airing in more than 75 markets throughout the country—over 15 years ago. But during that time, he learned the basic principles of entrepreneurship and some liberating lessons about ownership. He later referred to these lessons when starting and operating AHN.

I had no entrepreneurs in my family, so I had nothing to go on. My grandparents were working-class people with a sixth-grade education, so I didn't have a basis for understanding how to apply intellectual work into capital. So when the pageant came along, that's when I became an entrepreneur. Obviously, there were a lot of details about ownership that I didn't pick up while doing the pageant that were new to me when I started African Heritage Network, but I learned the basic elements [and] that allowed me to move forward with greater ease when deciding to launch AHN.

It all began in October 1984.

Mercado-Valdes was a senior in college. And, like many undergraduates soon to enter the "real world," he was thinking of ways to squeeze out the last bit of fun from his carefree youth. In a brainstorming session with his four Kappa Alpha Psi fraternity brothers, Mercado-Valdes came up with the idea to create a beauty pageant. To this precocious student, it was hardly a way of pursuing a lifelong dream of becoming an entrepreneur. At the time, he wanted to go to law school and become a big-shot attorney. Holding the pageant was, for him, simply a way to get more young black women onto the University of Miami campus, where the black population was only three percent, and where the sisters who were there only fussed over the football players. To fulfill his goal, he suggested to his frat brothers that they get all of the black college campus queens featured in *Ebony* magazine to compete for prizes and the title of Miss Collegiate Black American (the name was later changed to Miss Collegiate African American). If nothing else, it would give them leverage over the jocks. He had no money, no contacts, no business savvy, and no clue about how to put on a pageant. Nevertheless, Mercado-Valdes figured that if he just started something that he was passionate about, and built on that, he would have a good chance of making it a success. He would use this approach nine years later, when starting African Heritage Network.

> *As a business owner, I believe that if you simply transform that which you really have a lot of passion about and like into a workable plan for business and capitalism, you can do well. At 21, my passion was for girls. I thought a lot about girls, all the damn time, constantly, every day. I was too short to be a pimp so I knew that wasn't going to work. Plus, I thought I would really look stupid in that green hat with the feather that most pimps in the old black movies wore, so I figured I would give the pageant a try to achieve my goal, which initially at that time was just to meet girls.*

Mercado-Valdes and his frat brothers thought that the best way to convince the schools to allow their campus queens to participate in the pageant was to present their idea in person. They sent letters to many of the nation's historically black colleges and universities, notifying them about their intended visits. Mercado-Valdes had met Miss Fisk University at another pageant held in Miami, so he was able to persuade her to serve as the honorary queen for the Miss Collegiate Black American Pageant. So, with $200 and a gas credit card among them, the five frat brothers set out in Mercado-Valdes's red Camaro (a gift from a family friend) on a nine-city tour of black colleges.

None of us really knew what we were doing, so our business plan was simple. Get to the campus. Pitch our idea to the student body presidents. And hope that they say yes. Then when it was time to go to sleep, crash with frat brothers. Of course we didn't know who they were, but we figured that they would let us stay with them because we were all in the same fraternity.

The first stop was Bethune-Cookman College in Daytona Beach, Florida. Dressed in their Chess King suits, skinny ties, and pointy boots, the young men walked about the campus talking with students. Nearly all of the frat brothers continued to beam about the opportunity to meet a bevy of beautiful black women. Not Mercado-Valdes. His mission changed soon after his arrival. From the moment he got there, Mercado-Valdes was struck by the students' pride in their culture and their knowledge about so many black historical figures. Even though he had attended a university that had what was considered to be a first-rate and well-rounded curriculum, names like Maya Angelou, Phyllis Wheatley, and Paul Laurence Dunbar were foreign to him. Mercado-Valdes began to realize that doing the pageant was far more than just a means of meeting women. More importantly, it was a unique opportunity to build a business that would perpetuate the African American experience while rewarding the women for their academic excellence. Right then, Mercado-Valdes changed the focus of the pageant from beauty to brains; eliminated the traditional bathing suit competition, which did nothing to illustrate the contestants' intellect; and required a 3.0 grade point average (GPA) for all its participants. Looking to the future, Mercado-Valdes envisioned creating an annual event that would be televised nationally.

After Bethune-Cookman College, the gang headed to Edward Waters College in Jacksonville, Florida. Then it was off to Florida Agricultural and Mechanical (A&M) University in Tallahassee. Next came Spelman College, Tuskegee Institute, and Alabama

State University. At virtually every stop they made, the students were greeted with luncheons and receptions.

The student body presidents and leaders thought we were a big deal. They didn't know that the Miss Collegiate Black American Pageant was headed by a bunch of college kids who lived in the dorms at the University of Miami because they received professionally typed letters on stationery that said: "We're coming to your campus. We'd like to have a reception, meet your president and your queen and officially invite her to our next year's pageant." Half of them didn't realize that there hadn't been a pageant the year before. Of course not everyone gave us a warm reception. There was some college administrators who rolled their eyes and said, "Who are these kids?" But I was serious about the business and determined to make it work. Visiting the black college campuses made me realize that by living in practically all-white environments from the time I was 11 to 20 years old and by attending a predominantly white university, I had been missing out on the African American experience. Yeah, I was black, but I was raised white. And I knew that I wasn't the only one. Therefore, I decided, from that point on, that I wanted to spend the rest of my life building a business that would do nothing but perpetuate the culture of African people. That became my new passion. I didn't want the next generation of black kids who had dreams of becoming entrepreneurs one day to think that in order to be successful they would have to give up everything about their being black. I thought that if I could make the pageant a success, I could show them that they wouldn't have to deny who they were.

Rule 2: Borrow Credibility Until You Can Build Your Own

By the time the tour ended a month later, Mercado-Valdes and his clan had visited tens of black universities and colleges and received dozens of commitments from campus queens. They collected proclamations from several mayors and snapped photographs of their honorary queen with such renowned black figures as the Reverend Jesse Jackson and Andrew Young. They even posed their honorary queen with former Alabama Governor George Wallace. After weeks of burning up the roads, all of the preliminary work had been done. Now they needed money to put the pageant in motion.

Mercado-Valdes decided to approach the Miami City Commission and the Dade County Commission for funding. It seemed the perfect place to search for seed money, especially since both panels had just voted a $2 million grant to bring the Miss Universe Pageant to Miami for a three-year period. But getting the money wouldn't be easy. After all, Mercado-Valdes and his cohorts were just a bunch of college kids from Miami. To the outside world, they were nobody. They had no business experience and no concept of the cost of putting on a pageant, and they lacked a detailed blueprint of how they would carry out the event. It was highly unlikely that any financier, government or otherwise, would fund an idea that seemed destined for failure. Mercado-Valdes knew that he would need a few established allies on his side to lend support to his idea. More than anything, he needed the credibility that they could bring to the pageant. The question then became: How would he get it?

Having worked as an intern in the City Council's Office several years before, Mercado-Valdes met a lot of local politicians, businesspeople, and other professionals. Like any savvy entrepreneur, he began to work his contacts. First, he approached George Knox, then a hotshot Miami attorney and fellow frat brother. Playing the politician, Mercado-Valdes made his pitch.

The only reason Knox met with me was because we were in the same fraternity. But there was a political issue that I used, to convince him to support my idea. I had anticipated it and used it to give me leverage. I told Knox that, despite the fact that I lacked a track record, lived in a dorm room, and didn't pay taxes, the commissioners were going to fund the pageant because it would be difficult for them to explain to the black community why they gave $2 million to Miss Universe and not a penny to Miss Collegiate Black American in an election year and right after Miami had just experienced some of the most devastating riots in the city's history *as a result of a cop killing an African American. He couldn't argue with that.*

Impressed by his idea as well as his ability to articulate his vision for the business, Knox agreed to represent him. Mercado-Valdes also obtained the support of then State Secretary of Commerce Jeb Bush, and several more of South Florida's most influential figures at the time, to help form a board of directors. But he didn't stop there. He also went after one of New York's top guns, the chairman of Unity Broadcasting, Eugene Jackson.

For several months, Mercado-Valdes tried to schedule a meeting with Jackson. The appointment was made, then postponed, made, then postponed again. By February 1985, Jackson was ready to meet. He scheduled a 3:00 P.M. meeting with the young entrepreneur, so Mercado-Valdes bought the cheapest possible plane ticket to New York and got ready to make his pitch. Then Jackson rescheduled the appointment again. It was now set for the day after the original date, but Mercado-Valdes had already purchased his ticket. Being short on cash, he was unable to buy a new one, so he flew to the Big Apple anyway. He figured that he could stay with friends until his meeting. But when he got to the city, his friends were either unavailable or nowhere to be found. Mercado-Valdes had $50 in his pockets and about 18 hours to kill.

One of the problems I had as a new entrepreneur, that I know other new business owners experience, is that I had no credit card and I had no money. Therefore I had to improvise and be creative when it came to some of the things I needed to build my business. When I went to meet with Eugene Jackson, I didn't even have a coat. Because I had grown up in Miami, I was used to warm weather. I knew that going to New York in February meant that it was going to be cold, so I borrowed a coat from one of my frat brothers, but it had no lining so when I got there I was freezing. My meeting wasn't until 9:00 o'clock the next morning, so when I couldn't contact any of my friends who lived in the city, I spent large portions of the night at Chock Full o' Nuts. At 3:00 or 4:00 in the morning, the guy in the restaurant finally threw me out because I couldn't afford another cup of coffee.

After that, I just walked around for a few hours in ten-degree weather in Central Park. I walked and walked and then sat down, and walked some more trying to stay warm. When 7:30 A.M. rolled around and Unity Broadcasting opened up the building, I went inside and just sat there and waited for my meeting to start, which didn't actually take place until 11:00 A.M. It was rough getting through that night, but I was driven by my passion to show the economic viability of portraying the African American experience and determined to obtain the credibility that I lacked—and needed to make the pageant work.

Once inside, Mercado-Valdes, always smooth of tongue, was able to convince Jackson to become a member of the pageant's board of directors. Jackson also agreed to eye the progress of the event. With another solid commitment under his belt, Mercado-Valdes headed back to Miami to make his pitch for the cash, only he did none of the talking.

While doing the pageant, I learned a lot about borrowing credibility. Maybe it was just something that I instinctively understood, but I knew that if I was willing to let other people take the credit, I could get a hell of a lot done. I knew that my being out front would not have helped my cause because of my age and lack of experience. So, after I put together the brochure for the pageant and assembled a board of directors, I sent Knox to stand before Miami's City Council to ask for the money. They had no idea that they were voting on a proposal for $2 million for a bunch of kids living in a dorm room at the University of Miami. They just saw this organization, the Miss Collegiate Black American Pageant, with local community leaders on its board of directors, and this big-shot attorney, George Knox. They had no idea a college student was behind it all. So through his credibility and that of the other businessmen and politicians, we were able to get some funding.

The amount was nowhere near what he requested. But Mercado-Valdes obtained $35,000 from each commission and raised another $5,000 on his own. With the financing issue out of the way, it was time for production. Working another contact, he was put in touch with Peter Runfolo, who had served as production manager for the movie *Superman* and agreed to produce the pageant. Unfortunately, Mercado-Valdes was about to learn a harsh lesson about loyalty and commitment.

> *At the time, I was excited about Pete joining the pageant because he was involved with such a big movie like* Superman, *so I knew that he could make the event great. But three weeks before the production, he got a job as production supervisor of a movie called* Invasion USA, *with Chuck Norris, so he quit—and after I already paid him $5,000! And not only did he quit on me, so did my entire staff. He took all my damn staff with him and paid them each $300 a week. So suddenly I had lost all of my help. I was broke, trying to put on my pageant with no staff, and here are my frat brothers walking around wearing big snakeskin boots. The funny thing was that I created this opportunity for all of them and they just left me to do this movie for somebody they didn't even know. They felt no loyalty towards me. My frat brothers didn't see the vision I had for the pageant. They didn't have the long-term passion for it and didn't recognize the long-term potential of investing in our culture and perpetuating it outward. We had done the pageant up to that point as partners, so when they left, it frustrated me, but they gave me back their shares. The good news was that I got to own 100 percent of the business myself. The bad news was that it was 100 percent of zero.*

Frustrated but not panicked by the mass exodus, Mercado-Valdes booked the Miami Marine Stadium, an outdoor arena, to hold the pageant. He got several community groups to help organize the production, and he even talked Eastern Airlines, which was operational at the time, into providing free airline tickets for the 23 contestants. Mercado-Valdes also recruited local radio personalities as hosts, and took local rappers and dance groups off the street to provide the musical entertainment.

The pageant took place in April 1985. By all accounts, it was tacky. It rained off and on, so it took seven hours to complete. But the community looked past the cosmetic blunders to realize the long-term importance of holding the pageant. Here was a positive portrayal of intelligent African American women pre-Oprah Winfrey, pre-*A Different World*, and pre-*The Cosby Show*. The city's youth could use the women as a mirror to reflect what *they* could become through education and self-pride. For that reason, to the Miami community, the pageant was something worth holding onto. Going into year two, Mercado-Valdes, on his own, was able to convince the City Council to double his budget. He solicited more sponsors and obtained professional entertainers to participate. By this time, Mercado-Valdes had nabbed his political science degree, but by then it was just a piece of paper.

By the second year, the pageant had become who I was. It became so much of who I was that I couldn't imagine my life without it, and that's bad. I think that one of the difficulties entrepreneurs have is not being able to imagine their lives without their companies, and I think that drives a lot of them into very desperate situations that can really be dangerous. It's great to control your business, but you shouldn't let your business control you. Of course you can probably look at entrepreneurs whose businesses became a part of who they were and now they are, like Bill Gates. But by the same token, you can look at people whose businesses became a part of who they were, and because they became so absorbed in the company, they never recognized when it was failing so they didn't jump ship in time. As a result, they ended up drowning with everybody on board instead of having an exit strategy that might have allowed them to sail again. In my case, I felt it was too early to jump ship. Everybody else thought that I was just wasting my life, my energy, and my skills. And even though people were saying, "You are impressive, but this is never going to make you any money. You should work for me," I couldn't abandon the passion I held for the pageant. If nothing else, having this entrepreneurial spirit has gotten me a lot of good job offers. And I can't tell you, on the nights that I was deciding between gasoline for my car and a Burger King sandwich for dinner that taking that $25,000- or $30,000-a-year job, which at the time was plenty of money for me, wasn't given serious consideration. But when you've been a nobody your whole *life, at least in your own mind, and suddenly you can pick up the morning newspaper and read about how the entire community is calling you "gifted," something nobody has called you since you were in the fourth or fifth grade, and people are giving you a modicum of respect for the first time in your entire life, you can't let go.*

Rule 3: Be Honest with Yourself and Others About What You Can and Cannot Do

The pageant was slowly building a name for itself. Mercado-Valdes, who now lived in a three-bedroom apartment with two of his former high school buddies, was still penniless but was convinced that the pageant would soon pay off.

While standing in line at his neighborhood bank (to smooth-talk a teller into not bouncing checks he had written against an empty account, to pay bills), he ran into Eugene Jackson. Jackson's business was in New York, but the millionaire had a mansion in Miami to which he traveled on weekends to stay with his family. Mercado-Valdes had not seen Jackson since their first meeting. He took the second chance encounter as an opportunity to talk with him about getting more involved with the pageant. Fortunately, Jackson's newest venture, World African Network, a cable television network, created synergy with Mercado-Valdes's goal to bring the pageant to television. The two decided to partner in the pageant, splitting the shares 51–49 in favor of Jackson. Perhaps not a smart move for Mercado-Valdes; he would later find out that he was getting far less than his share. But at the time, it seemed to be the best way for him to turn his publicly funded pageant into a corporate powerhouse. Sponsorship was essential to the pageant's survival, and Mercado-Valdes knew that he would have to get bigger players if he wanted to stay in the game. He needed corporate funding, and Jackson was just the man to get it for him.

As part of the deal, Jackson agreed to fund part of the pageant and introduce Mercado-Valdes to some of his advertising colleagues as a way to raise the rest of the needed capital. In March 1987, Jackson took his protégé to New York to get the ball rolling. Mercado-Valdes met with Byron Lewis, CEO of UniWorld Group Inc., and several of his clients; they agreed to sponsor the pageant that year. The pageant still had not aired on television, but Jackson had taped it to have as a pilot show once he finally did launch his cable network. But when the curtain came down, Mercado-Valdes found that he had alienated those who risked their money, credibility, and clients to help him.

> *I made a complete fool of myself when interacting with Uni-World and burned some bridges that took ten years to repair because I just didn't know what I was doing. My ability to articulate a vision of what I wanted surpassed my ability to execute in such a way that Eugene didn't notice that I really didn't know what I was doing when we all met at UniWorld, and neither did Byron. They had no idea that I had no clue when it came to dealing with large advertising firms and senior account executives of major accounts like Coors and Kodak—and the kinds of things that were required to satisfy clients—until after the damage was already done.*

Because Mercado-Valdes lacked a staff and the expertise to carry out the kind of event to which UniWorld's clients were accustomed, UniWorld had to send some of its people to Miami to help organize the pageant—a definite no-no when it came to sponsorship.

> *I think that was ultimately the thing that made them feel that I was not someone that they wanted to be associated with. They felt that we misrepresented our capabilities. True, I didn't have a clear sense of what a client looked for when sponsoring a promotion. But I was cocky and arrogant, and felt at the time that being able to walk in the door with a media legend like Eugene Jackson and just articulate my vision was enough. But I quickly learned that it wasn't. I also learned that sometimes faking it until you make it has to have its limits, depending on the level you're dealing with. I think that it is better to be humble and act like you ain't got nothing when you're dealing with a mid-level person who's like you and older than you, than it is to try to demonstrate to that person that you are a big shot and then let them see things that clearly demonstrate that you are not. I played the big shot and got burned. And the setback*

was that none of them was too anxious to get back in it when 1988 came. So, for the next two years, I kind of drifted, and my business came to a standstill.

Rule 4: Don't Let the Rough Times Rule. Let the Potential for Success Motivate You to Forge Ahead

If anything, the next couple of years tested Mercado-Valdes's faith in his business. Although the pageant was on hiatus, he vowed that he would bring it back with new advertisers and that it would debut on television in the next couple of years. Jackson believed in his young protégé, so he offered him a job at Unity Broadcasting and charged him with the task of resuscitating the pageant. With $200 in his pocket, Mercado-Valdes moved to New York in the fall of 1987. But after just a two-day stay at a transient hotel, he exhausted nearly all of his money and ended up sleeping on the couch in Jackson's office.

I had developed a system in which I would leave with everyone else, go to the McDonald's nearby and sit for a while, then come back and talk the security guy into letting me back into the building to finish up some work. That worked for five days. Then one day when I came back into the building, as it had become my routine, the security guard wouldn't let me in. He told me that unless I had a key he could not let me go upstairs. To this day I don't know if someone found out and told the security guy what I was doing. All I knew was that I had no money and no longer had a place to sleep.

Although Mercado-Valdes was making $1,500 a month working for Jackson, he had not yet received his first paycheck. Too embarrassed to let him know of his situation, Mercado-Valdes then took up residence in Central Park. He became homeless and ended up sleeping in a cardboard box, but nobody knew.

Eugene had a private bathroom in his office so I would get up very very early, about 4:00 A.M., go into the office, and sneak in a quick shower. Then I would put on one of the two silk suits that I owned at the time and kept in his office closet, and start playing the role of corporate executive. Everybody just thought that I was a highly motivated little employee who got to work very early every day. And while I was a highly motivated worker by day, by night I was just a common homeless person. I would stay in the office as late as I could and then just go back out into the street.

After work, Mercado-Valdes hung out with other homeless folks. He played cards with them and talked with them. Then one night he took a walk that brought him the closest he had ever come to giving up on the American Dream.

I heard of Trump Tower, so I decided to walk past it. When I did, this doorman—who to this day, even though I now live on the forty-third floor of the building, still denies that it was him I saw that night—comes out and tells me that I can't stand by the resident entrance. He tells me to run along or he is going to call the police. At that moment, I thought, "Oh my God, I'm homeless. My grandparents are dead. I have nothing in the world. And even a white door-man doesn't want me standing in the same area where he is standing." I thought maybe I should just die because that would be easier.

Mercado-Valdes was homeless for a week. Admittedly, it was the toughest time of his life as an entrepreneur. And although he wanted to give up, he was comforted by the thought of who he could become rather than who he was at the moment.

In order for me to survive, I had to adjust my consciousness to be Eugene Jackson's partner: a young, black, and gifted soon-to-be superstar. And I had to live in that reality mentally instead of living in the real reality, which was marked by the fact that I had no money and I had no place to live, because if I lived in the real world, I would have committed suicide. Part of what I think most entrepreneurs have that drives them and that distinguishes them from others is their ability to live in a suspended animation: their ability to view or collect something in their brain and begin living in it before they get there. By living in there before you get there, the journey there is less painful because mentally you're in the shade so the heat doesn't hurt as much because you've convinced yourself that you got a hat on.

Reminded of his passion and his purpose, Mercado-Valdes pulled himself up by the bootstraps once again. After getting a call from a friend who had worked on the pageant with him in Miami and who now lived in New York, Mercado-Valdes suddenly had a place to stay. By February 1988, he had inherited the small $350-a-month rent-controlled apartment after the friend moved to California. Now, with a permanent home, Mercado-Valdes could focus squarely on putting the pageant back on track. It would cost at least $700,000 to bring it to television. He approached several advertisers, using his smooth tongue to get him in the door. But he could not mask his lack of experience in the television industry.

There was a lot of hostility, not so much towards the idea, I believe, but towards my ability to get it done. Also, I was forging into an area where the only other known black televised pageant had been of considerably inferior quality. Everybody knew how tacky the Miss Black America Pageant was. In fact, it had reached such a tacky level for so long that no one could envision a black pageant being produced on a level of quality that was consistent with top television standards. So it was a challenge for me to convince advertisers that I could make it work.

He couldn't. And when the Miami City Council pulled its funding, suddenly he had no options. The pageant was put on hold in 1988.

Mercado-Valdes kept himself busy by poring over books about syndication and meeting with syndicators, as if he was prophesying the launch of African Heritage Network. Jackson continued to work on starting World African Network. A longtime Republican and a friend of Jeb Bush, he took a brief break that year to work on the Bush/Quayle campaign in Washington, DC. Afterward, he was offered a job with the Department of Housing and Urban Development. But, staying true to his passion, he headed back to New York to revive his pageant.

After suffering a failed attempt at getting Disney to back the event in 1989, Mercado-Valdes was once again without support. But he didn't give up. In the summer of 1990, he cut a deal in which Universal Studios in Los Angeles would host the pageant. He secured advertising commitments from several UniWorld clients (despite the earlier disappointment, Lewis was still a close friend) and from Comer Cottrell, CEO of the Dallas, Texas based Pro-Line Corporation (one of the nation's largest black-owned companies). He then taped the first telecast of the Miss Collegiate African American Pageant, which aired in about 70 markets nationwide via Unity Broadcasting's World African Network division. The pageant lost money that year—$300,000, to be exact. But in its third televised year, it generated more than $600,000 in revenue and created a positive buzz among the viewing public. Securing sponsors was no longer a problem. Mercado-Valdes was able to sell out the show's commercial time eight months before its taping.

Pleased with the pageant's success, Mercado-Valdes developed another lucrative idea. He called it S.T.O.M.P.!, a nationally televised step-show competition between teams from black fraternities and sororities. Together, the two shows earned $1.4 million in 1992. Mercado-Valdes's share in the business was looking better and better, or so he thought. Even though he owned 49 percent of the pageant and did the ad selling, he saw next to no profit. Jackson still treated him as a salaried employee and controlled all of the money. By this time, Mercado-Valdes was making $50,000 a year, but he rarely was paid as scheduled. Jackson was on the downswing of his prominence and was experiencing financial difficulties. Mercado-Valdes decided that it was time to part ways.

Rule 5: Know When to Say Good-bye to a Bad Business Relationship

Like most successful business owners, Mercado-Valdes was always thinking of the next good idea. After the pageant and S.T.O.M.P! aired in the spring of 1992, he began to develop another concept, based on a long-held passion.

A movie enthusiast since childhood, Mercado-Valdes liked old black pictures. He had grown up with films like *Carmen Jones* and *Porgy and Bess.* As an adult, he realized how difficult it had become to find these and other black classics. He could not locate them in video stores or on television. Mercado-Valdes perceived a great way to revive these types of movies: create a company that would license the films, package them in a movie-of-the-month format, and offer them to television stations across the country. He named his newest venture African Heritage Network and began doing his homework. The pageant had given him some knowledge of syndication, but Mercado-Valdes needed to learn more.

> *I never really thought about how movies ended up on television, and most people don't even think about it. They just turn on a particular channel and there's a movie. They don't know how it got there, they just know that it's there. So I went and found out more about the movie packaging business: how it works, and how people could get involved. I talked to syndicators and attended television conventions that discussed syndication. Of course, AHN wasn't the first to develop the concept of movie packaging. There were lots of white movie packages airing before I even conceived my idea, but no one had ever done an all-black movie package, so I created a niche and I was excited about the niche. After crunching all the numbers, I figured that, if my plan worked, I could make anywhere between $700,000 to $800,000 a year from this venture.*

Naturally, Mercado-Valdes went to Jackson with his idea because Jackson had been his financier for the past five years. He felt a sense of loyalty to his business mentor. But, protégé or not, he approached him with some specific conditions about joining forces on this venture. The shares had to be split 50–50, and he wanted to be able to control the money because, as things stood, he could not write a single check. Jackson agreed to the terms, which had yet to be outlined in writing. But by September of that year, Mercado-Valdes decided to proceed without him. Part of his decision was rooted in the fact that three months had passed and he still had not been paid for work done at the pageant that spring. Hurricane Andrew hit Miami and devastated the neighborhood in which his mother lived. She needed $600 to make repairs, and Mercado-Valdes couldn't help. He simply did not have any money. He realized that he could no longer be subordinate to Jackson.

Eugene is a great man and I will always be eternally grateful to him for the support that he played in my life as an entrepreneur, but he lacked character as a partner. He had a bad habit of never wanting to pay his partners their share, and it was something that he had done to previous partners before me. His attitude was "Once I have the money, it's mine." He never paid the pageant bills on time—or the people that helped out. I watched people get paid almost eight months after they did the work. I watched him take advantage of people over and over again, but I never thought that he would do it to me. But he would go months without paying me, then not even call to ask how I was doing. Meanwhile, he's got a Rolex watch and he's riding around in limos and eating the finest food. He never once said, "Well, I know I haven't paid you in a couple of months, but are you okay? Can I pawn something?" By 1992, I was sick of it. Fewer and fewer people wanted to work for the pageant unless they got paid up front. He was ruining the reputation of the event and destroying . . . credibility that took a very long time to build. So when I came up with this new business idea that clearly looked like a pot of gold, casting loyalty aside, I just decided to go out and raise the start-up capital my damn self and do the business on my own.

Rule 6: Develop Clear Strategies to Make a Smooth Start

Mercado-Valdes has never been one to let grass grow beneath his feet, so he didn't waste time getting started on his newest venture. Collaborating with an attorney friend, he put together a business plan for African Heritage Network and incorporated the company. Then, to raise funding, he pitched the idea to Comer Cottrell, a longtime business associate. Cottrell had been sponsoring the pageant for the past three years, so he knew that Mercado-Valdes could successfully grow a business. Excited by the new idea, Cottrell loaned him $350,000 to jump-start AHN, invested $25,000 in the business, and took a 25 percent equity stake in the company.

Mercado-Valdes set up his office, ironically, in Jackson's New York condominium. He worked the phones, talking with studios, television stations, advertisers, and distributors. There was a lot to do. For starters, Mercado-Valdes had to decide which movies he would air. He also had to develop a list of the television stations to which he would offer his movie packages, solicit advertisers willing to push their products during the network's presentations, and find a company to distribute his product. Deciding which films to package required no particular strategy at first. Mercado-Valdes thought that he would just select the least expensive pictures—the only ones he could afford. But he quickly learned that getting studios like Warner Bros., Paramount, Twentieth-Century Fox, and Viacom to open up their libraries for access to *any* movie, no matter what the cost, was not that easy.

> *Getting access to studios was the toughest challenge. Many studios didn't want to give up their product to an unknown company. In fact, many of them have a general policy that says that they don't give up their projects to subdistributors who compete with them. So the first challenge for me was to convince them that I was not competing with them. The second challenge was convincing them that I had the ability to pay for the titles. I had to convince them to go ahead and let me license the movie and that I would pay them when the time came, before the movie aired.*

Besides persuading the studios to grant him entry, Mercado-Valdes had to deal with the issue of movie availability. He couldn't just cherry-pick his favorite African American films, write a check, and then walk out the door with the reel of film. Movies are sold in packages, and they have certain available windows for syndication. Syndicators plan their schedules well in advance. A customer may want to air a picture, particularly a popular one, next month, but it may not be available until the following year. The idea of having to wait for certain pictures concerned Mercado-Valdes, but not for long. He developed a strategy for getting solid pictures: He chose classic titles that were 20 years old or older.

Most likely, these films wouldn't be the first picks of his competitors because they weren't recent works. Mercado-Valdes chose *The Final Come Down, Go Man Go, Adios Amigos, Carmen Jones*, and *The Black Brigade* to begin the rollout of the "Movie of the Month" series for the first five months. He paid $25,000 for *The Final Come Down*, but the others cost $15,000 a pop to license for a period of one month.

Mercado-Valdes hoped that the "Movie of the Month" series would reach millions of viewers, but he was particularly interested in attracting the African American market. At that time, statistics covering all movie categories indicated that African Americans accounted for 2.8 million tickets sold at the box office for classic movies, and, compared to any other viewing group, they spent 40 percent more time watching them on television.

> *When building our TV station list, our strategy was this: Rather than compete with the general market companies on their terms, we would help create new terms by concentrating only on reaching large percentages of the African American market. Essentially, we wanted to go after markets in which African Americans constituted a significant portion. . . . With the types of movies that we were showing, we thought we would be better off trying to clear [i.e., attract] stations in areas like Jackson, Mississippi, rather than in Portland, Oregon. So we devoted our efforts towards developing a station list that was reflective of our target audience. In the end, the strategy helped us because, despite our low general market ratings, we were, from day one, getting high concentrations of African American viewers.*

Like the studios, not every station was excited about working with a newcomer. At first, many stations were reluctant to agree to take any product from Mercado-Valdes for fear that he would not deliver. But he knew that he could pull it off. The formula was perfect. If he could just get advertisers to see the value of his idea, he could gain greater leverage with the stations. But that was easier said than done. At the time, getting advertisers for ethnic programming was not an easy task. The television budgets in minority media were limited, and Mercado-Valdes stood in line behind several established ethnically-oriented shows such as *Ebony Jet Showcase* and *The Apollo Comedy Hour* for available ad dollars. If anyone was going to get the lion's share of the budgets, it was going to be the incumbents. Mercado-Valdes searched the client rosters of UniWorld and Burrell Communications Group Inc. for companies willing to buy or barter time during his movie package. He came up with a few pretty sizable accounts, including Procter & Gamble and Pro-Line Corporation.

Next, he needed to find a host to introduce each movie and talk about its theme, content, and cast. Mercado-Valdes asked some of Hollywood's finest entertainers. First, James Earl Jones. Then Danny Glover. When both turned him down, he asked Ossie Davis and Ruby Dee. They accepted, and on December 23, 1992, Mercado-Valdes taped the lead-in to his movie package at the famed Apollo Theater—ironically, a venue that would later raise questions about his credibility as a business owner.

Working with Baruch Entertainment, a Washington-based distributor, African Heritage Network's "Movie of the Month" series debuted in January 1993 and was aired via 73 stations across the country.

Rule 7: Learn How to Delegate, But Treat Your Employees Like Assets, Not Paid Labor

Like many new businesses, African Heritage Network got off to a slow start. Mercado-Valdes concentrated on building his station list and generating more advertiser support. At the time, only 30 percent of his commercial spots were sold. But that soon changed. In June 1993, Mercado-Valdes shelled out $75,000 to air a more popular picture: *Lady Sings the Blues.* The film, starring Diana Ross in a portrayal of the life of sultry songstress Billie Holiday, boosted the "Movie of the Month" ratings and raised the eyebrows of many advertisers who now believed that Mercado-Valdes could consistently deliver good numbers. That summer, the series became the number-two black syndicated show in the category of ethnic-targeted programming. And by the end of the first year, AHN had reached 80 markets covering about 75 percent of the country and 88 percent of all black households that had television sets. The company generated $1 million in revenue—a nice sum for a business still finding its way. But Mercado-Valdes lost $300,000. Admittedly, he wasn't too concerned.

I had more bills than I had revenues, but at least it was mine. I had my own paycheck and I was starting to see cash flow, my own cash flow, coming into my accounts. I was a liberated slave.

As AHN took flight, the business relationship between Mercado-Valdes and Jackson grew weaker. They came together for the pageant and S.T.O.M.P!, both of which continued to air each year, but barely spoke. Meanwhile, Mercado-Valdes steadily grew his syndication company. In 1994, he began airing more quality movies, including *Def by Temptation, The Autobiography of Miss Jane Pitman, The Great White Hope,* and *Sounder.* He sold 65 percent of his advertising inventory and raised revenues to $2.2 million. That year, he also began hiring some help—not an easy task for someone used to wearing all the entrepreneurial hats. He rented office space at UniWorld and brought in his first employee, a friend from Miami, who served as the company's general manager. Mercado-Valdes also hired a Chief Financial Officer and a computer whiz, who ultimately became the director of broadcast operations.

It was hard letting go of some of the work, and it's still very difficult letting others do what I used to do. After all, it's hard to find a salesperson that you think sells as well as you; but as the business began to grow, I had to delegate authority—and it's important that business owners realize that. We've got 17 employees now, and I admit that I am still a bit of a micromanager in the sense that I insist on signing the paychecks and having major decisions run past me, but I basically tell my employees to do what they do best and leave them alone. When recruiting a staff, you have to find people that you trust, and assume that they are going to be doing things differently than you and thinking differently than you or they would be you. You have to be reconciled with the fact that you're not going to find somebody exactly like you, but more likely to find somebody complementary to you. Then you have to be patient and give the employer–employee relationship time to work.

Mercado-Valdes appreciates the value of his staff and is known for compensating his workers very well. Although AHN is a small company by syndicate standards, the average salary is $60,000, and several employees make six-figure incomes. Mercado-Valdes even creates special packages with perks for his front-desk receptionists.

> *When I started AHN and I began to build my staff, I had to pay my employees well because I had the experience of working for someone who didn't seem to care about that stuff. Eugene [Jackson] didn't have a real good sense of loving his employees and appreciating the fact that they were assets to the company and that they should have been treated like assets. Employees are like the flowers in your home. If you don't plant them right, water them, and treat them right, they won't look pretty for you. So I've always gone to great lengths to make sure my employees are happy. In the seven years of my doing business, I have never missed a payroll, and I am very proud of that. I think one of the deficiencies of traditional black businessmen is that they don't figure out that a well-paid happy employee works harder and stays with you longer.*

By 1995, not only did Mercado-Valdes have a happy staff, he also had his own offices in Manhattan's Tribeca district and was running a company with $4.5 million in revenues. Advertiser support was up, and among the blue-chip companies added to his roster were: AT&T, Ford, Burger King, Colgate, and General Motors. He repaid Cottrell for the start-up loan and, with his and Byron Lewis's help, devised a way to gain full control of the pageant from Jackson. The rapid success of the company indicated that AHN was here to stay, so Mercado-Valdes decided to expand his operation by adding a second movie package. Unlike the first package, which had aired old black classics late at night, the new package would license more recent films and air them during prime time. Mercado-Valdes called the newest addition to his company African Heritage Primetime Network. The quarterly special telecasts featured films such as *Crooklyn, Soul of the Game,* and *The Tuskegee Airmen.*

Through the two movie packages, Mercado-Valdes airs 24 movies per year. The "Movie of the Month" series reaches 87 to 88 percent of all black TV households, and AHN Prime is seen by 95 percent of the same demographic. Both packages are aired in 75 to 80 percent of the entire country.

Rule 8: Use Acquisitions to Grow Your Business

Since its inception, AHN has doubled its revenues every year. In 1996, the company realized $8 million in revenue. Mercado-Valdes operated the pageant and S.T.O.M.P! that year, but he decided that it was time to bring those events to a close. The economics of producing both television specials had changed drastically, and Mercado-Valdes was losing money. Besides, the rags-to-riches business mogul was looking toward greener pastures.

I realized that I was spending half my year putting together and rounding up campus queens and steppers, for crying out loud, when I could be meeting with CEOs and COOs on driving the black market. Which would you rather do?

Acquisition became very important to Mercado-Valdes. He knew that it would foster continued and rapid growth. In 1996, he purchased the ad sales rights to the gritty police drama *New York Undercover*, a program that he now also distributes. He also bought the rights to Kensington Publishing Group's Arabesque Books, the first (and only) romance line from a major publisher that features African American characters in books written by black women. Mercado-Valdes, who obtained the rights for $10,000, had planned to make original television movies based on the novels, but he could not fully get the venture off the ground. He ultimately gave the rights back to the owner of Kensington without asking for one dime in return. Later, he found out that Robert Johnson, CEO of Black Entertainment Television, purchased the entire company and duplicated his idea.

That's business.

But Mercado-Valdes was far from giving up on new projects. In 1998, the company was up to $10 million in revenues, and he set his sights on obtaining the rights to the highly profitable television show *It's Showtime at the Apollo*, a competition among amateur entertainers. But Mercado-Valdes's attempt to do good business was met with an unexpected free-for-all of harsh words and aggressive attempts to destroy his credibility as an entrepreneur. When several of Harlem's business owners and local politicians, who have always closely guarded the Apollo from so-called "outsiders," found out that he had put up a $1.5 million bid, they accused Mercado-Valdes of acquiring the money through illegal activity.

> *We bid on programming all the time. We bid on* New York Undercover *against Don Cornelius (producer of the highly successful and long running dance program* Soul Train). *I won, but Don Cornelius didn't go around calling me a drug smuggler afterwards. I won and there were no hard feelings. But with the Apollo, they literally tried to destroy me.*

Mercado-Valdes lost the bid but gained even greater exposure for his company. In 1999, he picked up three new series for syndication, including his first Latino program. He also acquired the ad sales rights to the sitcoms *Moesha, Malcolm and Eddie,* and *The Steve Harvey Show,* as well as the musical program *Russell Simmons' OneWorld Music Beat.* Mercado-Valdes made these acquisitions in a period of just four months. By adding them, he estimates that company revenues will grow to $40 million in 2000.

Rule 9: Revel in Your Success, But Never Rest on Your Laurels

What will he do for an encore?

Mercado-Valdes never seems to be at a loss when it comes to developing new and exciting ideas.

> *I am constantly thinking of the next idea. If I have any skill or gift as an entrepreneur, it's that I never actually enjoy what's happening now. I'm always thinking about what could happen in the future.*

And the future looks extremely bright. Mercado-Valdes plans to build a black movie studio, acquire radio stations, and eventually take his company public. But you can bet that, even then, he won't rest. And not because he's greedy or has a need to feed his ego. He simply wants to stay in the game for as long as he chooses to play.

There are a lot of people who never grow their businesses because they are kind of comfortable and happy with where they are. But one of the difficulties with getting comfortable and happy is that you never know when that particular thing with which you are comfortable is going to become a dinosaur. If you want to stay in business and stay competitive, you have to constantly be thinking ahead and saying, "OK, the business I'm in now may not be the same (or around) in five years—not because I made a mistake but because things change dramatically." With my particular company, the FCC could wake up and create a rule that makes it even harder for me to do business. Therefore, the fact that I did everything right—the fact that I bought low, sold high, developed clients, developed relationships at the station level, developed relationships at the studio level, and developed relationships with producers—could become meaningless. So you should always be thinking about expanding and growing tentacles to your business, because you never know when the idea which has been feeding you is still going to feed you three or four years down the road.

And who better to know that than Frank Mercado-Valdes.

7

ROSCOE ALLEN
ROSCOE ALLEN COMPANY
The Other Mr. Peanut

I never approach a buyer thinking that I should get special treatment because I'm black. I know that I have to compete like everybody else.

Only six months had passed since Roscoe Allen, Jr. landed his first two major clients for his peanut manufacturing company. Now he was out to score again.

In January 1997, Allen drove two hours from his modest facility in Ocilla, Georgia, to Jacksonville, Florida. He planned to make a sales presentation before the vice president of merchandising for Winn-Dixie Stores, Inc. This major southern supermarket chain had more than two million customers and nearly 1,200 outlets across 14 states and the Bahamas. Allen wanted the chain to put his brand of peanuts, whole cashews, and mixed nuts, produced under his *GUBA's* label, on store shelves throughout its 11 divisions. Winn-Dixie supermarkets were already stocked with major brands such as Planter's, but Allen was certain that there was also room for his label. It offered the same quality as the others, but was cheaper in price (25 to 30 percent less than other brands).

Two of the nation's largest supermarket chains—Publix and BI-LO—had already begun selling GUBA's (a derivation of the African Congolese word *Nguba*, which means *peanut*). Allen believed there was little chance that Winn-Dixie would pass up an opportunity to carry such a competitive product. The offer

143

simply made good business sense. But when he entered the executive conference room of the Winn-Dixie headquarters, he learned that his track record of successfully selling to other chains did not matter. The only thing that the supermarket giant could see was his skin color.

Making my sales presentation was tough at first. The vice president seemed to be very irritated when I arrived. And before I could even get started, he said, "Let me talk first, Roscoe. You sit down and listen." He said because I was an African American-owned company, . . . he really didn't want to do business with me. Then he said, "If you think you're going to come in and push your product in here, you've got another thing coming. We'll fight you in court."

Allen was dumbfounded by the harsh outburst. Where had it come from and how could he calm the situation? He wondered whether he might be feeling the effects of a storm that had previously brewed between Winn-Dixie and other minority business owners.

He was right.

He seemed to be getting very heated so I said, "Wait, wait. I know that I'm black and perhaps that is what has gotten me in the door to see you, but I've come here to tell you about my peanuts and show you that I can give you a competitive price and a quality product. That's it." After he calmed down, he told me that, in the past, a lot of African-American entrepreneurs would meet with him, then try to make the store carry their products, regardless of the quality and price. In dealing with grocery store managers over the last several years, I have found out that a lot of minority-owned companies go into meetings expecting the client to do business with them just because they are minority. But I think that's where we go wrong when approaching major companies. We try to live in the past and get retribution for wrongs that were committed against us years ago, instead of focusing on how we can give the client a product that is just as good as, if not better than, the ones they are already carrying. I think that we have to focus on today's *business environment and figure out how we are going to compete now and in the future. So when I make a sales presentation, I push my company on three things: price, service, and quality. I never approach a buyer thinking that I should get special treatment because I'm black. I know that I have to compete like everybody else.*

By keeping a cool head and a professional attitude, Allen was able to convince Winn-Dixie to try his products in one division at a time. About two weeks after the initial meeting, GUBA's hit the shelves of 250 stores in Florida. By the end of 1997, his label had entered nearly all of Winn-Dixie's divisions. Today, his products—which include salted peanuts, mixed nuts, cashew halves, whole cashews, and pecans—are sold in about 4,000 stores, all of which are in the top ten supermarket chains in the nation. And after just four years in operation, company revenues have reached $5 million. Not bad for a guy who used to sell used cars for a living.

The Roscoe Allen Company, the South's first and only African American-owned peanut manufacturing plant, is a small operation situated among the flowing acres of farmland in Ocilla, but it is very efficient. Everything, including the roasting, salting, canning, labeling, and packing of nuts is done on the premises of the 20,000-square-foot facility, which includes a processing plant and a warehouse. Allen also operates a mail-order business for sales of GUBA's products. There are no idle hands or machines in this shop. Forklifts buzz about the floor almost daily. The metallic sounds of the assembly line fill the air as batches of peanuts sift through a huge hopper and aluminum cans whiz through the conveyor. In an eight-hour shift, workers can churn out nearly 18,000 pounds of nuts, which translates into about 800 cases of finished product per day. Afterward, Allen ships his product to stores via several trucking lines.

There's a lot of activity throughout this small peanut empire. Orders are filled and shipped in just five days, even though, from the outside, it doesn't appear as though much is going on. The beige and green metal-sided building is located several hundred feet in front of a correctional facility for youths. The parking lot is a bed of dirt and gravel. The entrance is a single unadorned door. There is no identifying sign pointing the way to the company. Then again, none is really needed. Once inside the facility, it's clear what makes Allen's venture so visible—and it has nothing to do with aesthetics.

Like most business owners, Allen, now 40, has gained a strong foothold in his industry because of hard work, determination, persistence, confidence, and humility. Nonetheless, the ex-Marine, who was named Georgia's Small Business Person of the Year in 1998, is not your average manufacturing executive. There's no "President Only" parking space out front. He doesn't confine himself to a plush office where he sits behind a mahogany desk and pushes papers. Nor does he bark orders to employees through memos typed by a dutiful and overprotective secretary. Allen, who, on most days, sports jeans, a golf shirt, and a baseball cap (unless he will be meeting with a client) takes a hands-on approach to running his business. Speaking in a thick Southern drawl, he often answers the telephone himself. And he frequently works on the assembly line—hairnet and all—alongside his staff of 11 employees. Allen likes to manage from within the trenches and not just from behind the desk. He boxes cans, wraps pallets of peanuts, and even loads the delivery trucks. No job is too menial for this CEO. He proudly wears the hats that most executives would refuse to even think about putting on. He's got sales covered, too. Instead of hiring a salesperson or a food broker, which he can clearly afford to do, he packs up his presentation and product samples and travels thousands of miles each month, to meet with purchasing agents.

Sure, I could get a salesperson, but I'd rather assume the role myself because no one knows my business better than I do, and by playing the pitchman it gives me greater credibility. I think it is critical for minority business owners to sell their companies themselves, especially when first getting started, because some large firms don't think that small businesses can compete with the big boys. We need to go out and push our own products so that we can prove our ability and willingness to compete, no matter what the size of our companies.

Rule 1: Make Sure the Business You Choose Is the Right Business for You

Allen began competing long before he opened the Roscoe Allen Company. Playing the role of contender began more than 20 years ago, on the basketball court at Coffee County High School. Although he was tall and brawny as a teenager, his opponents were bigger and swifter. But, with his fearless approach and his refusal to acquiesce because of size, young Allen became an athletic wonder. His confidence, ability, and skill earned him a basketball scholarship to Troy State University in Alabama. This was his ticket out of the small rural town of Douglas, Georgia, where he was born and raised by his mother, who worked as a nurse's assistant, and by his grandparents. But after earning his high school diploma in 1978, he turned down the scholarship—a decision that he would later regret— and went to work at a local flower nursery.

Sound strange?

At the time, Allen didn't think so. He had worked his way up from watering flowers and unloading delivery trucks to becoming the company's shipping supervisor. Then he got word about the scholarship. Allen enjoyed the job and was making good money, so he saw no reason to give it up for a college education that he really wasn't interested in pursuing, or for a slim shot at the pros. But the nursery closed just one year later. In 1979, Allen was working on the assembly line of a canned soup company and hating every minute of it. The money was fine; with it, he was able to purchase a brand new Z28 Camaro. But after just six months on the job, Allen jumped ship to work as a machine operator for an airplane manufacturer. This job held no more promise for a lifelong career than the one before, but it was at least bearable. By 1980, he had had enough of the blue-collar job market. He entered the Marines, hoping to carve out a more professional career. But, in a fall during training, he damaged the nerves in his left foot. He was discharged one year later. Allen was now back where he started. He had to make a living, so he began working at Intermetro Industries, a food supply manufacturing company in his hometown of Douglas. Then he got a life-changing phone call. A buddy whom Allen had met while serving in the Marines had started a used car dealership in Valdosta, Georgia. The town was just 45 miles from where he would later start his peanut company. The buddy wanted his old bunkmate to work for him, learn the business, and then join him as a partner. If everything worked out, the two would open up a second dealership in Douglas.

For as long as he could remember, Allen had always thought about becoming his own boss. At age 13, he talked with his stepfather, a forklift operator and car salesman, about *ownership*. He was never particular about the type of company he hoped to own, so the used car business seemed to be as good as any. Allen accepted the unsalaried position and began taking classes to obtain his wholesale dealership license. He started selling cars in 1991, but he continued working at his day job. From 6:30 A.M. to 2:30 P.M., he worked at Intermetro. For the rest of the day, and on weekends, he attended car sales auctions to purchase inventory and then sold Jaguars, Mercedes, Volvos, Saabs, and other imports. Allen's commissions ranged from $500 to $1,500 on each sale, so it seemed he had found a good entrepreneurial endeavor. Then one day, while taking a routine road trip to a car sales auction in Albany, Georgia, Allen was struck by an even better business idea.

He always passed through Ocilla when he traveled to the auctions in Albany. This day, Allen noticed something amid the acres of farmland that had never grabbed his attention before. He had no idea why it had caught his eye on this trip, but he had to find out what it was. Peering out the car window, he saw a dilapidated structure surrounded by weeds and bushes. It looked to be some sort of manufacturing plant. Having worked in a few factories over the years, Allen could spot one a mile away. His curiosity prodded him to investigate. Playing private eye, he called a childhood friend whose father was the city commissioner in Ocilla, and asked for some background information. (The friend would later become a central figure in his company.) The building was an old peanut manufacturing plant. Allen decided that he would try to produce his own label.

I figured that if Wally (Famous) Amos could make chocolate chip cookies and compete successfully with Nabisco, Keebler, and other major labels that produced the same product, I could market my own brand of peanuts.

The timing for finding the plant and developing a new idea could not have been better. Used car sales were booming, but Allen's partner-to-be was becoming jealous of their business relationship. Allen, working only part-time, was moving more cars than his associate, who was working full-time. According to Allen, the owner was also asking him to compromise his integrity by selling inventory that was in poor condition. Knowing the importance of credibility in operating a business, Allen could not agree to sell damaged goods. By this time, he was married and wanted to reduce the amount of time spent away from his wife, so he decided to put the brakes on his intended venture. He kept his job at Intermetro while he explored the idea of processing peanuts, but by 1995 he had stopped selling cars altogether. Partnership or not, Allen realized that it just wasn't the right business for him.

If there is any lesson that I learned from working in the used car business, it is: Make sure that whatever business you have chosen to pursue is actually what you want to do. I hadn't really given any thought to the used car business before getting involved. It sounded good and seemed like a great venture for the future, but it turned out to be something that just wasn't right for me. When choosing a business, it should be one that you can see yourself being involved in for an extended period of time. Given the nature of the used car business and the type of outfit that my potential partner wanted to run, I couldn't see myself having any longevity in the company.

Rule 2: Research Your Industry Before Setting Your Wheels in Motion

Some people might think it's strange to build a business in a place like Ocilla, which has only two traffic lights, one major hotel, and barely 3,000 residents. But when the area is known for its agriculture and the business is rooted in one of its cash crops, the location makes perfect sense. Allen admits that he knew nothing about the peanut industry when he decided to take a crack at manufacturing his own label. But he was eager to learn, and he believed that he could find his fortune in a market dominated by Planter's.

In 1995, Allen started putting the first pieces of his peanut business in place. After contacting the owner of the facility, he toured the grounds to survey what types of equipment, if any, were already inside. The plant had been vacant for two years, so much of the machinery was tattered and a bit rusted. Still, the roaster and the canning assembly line system were good enough for him to make a start, so Allen decided to lease the plant. His next step was to learn all that he could about manufacturing his product. For that instruction, he traveled to nearby South Georgia College and spent hours in the library, poring over stacks of books. He researched the entire snack industry and noted the various kinds of nuts he could offer. He listed the equipment needed to process peanuts, the number of U.S. peanut-manufacturing companies, and the number and types of supermarket chains nationwide. Allen left no stone unturned. Meanwhile, D.W. Harper, the childhood friend who had revealed to him the purpose of the plant, did a little digging of his own. Harper, a former accountant, checked major business publications like *Black Enterprise* for articles about start-up financing, pricing, targeting a customer base, and other issues that would help Allen fuel his venture. Allen had mentioned nothing about taking on a partner in his business, but Harper was more than happy to help a friend get started. Harper had met Allen in 1976, when they played on opposing basketball teams in high school. He remembers their first encounter well.

> *I was on a fast break, an easy layup. I coasted in to make the play, and when I looked back at the goal to watch the ball go in, all of a sudden this guy with a big afro as big as the basketball jams the ball against the backboard and blocks my shot. After the game, I started kidding him about how he spoiled my easy layup. We became friends after that and have stayed friends ever since.*

Allen had yet to set the assembly line in motion or obtain a single client, but he was already putting his organizational structure in place. He assigned Harper as the company's office manager, and put him in charge of the financial aspects of the business: handling payroll, accounts receivable, inventory purchasing, and other back-office duties. He recruited another friend, a former farmer, to oversee the plant operations once the manufacturing facility was up and running. Allen handled sales and marketing. These assignments were only the beginning. There was still a lot of work to be done, but Allen was primed and ready for the long haul.

Putting the finishing touches on his business plan, he prepared himself for what would become his biggest challenge: raising capital.

Rule 3: When One Financial Door Is Closed in Your Face, Open Up Another

Allen needed at least $50,000 to get his business off the ground. Like most new entrepreneurs with no personal savings to invest, he headed straight for a bank, and then another bank, and then another bank, and another. Allen was denied startup financing from banks in four different South Georgia counties.

I remember going into NationsBank (now Bank of America) in Fitzgerald. I went in there, laid out my business plan and my financials. I had good credit and all of my papers were in order, but they said that they didn't understand the business plan and that they couldn't see how I could pay back the money I was asking to borrow. The rejection bothered me, but I didn't let it stop me so I went to another bank in a different county. This time, I invited the president of the bank out to the plant to take a tour. I showed him the entire facility and, in addition to presenting to him my business plan, I explained what I intended to do and the types of supermarket chains I intended to go after, but none of it mattered. He said that the bank needed to have sufficient collateral in order to grant me the loan. I was stuck again.

Allen was also given the cold shoulder by a state government lending agency. He was told that their program was "not a giveaway program and that the loans had to be paid back."

I understood that. I filled out my application like everybody else, and I understood the terms of the loan, but all they could see was a black man standing before them, not a businessman.

After attending a Black Expo event in Atlanta, Allen found a financier willing to support his venture. He had obtained information about the Business Development Corporation of Georgia, a Small Business Administration (SBA) preferred lender with a solid track record of funding minority-owned businesses. Allen met with the organization's senior vice president and, after just four short weeks, his loan was approved.

Allen used the money to acquire a 15-month lease for the peanut plant, trademark his product name, and commission a designer to create a label. He also purchased a small amount of inventory for preparing product samples for potential clients, and he put in a new conveyor line.

Without the SBA, I would have never been able to open my business. I would suggest to any minority entrepreneur who wants to start a business: "Go to the SBA for financial assistance because they are in tune to your needs and are willing to help the little guys."

Next stop: Center shelf of the snack aisle at a supermarket near you.

Rule 4: Be Fearless in Your Approach to Sales

By the spring of 1996, Allen was ready to take his product to market, but not just any market. He wanted the biggest and the best. Forget the facts: His company was half the size of his competitors, he had an unknown product, and there were no previous sales. Allen was not going to settle for shelf space among the mom-and-pop outfits—the area that is an easier target for fledgling businesses. He headed straight for the top ten supermarket chains in the nation.

After thoroughly studying the peanut manufacturing field, I knew that if I wanted to stay in business, I would need to tackle the large grocery stores first. I found that not only would they help me meet my overhead, they would also give me easier access to other large supermarkets. Now there's nothing wrong with going to the smaller stores as well. In fact, today I do business with some mom-and-pop stores that have only 50 shops. But if you are in the manufacturing field, you need to get the large companies in the beginning because when you approach other large buyers they will want to know who you are doing business with and what types of supermarket chains you have on your client list. If you have a Winn-Dixie, Albertson's, Kroger, or some other big name under your belt, it will play a big role in your getting future business that much more quickly.

Allen took on the top supermarket chains with the same focus and attitude that he had when playing high school hoops. He was fearless in his approach and confident in his ability to produce. Referring back to the list of supermarkets he had compiled during his market research, Allen scrolled the names and plucked out those he would approach.

First up, Publix.

At the time, with about 550 stores throughout Florida and Georgia, it was the sixth largest chain in the United States. Publix had a solid reputation, a criterion that Allen considered before doing business with any company. But it was also a good pick geographically. As a small manufacturer with minimal cash to spend on shipping costs, Allen had to select stores that were in close proximity to his facility. Few Publix supermarkets were more than a five-hour drive from the back door of Allen's facility, so delivery was pretty swift. With his first target in place, Allen moved in for the kill. He called the executive offices at Publix headquarters in Lakeland, Florida, and introduced himself. Afterward, he faxed information about his company to the chain. Impressed by his confidence and intrigued by his product, the category manager in charge of snacks requested a meeting. Allen wasted no time preparing his sales presentation and product samples.

I ran (on the assembly line) about a 100-pound bag of nuts I purchased wholesale from the Georgia Peanut Company in Albany. We didn't buy materials in large quantity at first because we hadn't made any sales yet, so I bought just a few cans from a local can company and I ordered about 100 labels. We didn't even run the labels through the label machine. Using a glue stick, we just put them on the cans by hand, then ran them through the can line to put the lid on. That's how I got my samples done.

He bought a new suit, rehearsed his presentation with his wife as his audience, packed up the car, and headed for Lakeland. Although this was Allen's first sales pitch in front of supermarket executives, no butterflies were swirling inside his stomach. Allen was certain that his experience in selling cars would serve him well. With his head held high, he walked in the door. "You're a peanut manufacturer," said one of the executives, obviously surprised that Allen was African American. Allen was neither shaken nor shocked by the group's reaction. "Yes sir, I am. This is the first supermarket chain I have approached, and I am excited to tell you about my product," he answered.

My advice to small business owners, or any entrepreneurs for that matter, is that when you go into a company to make a presentation, walk in with the attitude that you have come to compete, like everybody else. You can't walk in the door as a minority businessman or even a small businessman. You have to believe that you are just like the next guy and that you can hold your own. Then you have to be able to convincingly convey that to the buyer. I knew that I had a quality product and a good price that no other label could match, so I had no reason to fear being turned down because I was not a Fortune 500 company.

For the next hour, Allen talked peanuts, price, and profits. The buyers tasted his product and, by the end of the meeting, issued Allen a verbal agreement to try GUBA's in 100 Publix stores throughout Miami. They also promised to spread his label throughout all the Publix stores if the first wave of product sold well. Allen requested 14 days to get the product to their distributor's back door, then drove back to Ocilla smiling from ear to ear. Back at the office, he waited for the fax they promised to send and then waited some more. Six days passed. On the seventh day, he received the $80,000 order. But instead of having two weeks to fill it, Allen now had only one. He had no staff other than his first two recruits, no supplies in house, and no truckers in place to haul the load. He had 4,385 cases to prepare, with 12 cans per case. You do the math. But Allen didn't panic. He kept a cool head and just worked fast.

I couldn't believe my eyes when I saw how many cases they ordered. But I knew that I had no other choice but to fill the order. I didn't want to call them back and tell them that I couldn't do it, because I would lose their business and ruin my company name. So I put an ad in the local paper to find a few additional employees. D.W. and Walter Hudson, the plant manager, got on the phone and called label companies and can companies. I called the peanut shelling companies. We didn't have any of these supplies yet because we didn't have any customers prior to getting Publix. In anticipation of the business to come, I had already put together a list of different suppliers before the order came down. And I'm glad that I did because it helped to speed up the process of getting the materials that we needed.

Allen worked on the assembly line, along with his five employees. He hired three additional workers through his ad. They worked 15-hour days every day: roasting, salting, labeling, and canning peanuts, mixed nuts, and cashews. On the Friday before the deadline, Allen paid a truck driver $100 to get the cases to Publix on time.

He did.

In June 1996, GUBA's hit the shelves and sold out within two months. Allen's label was a hit. Making good on their promise, three months later Publix distributed his product to all of their stores. The gates were opened for other major clients to walk through. Allen was ready to make his next move.

My strategy to attracting and getting into the major chains was simply that I would approach one during one particular month, present to them a quality product at a price that they couldn't refuse, and then, when I obtained their business, move onto the next chain the following month.

In October 1996, Allen approached BI-LO. By the end of the year, his product was, without incident, in 260 BI-LO stores throughout the South Carolina market—undoubtedly because of his business relationship with Publix. Allen experienced few problems when he attracted his first two clients. But when he approached Winn-Dixie in January 1997, trouble began to brew. Buyers at the chain accused Allen of trying to force his product into their supermarkets by playing the race card.

The first thing I tell people when I go to do a presentation is that I'm not there to do business because I'm a minority. Supermarkets look for price and quality. So my goal is to give them a good product at a competitive price so that they can then sell it to their consumers at a reasonable price. I'm not trying to make them feel some sense of obligation to do more business with blacks because we have been shortchanged in the past. That's just not good business, and it's not the way I operate.

Staying true to his credo, Allen managed to obtain access to Winn-Dixie, but not every division. Unlike the procedures at Publix, product purchasing at Winn-Dixie was left to the discretion of the category manager in each division. Therefore, entry into one store did not automatically guarantee admittance to all the others. Allen identified three divisions that just wouldn't budge.

I tried to get into the Alabama, New Orleans, and Kentucky divisions, but I was unsuccessful. I think part of the reason had to do with the fact that some category managers don't care about making the best business decision for their company. Some of them have been doing business with the same suppliers for so long that they just don't want to change, even if another manufacturer, like myself, has a cheaper priced product. But I think the other factor has to do with discrimination. I have gone to several supermarkets like Winn-Dixie. I've met with them and let them sample my product. They've told me that I have a quality product and a good price, but still turned me down, and I can think of no other reason except for the fact that I'm black. If a company has a good price and a good product, why not do business with them?

After all, a peanut is a peanut no matter who's selling it.

Rule 5: Don't Be Afraid to Get Your Hands Dirty

By 1997, company revenues had reached $1.3 million, and Allen was living in purchase-order paradise. He added Albertson's, Food Lion, and Kroger (the number-one supermarket chain in the nation) to his client list. GUBA's was clearly becoming a favorite across several states and, surprisingly, all without a single advertisement. Allen promoted his products through a few in-store demonstrations, but, without enough money to launch a full-fledged ad campaign, he relied on the product's packaging to spread the word about his peanuts.

When I first started the company, I knew that I would not have enough money to advertise in the newspaper, on radio, or through some other form of media. That's why I spent so much time choosing a label. In fact, I changed the label at least three times before I made a final decision about which one to use. I wanted something that would stand out on the shelf so that consumers could clearly see it and want to at least pick it up for a closer look, if not to ultimately choose ours over another brand.

It was an inactive approach to attracting customers, but it worked. GUBA's, packaged in an aluminum can with an African inspired design printed on the label, intrigued potential customers who wanted to know exactly who was the other Mr. Peanut. As a result, the product flew off nearly every shelf on which it was placed. And with the influx of new supermarket chains flocking to his company just one year after its inception, TV advertisements or not, it looked as if the Roscoe Allen Company was here to stay.

Allen was excited and motivated by his rapid success, so he purchased the peanut plant that he had been leasing and went back to the Business Development Corporation of Georgia to obtain a second SBA-guaranteed loan, this time for $250,000. He used the working capital loan to purchase new equipment and bring on additional staff. But securing extra hands did not keep this driven and energetic entrepreneur from maintaining an active role in his growing peanut empire. Dressed in his blue-collar digs, Allen continued to work on the assembly line alongside his employees. To this day, he still doesn't mind getting his hands dirty.

I go out on the line all the time and work with my employees. They like it. Sometimes, when you are the president of a company, your employees really look at you as if you are so far above them, almost as if you're not human. But if you get out onto the floor and you get dirty like them and sweat like them, you're no longer just the boss, and they don't think they are beneath you just because they're the employees and you're the employer. Developing a more interactive relationship with your employees also creates more loyalty among them. They come to work on time more often and are just happier, more productive people. So I will get out there in that production room in a minute and do anything from sweeping the floor to loading the delivery trucks. It makes them happy and it keeps me humble.

Allen prides himself on developing solid working relationships with his employees. He enforces an open-door policy with his staff. Each morning, before starting his day, he checks in with the troops to discuss any questions or concerns. To Allen, using a little TLC—teamwork, leadership, and communication—among employees has made all the difference in the world.

One thing I learned about business is that you need a good staff. I don't care how big your company may be, if you don't have good workers and if those workers are not pleased with their jobs—or you—your company is not worth a hill of beans.

Rule 6: Eye Your Product's Progress on a Regular Basis

Allen has always kept a careful watch over his employees, but he has also kept a close eye on his product. After all, if he doesn't, who will? Not Food Lion, as Allen found out soon after getting the supermarket chain's account in 1997. When Allen first approached Food Lion, he thought that the chain would become one of his best customers—and with good reason. Like the other supermarkets that had become clients, Food Lion was at the top of the food chain and had a bevy of stores just begging for a new and competitive product—or so he thought.

Allen experienced several problems when dealing with the chain. First, there was disagreement over use of a food broker—an intermediary (between the buyer and the seller) who pitches new products to potential clients. Allen did not use a broker unless the supermarket chain requested one. Why pay someone to do something that he could do—and had been doing—himself? But Food Lion insisted, so Allen agreed. The relationship between the two soon soured. The broker failed to perform and was cut loose. Allen was back to square one, so he met with Food Lion executives for a second time to make another presentation. Then he waited for a response. Three weeks passed without one word from the chain. Always aggressive but never pushy, Allen called the chain's headquarters for a status report, but was given no definitive answer. After several follow-up calls, his products were finally placed in one of the chain's divisions in Plant City, Florida. Allen obtained a small number of stores—59, to be exact—but it was a start. Having now gotten a foot in the door, Allen figured that it would be easier to gain access to the other divisions. But, as he soon learned, that wasn't the case.

GUBA's barely moved off the shelves at Food Lion. Yet the people at Albertson's, a chain that had the same amount of stores and was in the same division, couldn't keep enough of them in stock. Allen decided to investigate why.

> *I made an appointment with Food Lion to find out why Albertson's, a supermarket chain that shared the same division and the same number of stores, was ordering 15 times as much product as Food Lion. My theory was that Food Lion was not putting my product in all of the stores in that division, because if they did, there was no way in the world it wouldn't sell, and the sales report from Albertson's was proof of that.*

Allen's theory was right. He also found out that Plant City was Food Lion's lowest selling division.

Food Lion didn't want me to succeed, because if they did, they would have put me in a better division. I should have asked for more details about this particular division from the start. But I didn't. I just figured that it was one of their best, so one of the things I learned from that experience was to not make any assumptions. I also learned to not just take for granted that these supermarket chains are stocking products as they should and where they should. It's important to always track, on a regular basis, how well your items are selling, so if you are faced with a situation in which one store is telling you that your stuff is not moving, you can pinpoint the problem and correct it.

Food Lion is far from being a favorite client. In fact, it is one of the company's worst. But Allen is not worried. In the next several years, there would be a lot more where that one chain had come from.

Rule 7: Position Yourself for the Long Haul: Expand Your Products and/or Services

By year three, there was no stopping Allen. His client list grew bigger and bigger.

- Wal-Mart.
- Harris-Teeter.
- H.E. Butt Grocery Company.
- Harvey's Supermarkets.
- Ingle's Markets.
- Jitney Jungle Stores.

Allen was racking up supermarket chains faster than the famed Chicago Bulls had earned championship rings. But, never one to rest on his laurels, he knew it was time to grow the business through product development. Other snack manufacturers were debuting new items, so Allen followed their lead by adding pecans and cashew halves to his line. He also began assisting other small manufacturing concerns by processing products that the companies could not afford to handle themselves. Through his efforts to strengthen the company, which will soon add a honey-roasted and dry-roasted line, Allen proved that he could get the job done. Contrary to popular opinion, it seemed as though size didn't matter. But a few skeptics still felt that it did.

When I went to Stop & Shop Supermarkets in Boston, Massachusetts, in 1999 to make my sales presentation, they said, "Well, Roscoe, you already have Winn-Dixie, Publix, Kroger, and Albertson's doing business with you. Can you run the product for our stores as well? Can you handle all of the volume?" I told the guy to just cut the purchase order because I would deliver the product to his door, guaranteed. It amazes me that some companies, despite the number and types of clients that I have, still think that, just because I am a small business owner, I can't handle more than two customers at a time. It's just not so.

Can Allen change their minds?
He thinks so.
How?
By serving even more customers and serving them well. Given his track record, consider it done.

8

VERA MOORE
VERA MOORE COSMETICS

Madam Makeover

When starting a business, people want to reap the harvest but they don't want to plant the seed and till the soil. I'm here to tell you that if you can't do it all, you can forget it.

Green Acres Mall, 1979.

It had everything Vera Moore needed to successfully sell her makeup and skin care line: a captivated audience, rain or shine; constant walk-in traffic; and lots and lots of black female shoppers—her customer base. But getting into the bustling shopping center in Valley Stream, New York, would not be easy. Moore already had two strikes against her: (1) she was a small business owner, a turnoff to major malls that generally bank on big chains, and (2) she was black. In its 40-year history, the Green Acres Mall had not a single African American tenant. Think Moore was worried about the circumstances surrounding her?

Think again.

A God-fearing Christian with all the tenacity of a presidential nominee, Moore boldly approached the mall's corporate management staff about acquiring space for her business. She filled out the proper forms, played Twenty Questions, and cut through all of the other required red tape. Then she waited for a response. Two months later, the mall began construction to add a second level to the building. Still no word. Always the aggressor, Moore contacted the corporate office again. She even wrote a series of letters. But three years down the road, she was still sending out

163

queries and making frequent follow-up calls to check on the status of her admittance. Finally, the mall decided to put Vera Moore Cosmetics in a small store on the second floor, near the food court. It was the only space left. The Mall representatives drew up the paperwork, and Moore readied her business—which had been temporarily operating out of a tiny nook in the hair salon that she and her husband owned—for the move. Meanwhile, another entrepreneur snatched up the area promised to her, and opened a jewelry store there. When Moore confronted management about the foul play, her contacts acted amnesic but they could not dispute the written agreement she had in hand. The mall had no choice but to create a space for her. With no other vacancies available, Moore was given 100 square feet of sales space inside the jewelry store. It was hardly the location that she had in mind, but it was a start. In 1982, Vera Moore Cosmetics became the first black-owned business to gain entry into the Green Acres Mall, a facility that today accommodates about 200 stores, as well as several carts and kiosks.

Nearly 20 years later, Moore is still a resident. These days, she operates from a kiosk not much larger than her original location. But business couldn't be better. Forget the fact that Fashion Fair, Estée Lauder, Revlon, Clinique, and other major cosmetic lines are sold in Macy's and JCPenny's, not far from her counter. Moore is not intimidated or shaken by the competition. She knows that her product will sell, regardless of her contenders. Some might interpret her attitude as one of arrogance or conceit. Moore simply calls it confidence in the quality of her line—a confidence built by the numbers and types of customers she has acquired over the years.

> *Most of the girls in the department stores in the Green Acres Mall are wearing Vera Moore Cosmetics. Even a lot of Mary Kay ladies have chosen to wear my line, and I don't even have a pink Cadillac to sell, so I know that I am providing a top-notch product that is wanted and needed. The foundations that I have now I will put up against any line out there. Now maybe I couldn't say that 20 years ago because I was just starting out, but, over the years, I've grown my business and I have refined and updated my products, so now I can.*

Moore's success stems from supply and demand. She launched her business at a time when many black women wanted but couldn't find makeup that made them look natural, soft, and supple—and didn't rub off at a mere touch. What the market offered then—and, in some cases, still offers now—were colors that completely ignored the complexity and diversity of black skin. Makeup made the black women appear chalky, red, oily, or greasy, and it ended up soiling their collar—or someone else's—before the end of the day. Vera Moore, a former Broadway and television actress, recognized this problem while appearing on the NBC soap opera *Another World.* That was 25 years ago, well before today's mainstream cosmetic conglomerates decided that it was time to create some sister-friendly shades and started touting smudge-proof slogans. A quiet trailblazer, Moore created, for black women, shades of makeup ranging from blue-black to bisque. Over the years, she put together a line of 20 different foundations "That Don't Rub Off on Your Clothes or His," as well as an array of pressed powders, concealers, lipsticks, eye shadows, blushes, and accessories for applying makeup properly. Realizing that beauty *is* skin deep, she simultaneously developed skin care treatments consisting of cleansers, toners, moisturizers, conditioners, and gels, and a bath-and-body line that included body scrub and crème bath products.

None of this came to fruition overnight. A lot of planning, developing, refining, and marketing was needed. And that took much more money than she had made during her days on stage and screen. To help raise start-up capital, Moore mortgaged her home and obtained a loan through the U.S. Small Business Administration (SBA) 7(a) Guaranteed Loan Program. As for marketing (something few startups can afford), she relied on word-of-mouth advertising and worked her contacts to get free publicity. Her strategy eventually led to a cross-promotions deal with Clairol. She also schlepped her products to one trade show after another, to see whether her target audience *wanted* the product she knew that they needed. When the masses answered "Yes," she worked tirelessly, catering to their every cosmetic and skin care need.

Moore was—and still is—a marketing guerrilla. She uses various promotional techniques to sell her products, but she also pays close attention to her customers and how they are treated. Providing quality customer service is a huge part of the marketing puzzle. For Moore, staying in the game goes far beyond selling a bunch of lipsticks in every color of the rainbow. It requires giving shoppers the time and attention they need to make smart choices involving their makeup and skin care needs. That's why every person who walks up to Moore's kiosk receives a warm greeting, a demonstration of her product line, and a crash course in cosmetics and skin care. She truly cares about her customers.

Moore could rewrite the book on customer service. Give her half a chance and she just might. Sitting still is not something Moore likes to do. She has a handful of employees and family members, including Billy, her husband of 27 years, to help out with the operation. But the bubbly beauty is always front-and-center. Visitors rarely see Moore sitting down during work hours, unless she is perched in front of her computer and answering customers' E-mail messages that have piled up in the "Ask Vera" section of her company's Web site. With the energy level of a fitness instructor, and wearing flawless and barely-there makeup, she bounces around her 150-square-foot kiosk, reloading lipsticks, lining up bottles of foundation, and servicing customers with her superstar smile. If she's not at the mall, she's in her office—handling paperwork or talking with distributors about placing Vera Moore Cosmetics in stores overseas. And if she's not there either, then she's probably out on the town spreading the word about her company through her community service projects. One of her more notable efforts involves a self-esteem program called STEP (Self-Taught Empowerment and Pride), held at New York's Riker's Island prison. By providing makeovers and advice on building their self-esteem, STEP helps prepare female inmates who are about to be released into the outside world.

Moore's entrepreneurial regimen is rigorous, but it is hardly esoteric. She insists that it's just standard stuff that every new business owner must endure.

> *People always ask me how I have been able to start and maintain this business. Some things that have happened to me I can't explain, so I give God the glory. But I share with them my stories about perseverance and sacrifice. When the Green Acres Mall first brushed me off, I didn't go away with*

my tail tucked between my legs, hoping to find another location. I wanted to set up my business there, so I went back again and again and again until I was given a space. To help save money, I sacrificed something as simple as food. Now I'm not saying that I didn't eat, but instead of having something like steak, I ate grits for dinner. Once the company was off the ground, I then worked 365 days for the first year— greeting people and nurturing the store because that's what it took to stay in business and to get where I am today. When starting a business, far too many people want to reap the harvest but they don't want to plant the seed and till the soil. I'm here to tell you that if you can't do it all, you can forget about entrepreneurship because it's not going to happen.

Rule 1: Put God First

Trust in the Lord with all thine heart; and lean not unto thine own understanding. In all thy ways acknowledge Him, and He shall direct thy paths.—Proverbs 3:5–6

This is Moore's daily credo for getting anything and everything accomplished in her life, and that includes operating her cosmetic concern. Moore is a go-getter with an electrifying personality. Her company has generated over $500,000 in revenue, a successful mail-order arm, international popularity, and an impressive client list that includes Lena Horne, Debbie Allen, and Phylicia Rashād. But she is also a humble entrepreneur who recognizes that, despite her winning personality, articulate speech, and stick-to-it-iveness, none of her accomplishments would have been possible without God.

Moore was raised as a Pentecostal Christian. Her family lived above a storefront church during the 1950s. Every Sunday, she took her place among the other parishioners in the pews after completing her Sunday School studies, so there was never any question about who was really in charge.

My mother always said, "You can't do anything without Him and you have to give Him the honor and the glory for each and every blessing." I learned early on that I must put God first in everything that I do, and that I must not compromise my faith under any circumstances. As a new business owner, you will come across a lot of situations that are frustrating and stressful. But if you put God first in your life and go to Him for the strength to go through hard times, or go to Him to ask that He transform obstacles into opportunities, you will be successful. I'm not saying that you shouldn't have a plan or strategy when starting your business; . . . you have to be focused when running your operation. But you have to have roots in order to grow your business, and Jesus Christ, the Son of God, is the root.

Moore's faith has carried her through difficult times in starting and operating her business. When the operators at the Green Acres Mall told her that they "forgot" about promising the space to her, she didn't panic or become frustrated. She just looked to the Lord. Some entrepreneurs create a business philosophy that puts strategies such as "outworking the competition" and "building strategic alliances" at the core of their companies. Moore relies on a much simpler axiom. It works, and she urges other entrepreneurs to try it for themselves.

In my company, I keep God as my center. I ask Him to give me grace and I stay true to Him. I don't get caught up in my success. I know that the Lord wants me to enjoy it, but it's important for me and other successful business owners to remember at all times how we got it and who gave it to us.

Rule 2: Create a Plan, Then Work Your Plan

Planning is a part of Moore's entrepreneurial work ethic. She learned it from her mother, a domestic worker, and her father, a porter, long before she decided to hang out her shingle. Growing up as the youngest of seven children in the Corona section of Queens, one of New York City's five boroughs, Moore remembers watching how her mother (after whom she is named) would schedule household chores. Vera knew that, every day, she had to rise early and catch the bus that took her to the big homes where she scrubbed floors. There was little time for morning housework and for getting her children ready for school. Each night, Vera zipped through her mental "To Do" list, making sure that her children's shoes were shined, socks were clean, clothes were laid out, and hair was combed. Moore vividly recalls sitting between her mother's legs each evening so that her hair could be braided. Then her mother would place a stocking cap on her head to keep her locks in place. When the sun came up, hours after her mother had already left the house, Moore and her siblings would jump into their clothes and head for school.

Management and planning were always important in my house, growing up. They were lessons that stayed with me throughout my entire life. So when I decided to start my business, I already knew how critical these two principles were. Undoubtedly, every entrepreneur needs to have a plan because it allows you to outline your goals and stay focused. But don't just keep it in your head. Put it down on paper. I didn't always have a written plan. In fact, a lot of things I committed to memory; but taking that approach can be dangerous because you run the risk of forgetting certain things. So document your plan because, without it, you will have no idea of where you want to go and how you are going to get there.

Moore comes from a very humble household. Neither of her parents was very educated, having advanced to only the fourth grade. The family often ate nothing but grits, gravy, and biscuits for dinner. And a pubescent Moore slept on the couch. But love, harmony, and understanding were always under her family's roof. For that reason, this feisty optimist has no sob stories to tell about growing up poor or without direction. From day one, Moore has been focused on her future. Before she finished junior high school, she knew what she wanted to do. Moore wanted to sing. Singing had been a part of her life since the first grade. Dubbed "the singing bird" by her elementary school classmates, Moore crooned in the church choir, at school plays, and in the glee club. To strengthen her God-given talent, she studied voice with neighborhood voice teachers. And by the time she graduated from the ninth grade, she had auditioned for and received a four-year scholarship to study opera, her first love, at the Sadisburg Academy of Music in Brooklyn, New York.

Moore sharpened her voice skills every Saturday at the academy, and she studied privately with professors from the famed

Julliard School of Music. Her talent landed her a part in the All-City Chorus, and Moore sang in the chorus at Carnegie Hall while still attending Flushing High School. The swift progression of her singing pointed toward the stage as her home away from home. Then her plans changed, as plans often do. Moore was fast approaching graduation day. With no money for college, she had to do what those in her family had always done to survive—work. But she didn't totally ditch her plans to become a songstress. After getting her diploma in 1963, she attended night courses to study French and German—two languages that are essential for singing the classics. But most of her time was spent working as a secretary at the United States Customs building in lower Manhattan. Moore started the job just days after all of the pomp and circumstance of graduation. She was excited about the position, but don't think for one moment that filing and typing, day in and day out, was a thrill for her. Moore had yet another plan in mind.

> *I made up my mind that I was going to save the money I made and buy my mother a house. My plan was to work for the federal government for five years, then quit. I figured that I would have enough money saved by then. So I stayed at home rather than moving out. When I got my check every two weeks, I gave my mother a little money for the rent, paid the phone bill, bought two weeks' worth of subway tokens, and the rest I put into the bank. Here again was the management and planning I had learned as a child. I ate at Chock Full o' Nuts every day for about four years, and had basically the same thing every time. I made sacrifices because I wanted to take my mother away from having to scrub floors in white people's homes. Her knees were pitch black because of it, so I made a vow to myself that if my mother was going to scrub anybody's floors they were going to be her own.*

As one year rolled into the next, Moore's bank account got bigger and bigger. She was also promoted from one department to another at the Customs building. Still, she never forgot about performing. A very animated thespian, she went to acting, singing, dancing, and drama classes every chance she could get. During her fourth year on the job, she was auditioning for parts on her lunch hour. She tried out for *Annie Get Your Gun* and *Hello, Dolly!* She didn't get a call for either show. But after a second call back for a bit part in the chorus of *South Pacific* at Guy Lombardo's Jones Beach Theater, Moore was on her way. She quit her job at the federal building a year ahead of schedule, put a $4,000 down payment on a house for her mother in a nice suburb, and began working on *South Pacific.* She performed in the summer production for two years. After the curtain came down, Moore appeared in several McDonald's, Kodak, and Pepsi-Cola commercials. She also did a "Million Dollar Movie" and several soap operas, including *A World Apart* (with Susan Sarandon, later an Oscar-winning actress), *Edge of Night*, and *Search for Tomorrow.* Then came Broadway. First, a part in *A Teaspoon Every Four Hours.* Then a spot in the chorus of *Purlie Victorious.* By 1970, she was back on the soaps playing Linda Metcalf, a nurse on *Another World.* Almost a decade would pass before she would start Vera Moore Cosmetics, but Moore was already becoming ownership material.

All of the work I did, leading up to starting my business, prepared me for entrepreneurship. Of course, at the time, I had no intention of starting my own company, but I was learning some of the basics and didn't even realize it. For example, when I played an extra or got a nonspeaking role in a movie, I would have to stay on the set for 10 to 13 hours each day and just sit there. That taught me patience, which is a very important characteristic to have as a business owner because your company may not take off as quickly as you would like it to, so you have to be willing to stay with it until it does. I also learned how to handle rejection and how not to let someone's saying "No" to me discourage me from pursuing my plan. Every actor knows that, in order to be successful, being able to handle rejection is key. And when I say key, I mean that if you can't handle it, forget it. I remember going to places where I had auditions and they called me back two and three times and I didn't get the part, but that happens. In theater, you don't always get the part. In fact, nine times out of ten, you don't get it, but you don't stop trying. The same thing applies to business. For example, when searching for start-up capital to start Vera Moore Cosmetics, I was rejected three times by banks, but I didn't just throw in the towel. I kept looking until I got the funds that I needed.

Rule 3: Find a Void in Your Market; Then Fill It

Moore was one of the first blacks to appear on *Another World* and the only African American on the set at the time. That distinction caused a problem with how she appeared on the daytime drama, but it also created a unique and unexpected business opportunity for the rising actress. The problem had to do with the colors her makeup artist was using on her. The cosmetics that Moore wore were in stark contrast to her caramel-colored skin. They gave her face a chalky appearance or they made her complexion look much darker than it really was. The same makeup was used for every actress on the soap opera, so Moore wasn't singled out for use of an inferior brand. She had no choice.

It wasn't about race. It was about supply and demand. When I appeared on Another World, *it was during a time that when you saw a black person on television, you would call your mother and say, "Mom, mom! Come here. There's a black girl on TV," and by the time she ran out of the kitchen into the living room, the girl was gone. My point is that there were few blacks on TV back then, so there was simply no makeup for us. The makeup the soap used was good makeup, but it just wasn't for black skin, so I knew that it wasn't going to work for me. . . . [The] line that was on the market at that time, that virtually every black woman was wearing, was too oily and greasy, and it rubbed on your clothes, so I didn't want to use that either. With no choices left, I decided to create my own cosmetics. I went to department stores and got different colors from different lines and mixed several products together to create colors that I thought were more fitting for my complexion. I brought what I made back to the studio and gave it to my makeup artist. I said, "This is what I want you to use on me from now on." She asked me what it was. I just said, "I don't know. I made it."*

With that amateur experimentation, Vera Moore Cosmetics was born in 1979. Moore continued to work on *Another World* using the colors she had created, but she also began to lay the foundation for her cosmetic line. She figured that if she was having a problem with the products that mainstream makeup companies were putting out, other black women were probably experiencing the same difficulty. Moore wanted to provide a solution. The lack of quality cosmetics for women of color gave her the opportunity.

Anybody that goes into business knows that they have to find the void in their market. You have to find your niche if you want to be successful. I knew that there wasn't a void for cosmetics because there were already plenty of makeup lines out there. But by working on the soap opera, I saw that there was a need for quality products for black women. Now I'm not trying to knock other makeup lines, but I knew that there was room for improvement for our women of color.

Moore worked with her makeup artist and learned about undertones and hues. Then she went to makeup manufacturers to get more products so that she could mix a batch of bases. After Moore created her colors, she and her husband, a cosmetologist, decided to test the market. Moore was certain that her products were needed, but she wanted to find out whether black women would be willing to use what she had to offer. Admittedly, Moore knew nothing about conducting a market analysis, but she knew enough to go where there was an abundance of black folks, her target audience. In 1980, she carried boxes of her products, which at the time included only a few foundations and shades of lipstick, to a beauty trade show in Florida. Moore set up a small booth and painted face after face after face. As she had anticipated, the women who stopped by were using only one particular brand (she refuses to name it, for fear of giving her competition free publicity) because nothing else on the market was created specifically for African American women. With only one product line, they had no choice. Moore was providing a welcome alternative. She proved that there was indeed a market for her line, so she began working with a chemist to refine her cosmetic concoctions. Once her products were given the scientific green light, she started selling them out of the hair salon she owned with her husband in Jamaica, a section of Queens in New York City. Moore set up a little area in the shop to display her products. After customers finished with their hair, nails, facials, and pedicures, she gave them a makeover. The response was overwhelming. Customers ordered products by the bunch. Before long, the budding actress, who had longed to build a career on stage and screen, was looking down a long, yet potentially lucrative road to entrepreneurship, and there was only one direction in which she could go—forward.

And she did.

Moore retired her nurse's uniform on *Another World* and began focusing all of her attention on building her new business.

I had no idea my acting career would someday lead into creating a cosmetic line for women of color, but it did; and when it did, I jumped on the opportunity to take it as far as I could go.

Rule 4: If Possible, Make Your Business a Family Affair

Moore wasted no time branding the Vera Moore Cosmetics name. She scrawled it across foundations, face powders, lipsticks, blushes, and eye shadows. But she also placed it on cleansers, exfoliants, moisturizers, and conditioners.

We started the makeup and skin care lines together. We just didn't put the makeup out there and then, ten years later, say, "Let's introduce some skin care products." We started off getting customers to talk about and realize the importance of taking care of their skin, and cleaning and moisturizing it properly, because healthy skin is important. We didn't want our customers using makeup to cover up their flaws. We wanted to try and help them correct their flaws.

Moore didn't begin with the extensive glycolic and camphor treatments that her line now includes. They took several years— and several thousand dollars—to develop and refine. But she did introduce some basic skin care products for her customers to try. Starting off her business with a full line—something that most small cosmetic concerns don't do—meant doubling the workload, but Moore was ready.

So was her family.

Unlike some business owners, Moore did not have to twist arms or promise huge payoffs to get her relatives to help out. From the very beginning, they rushed to her corner to lend support. The help wasn't financial; however, they contributed their time and expertise even if only to type correspondence or answer the phones. Moore recalls working side by side with her niece Gloria, who today handles the company's mail orders, wholesale accounts, shipping, and invoicing. Together, the two battled floods in the basement of the salon and filled orders under strict deadlines. Gloria also helped Moore prepare for the endless stream of Atlanta trade shows she attended to promote her products, and handled the switchboard when her aunt/boss was away.

The first couple of years were shaky, and sales weren't even high enough to mention, but Moore forged ahead. She knew that, with time and a new location, her customer base would improve. In 1982, after operating for two years in the hair salon, she moved to the Green Acres Mall. Although she had a new address and put one employee on the payroll, she still sought the help of her family. Moore's sister Betty created the company's first brochure. Only four pages in length and with little color, it was hardly a keepsake, but it helped spread the word about the business and strengthened its credibility.

Like many small business owners, especially those who are tight on cash, Moore got help from family members whenever and wherever possible. She had to mortgage her home and obtain a $65,000 SBA-guaranteed loan just to open her in-line store (a regular retail venue) on the second floor of the Green Acres Mall, so she had little left to pay outside professionals.

We didn't have much money. Now I know that people say, "Well, you were on a soap opera, so why didn't you have any money?" I always tell them, "Yes, I was on a soap opera, but I was a small fry on the soap opera so I wasn't making the big dollars." The money that today's soap stars make was unheard of back then. I used what cash I did earn to get Vera Moore Cosmetics off the ground, but it wasn't enough to keep it going so I had to get a loan to pay for the essentials and then cut additional expenses wherever I could.

When it came time to prepare flower arrangements for the counter or create "free gifts with a purchase" for potential customers, Moore called on her kin for some creative ideas. And they delivered. Betty would buy up bunches of silk flowers at a local craft store and make the arrangements herself. She burned the midnight oil wrapping ribbons around 500 miniature sacks filled with potpourri, lotion, and bath salts and beads. The finished product always looked like it came from a posh designer store, but it didn't cost designer prices.

Betty will come to the booth today and help me out with my presentation, and people swear that it is custom made. In fact, people ask me all the time what company does my flowers or other arrangements I may have on display at my kiosk, and I just say, "Betty Inc."

Rule 5: Do Unto Your Customers As You Would Have Them Do Unto You

Moore pushed her products out of her 100-square-foot store for ten years. During that time, she continued to refine existing products and develop new ones—and spent thousands of dollars in the process. Yet she still experienced negative vibes from some potential customers. They questioned the quality of her makeup and her actual ownership of the store. To them, being a black business owner, even in the 1980s, was too good to be true. Brushing off the feedback as pure jealousy and ignorance, Moore continued to press on, refusing to be shaken by the silly innuendos. Nothing could break her spirit. Having worked in the theater for many years, she knew how to handle backbiting. She ignored it and focused on the positives instead. She always has. Even after a major conglomerate bought out the entire second floor of the Green Acres Mall in 1992—an acquisition that could very well have jeopardized her business, at least temporarily—Moore didn't worry. She waited patiently as the mall operators began shifting tenants around. There was no telling where her store would land since the mall operators dictated where the tenants would go. Moore might have been placed in a dark corner of the mall, where the traffic is slowest. Or maybe sandwiched between carts filled with hot pretzels and frozen yogurt—not an ideal spot for a cosmetic concern. But after six months of operating out of a temporary space, she landed in a $45,000 freestanding kiosk (that's how much it cost to build) in front of Sears, where the traffic was—and still is—great. And she has been there ever since.

It hasn't been easy for Moore to successfully sell her products from a space not much larger than the rolling popcorn carts found at carnivals or sporting events, especially when a well-known 35,000-square-foot store that carries the same products sits right next door. But offering superb customer service, in addition to providing quality products, has been Moore's mixture for maintaining longevity among such labels as Mac, Bobby Brown, Prescriptives, Naomi Simms, and Iman. Many business owners neglect the importance of serving their customers well. But, like her faith, it's something that Moore takes very seriously.

And so do her employees.

Moore trains all of her workers to regard every customer as fine china. The littlest thing that could possibly drive a potential patron away is pointed out and politely but firmly corrected. Moore, a no-nonsense lady who has little patience for mediocrity, regards excuses as just excuses. As any business owner would, she expects her employees to arrive on time and to always serve customers with a smile. Anyone who approaches the glass counters at Vera Moore Cosmetics won't find gum-popping chatty teens filing their nails and waiting for five o'clock to roll around. Dressed in smart white jackets and wearing flawless makeup, the ladies stand erect, alert, and ready to serve. They even rush to say, "Can I help you?"—a greeting that seems to have become a rarity in stores where staffs have been cut in half and the number of customers has doubled.

Have you ever gone up to a cosmetic counter in a department store and you look around, but there is nobody at the counter to help you? Then when you finally do find someone to show you some product, they can't fully assist you because they have no expertise about the line. The person doesn't know how to apply the makeup because he or she is working as a floater and, just yesterday, was working in appliances. This scenario has happened to me far too many times. I never wanted the counter at Vera Moore Cosmetics to be like this, and it isn't. When my customers approach my kiosk, they are met by friendly and experienced employees who know my product and who can demonstrate my product. We treat our customers like they should be treated—like gold—because what sets your business apart from others, especially in this industry, is customer service, and we work overtime in that area.

The personalized attention that Moore provides for her customers is perhaps unparalleled. Although she is the CEO, she spends many days working at the mall, from open to close, talking with shoppers about their cosmetic needs and getting them to try her line. She takes her time with each customer, never rushing one away to hurry and get to the next. And a few days after each patron makes a purchase, she or one of her five employees places a phone call to the woman's home and asks how she liked the products.

I don't know any company that has ever done that to me.

Rule 6: Be Global-Minded, But Take Your Time and Focus

By 1998, company revenues had reached $400,000. Hundreds of women throughout New York and New Jersey, and some major film and television celebrities across the country, were using Vera Moore Cosmetics. Moore's company was here to stay. With confidence in her status as a major player in the cosmetics industry, she decided to take her business to the next level. In the fall of that year, she introduced a brand new catalog. The handmade brochure her sister had made years before would no longer suffice. She needed a colorful and detailed illustration of her line, with the prices indicated and an order form inside. Moore was thinking of expanding to mail order, and developing the publication was the key to making this additional arm to her business a success.

The reason we did a catalog was to grow our business. We knew that we were in Green Acres Mall, and people who lived in the surrounding communities would get to know us because they shopped at the mall. But we wondered how we could grow outside our community in Valley Stream, and let other people who lived in other states—and even in other countries—know about Vera Moore Cosmetics. The catalog is just one of many steps we have taken to build the business, and we have found that it is necessary in order for us to stay in the game. Of course, . . . to grow any business, you have to diversify. It's just like when you go into the theater as an actress, and when you finish auditioning, they ask you if you can sing. If you can sing, then they ask you if you can dance. The same principle applies to business. Once you have started one particular product and have earned success with it, the public then wants to know what else you can provide and you have to be able to deliver if you plan on competing.

The catalog, which is free and available on the company's Web site (www.veramoore.com), is 14 glossy pages in length and includes descriptions of each product, including the most recent additions to the makeup line and the new spa line.

Moore constantly looks for ways to spread the word about her business here and abroad. She continues to work with distributors to put her products in stores overseas—a process she began in 1997. Penetrating the international marketplace is never easy, especially for a small business owner. But, as always, Moore let the quality of her products do the talking for her when she decided to go abroad. And it worked. A London-based business owner, during a visit to relatives in New Jersey, read about Vera Moore Cosmetics in *Hair and Style* magazine. (Over the years, Moore has bartered services to get ad space in hair and beauty magazines.) The business owner stopped by the mall to talk with Moore and to sample her products. Immediately, she was hooked. A native of Nigeria, the woman was very dark and she had difficulty finding cosmetics that complimented her skin tone. Moore's line, which provides the true colors for all women of color, gave her what she needed. Knowing that other black women back home craved the types of cosmetics Moore had created, the visitor became a distributor for Vera Moore Cosmetics and began carrying the line in her store. That working relationship soon created a domino effect. Shortly afterward, Moore began working with a distributor in the Netherlands, who had read about her company in an advertisement that the London store had placed in a magazine. Moore also tried stores in Germany, but was unsuccessful. Throughout all of her efforts to take her brand overseas, Moore has come to realize that being globally minded is fine, but staying focused is key.

> *One of the mistakes I think that I made was that I went all over the place too fast instead of taking it one step at a time, getting a solid footing in one area, and strengthening my sales there before moving onto the next, but now I know that.*

Moore recognizes that the world is browning. And although some cosmetic companies are still determined to lump black women into color groups that disregard the complexity of their skin, she continues to provide cosmetics that cater to every complexion. And she doesn't plan to stop there. Providing makeup is just the beginning. In the near future, Moore plans to publish a book and produce a tutorial video that demonstrates how to properly apply makeup. Her customers have been asking for this advice, so Moore, the queen of quality customer service, is not about to let them down. Then there's the idea of putting out a Vera Moore bed and bath, accessory, and clothing line—complete with pants, sweatshirts, hats, handbags, wallets, towels, sheets, you name it.

> *Why not? There's enough room in the marketplace for more than one Martha Stewart.*

9

RENÉE E. WARREN AND KIRSTEN N. POE NOELLE–ELAINE MEDIA CONSULTANTS

PR's Dynamic Duo

If we put our name on something, we are going to get the job done.

The decision is unanimous.

Noelle–Elaine Media Consultants always gets the job done.

Says who? Say their clients.

When the Negro Baseball League decided that it wanted to put together its First Annual Negro Baseball League Awards Celebration Dinner to honor its players of the past, the organizers went to a public relations firm that seemed capable of coordinating the event.

They were wrong.

Then they met with a second PR firm to discuss the logistics.

Still no luck.

With time running out, they approached Renée E. Warren and Kirsten N. Poe, the founding partners of Noelle–Elaine Media Consultants (NEMC). At the time, the up-and-coming entrepreneurs had been in business for only about a year and had no event-planning experience. Providing public relations was their forte. But their reputation for excellence preceded them, and they got the job. The young businesswomen had less than three months to solicit sponsors, write the script, book celebrity talent, coordinate travel and hotel accommodations, and handle the press and promotions for the event. But they delivered, and nearly 500 attendees celebrated in rare style.

When Earl G. Graves, chairman and CEO of Earl G. Graves Ltd., and founder, editor, and publisher of *Black Enterprise* magazine, went searching for a public relations company to handle a book tour to tout his tome *How to Succeed in Business Without Being White*, he was quick to find one. But shortly after the tour began, he dropped the prominent company in disappointment. The firm was not generating enough publicity for the book, which reveals the secrets of Graves's success and provides a blueprint for other aspiring entrepreneurs. Enter Warren and Poe with their results-oriented rule:

> *If we put our name on something, we are going to get the job done.*

And they did. Immediately after taking over the book tour, they arranged television, radio, and print interviews for Graves in more than 25 markets. The book received critical acclaim nationwide and made the *New York Times* and *Wall Street Journal* best seller lists.

Since launching NEMC in 1993, Warren and Poe have built a rock solid reputation for getting results, no matter what the situation. They have resuscitated accounts that other PR firms had nearly killed. And they have shaped star-studded affairs both here and abroad, under nail-biting time constraints. Their expertise has earned them $1 million in revenue and a well-respected place among their PR counterparts.

Getting to a comfortable spot in the intensely competitive and highly unsympathetic communications industry wasn't easy for them, especially in the number-one media city in the nation. The partners started their company in Warren's New York studio apartment with no cash, one computer, one printer, and a Rolodex full of hopefuls. They didn't even have individual business cards, and they often shared clothes, just to get by. But their lack of inventory was masked by the quality of their work. Warren and Poe flexed their hustle-muscle every day and landed mainly through word of mouth, accounts that the industry said only large and seasoned firms could handle. When they put their names on the contracts, they proved the so-called experts wrong.

NEMC handles public relations, event planning, video production, sponsorship development, and fund-raising for scores of publicly and privately held corporations, national and local organizations, entrepreneurs, athletes, celebrities, and politicians. BET Holdings Inc., HBO, Wittnaeur International, Charles Schwab & Co. Inc., Sloan Financial Group, The Chapman Co., Citibank, Pepsi-Cola, and Disney are just a few of the major companies that have retained their services. The partners have also handled press and events for film legends Ossie Davis and Ruby Dee, The Artist Formerly Known as Prince, former South African President Nelson Mandela, first lady Hillary Rodham Clinton, famed attorney Johnnie Cochran, and retired General Colin Powell—among others. NEMC's client roster is as long and impressive as the guest list at a post-Oscar-awards soirée. But unlike some publicists and other media personnel who glean contacts from being in the right place at the right time, Warren and Poe didn't earn their credentials through lady luck. They contributed good old-fashioned hard work.

When they were launching the business, both women had full-time jobs at CNBC. Warren, a second-generation entrepreneur whose father once operated a real estate company, worked as a senior producer. Poe was a media relations manager. Each day, after leaving one pressure-cooker environment, they rolled up their sleeves and jumped right into another. Before the clock struck midnight, they fielded telephone calls, typed press releases, prepared press kits, and coordinated the logistics involved in putting together restaurant openings, dinners, and other affairs for their handful of clients. They used vacation time from their day jobs to manage the press for an event in Venezuela. To Warren and Poe, working hard was just as natural as breathing. They didn't know how *not* to work hard. And they still don't, even though they now have a strong team of seasoned employees and ambitious volunteers who can carry some of the load they once shouldered all by themselves.

From a spacious eight-floor suite off Madison Avenue in New York, Warren and Poe clock ten to 15-hour days. If they are not tucked away in their offices developing strategies for existing clients, working the phones to attract new ones, or writing proposals, they are flying from one city to the next to work an event. And not just from behind a booth. The dynamic duo always takes to the floor, racing—in heels, no doubt—from one room to another with headsets on their ears and scripts in their hands. Warren and Poe, both 35, are best friends who act more like sisters than associates. They share the same work ethic and drive to succeed. Perhaps that is what makes their 50–50 partnership a success. Some might see going into business with family or friends as a liability, but Warren and Poe have made their relationship an asset by capitalizing on their similarities and respecting their differences. They are like two different sides of the same coin. Both are competitive and committed to building a well-known and trusted company that can fulfill the communication needs of minority and mainstream clients. But they remain individual. Warren, tall and slender, is a talkative and gregarious extrovert who, more often than not, is the face of Noelle–Elaine in newspaper and magazine articles about the company. Poe, an equally statuesque woman, is "an introvert in an extrovert's clothes." She prefers to operate behind the scenes, and she cares more about doing her job well than she does about being seen. But don't mistake her preference to shun the spotlight as a sign of timidity. Poe is very confrontational and, like Warren, she is verbose once you get her going. Together, their personalities create a powerful entrepreneurial mix and an unshakable confidence in their company.

> *We would put Noelle–Elaine up against any other public relations firm out there. We have, and we always outperform the companies for several reasons, one of which is the fact that they train their employees to think that a media tour means scheduling three interviews. To us, a media tour means having at least ten interviews—and that's just in one day. Also, unlike some top-name PR agencies that get caught up in the glitz and glamour of the game and use it to create more celebrity for themselves than for their clients, we don't. You're not going to see our faces in the paper at our client's*

event because we are there to just do the work. So we do, and leave it at that.

Rule 1: When Opportunity Knocks, Open the Door

It's four o'clock on the Friday before Christmas, 1995. Like everyone else in the city, Warren and Poe are getting ready to leave the office and start the holidays. With their coats on their backs and their shoulder bags slung on their shoulders, they head for the door. Then the phone rings. It's an associate who works for The Artist Formerly Known as Prince. The Artist is ready to announce his departure from Warner Bros. Records, and he wants NEMC to handle the public relations ASAP. Warren and Poe were referred to the musician by the husband of a friend of a friend who developed a Web site for The Artist. Plus, NEMC had sent information about the company to members of his camp. This was their chance to prove themselves and land a plum account that would clearly open their doors for other celebrity clients. Accepting the assignment meant that the start of their holiday would have to be delayed, but they rolled up their sleeves and got to work.

I will never forget it. Renée and I were the only ones left in the office because it was the break for the Christmas holidays. But The Artist didn't care. He wanted to make the announcement right then and there. He didn't want to wait. We saw it as a great opportunity to show him what our company could do, so we took it. We got on the phone and called every contact we knew. We wrote a simple announcement and sent it to the Associated Press in Minneapolis and, within minutes, the story was on the wire and was picked up by all of the media. We also got in touch with national entertainment outlets such as MTV News and Entertainment Tonight. *By the time The Artist got home that very same night, he saw himself on the six o'clock news.*

Warren and Poe didn't get out of the office until four hours later, but the extra time they worked paid off. Their handling of the breaking entertainment news event was rewarded with management of other PR projects for The Artist, including his wedding announcement and highly talked about name change.

Recognizing a good opportunity when it presents itself, seizing it without hesitation, and then executing it to perfection—these traits come very naturally to Warren and Poe. Looking back at the professional road they traveled before starting NEMC, it's easy to see why.

Poe, a native New Yorker who once studied psychology before challenging herself to enter communications, started her career in the media one semester before graduating from college. In the summer of 1985, she interned at Manhattan Cable, now Time Warner Cable. That December, she received her degree in television, radio, and film management from Syracuse University's prestigious Newhouse School of Public Communications. A month later, she accepted a position (for which she did not have to interview) as a sales assistant at the cable company. She worked there full time for a year while attending graduate school part-time at New York University. In 1987, opportunity knocked, in the form of an unpaid internship to work in production for a public affairs program at WNBC-TV, the flagship television station of the National Broadcasting Company. Poe left her $13,000-a-year job at Manhattan Cable to work for free at the station. To some rookie journalists, the move may seem foolish. But, money or no money, Poe recognized its opportunities to learn different facets of her field as they came. She never knew when she would need solid production skills down the road. Besides, a somewhat prophetic and very confident Poe just knew that eventually the station would hire her. And it did.

Meanwhile, more than 250 miles south of New York City, Poe's partner-to-be was leaving the ivory halls of Old Dominion University, in Norfolk, Virginia, with a joint BS degree in criminal justice and speech communications. Warren, who longed to become a journalist ever since she had worked on her high school newspaper, now had several choices: (1) she could accept a position at the local newspaper, where she had interned while completing her undergraduate studies; (2) she could continuing working as an associate producer at the CBS-TV affiliate that had hired her to work part-time before she even got her degree; or (3) she could enter a postgraduate program in London, offered through Southern Illinois University, to analyze the British media.

Wanting some time off before entering the workplace full time, she headed for London for the summer. In the fall of 1987, Warren began working at the *Daily Press*, covering the courts and City Council meetings. After only eight months, she jumped to *The Virginian-Pilot*, a newspaper with a much larger circulation, and worked as a general assignment reporter. But that too was a short-lived position—six months to be exact. Warren, who was born and raised in Chesapeake, Virginia, was tired of living in her home state. She wanted a change. Determined to find a job before leaving her hometown, Warren traveled to a job fair held by the National Association of Black Journalists, an organization NEMC would later obtain as a client. She interviewed for positions in Chicago, New York, and Washington, DC.

In 1988, Warren accepted a position as a news assistant for Dow Jones & Company's wire service Professional Investor Reporter, and she moved to the Big Apple. Poe was still at WNBC, working her way through several of its departments, including program operations and sales administration. By this time, she had also received her master's degree (magna cum laude) in media studies, from New York University.

In 1990, Warren hopped to yet another job. This time, she landed at CNBC as an associate producer. Never having been the type of person who does one thing at a time, she also began freelance writing for *Black Enterprise* and *Essence* magazines, affiliations that would prove extremely useful when starting Noelle–Elaine. In October 1991, Warren and Poe (who had just joined CNBC as a media relations associate) met for the very first time. If it had been up to Poe, several months may have passed before their paths crossed. A mutual friend suggested to Poe that she should contact Warren once she got to CNBC, but she was in no hurry to make acquaintances.

> *Despite the fact that I own my own company and it happens to be in an industry that requires having an aggressive and outgoing personality, I'm really an introvert. So when I got to CNBC, I said to myself, "I'm not looking for nobody. Let me just get settled in my job because I'm not trying to be friends with anybody." I just wanted to do my work and go home.*

Not Warren. She couldn't wait to introduce herself to Poe, and when she did, the two clicked immediately and became fast friends. They hung out religiously; they were together so much that their coworkers could hardly tell them apart. The two even spent their vacation time together. For their vacation in 1993, they planned to travel to Aruba, but like most people in the beginning stages of their communication careers, the two were short on cash. So they came up with the idea of throwing a party at a Harlem restaurant to raise money for their trip. Warren and Poe had made lots of friends, and because of the nature of their work, they had also generated tons of contacts, so their idea was bound to be successful. The two spread the word about their upcoming bash. They charged about $10 a head, and over 200 people, including the vice president of CNBC, showed up in a snowstorm in March—on a weeknight! The two were on to something that could possibly make them millions. But the thought of becoming professional party planners had never even crossed their minds. Besides, by this time, Warren had become a senior producer at CNBC and was producing ten daily live financial news shows and two weekend shows. Poe, was promoted to media relations manager and was put in charge of all press-related activities for the 50-million-subscribers network. Neither woman was discontented with the direction her career had taken. But, after they returned from the islands, when the manager of the Harlem restaurant approached them about working on a PR project for Sherman Hemsley, star of the 1970s–1980s sitcom *The Jeffersons*, the two just couldn't resist.

After taking a long hard look at the industry, Kirsten and I felt that nobody was really representing our African-American counterparts from a public relations standpoint, so we saw the Sherman Hemsley project as a way to start filling that void. Although there were other PR companies out there, it was a niche that was untouched. Because we had become such close friends, like family even, and because of our professional backgrounds, we knew that we could work together to build this type of business. Kirsten had a solid knowledge of PR strategies and PR planning because that's what she did for a living at CNBC. I knew a lot of reporters, both African American and otherwise, because of the newspaper jobs that I held and the freelance writing that I was doing. Plus, I had acquired many producer contacts working as an AP [assistant producer], so we knew that we could make the business work.

Rule 2: Be Creative in Your Approach to Cut Down Costs, But Always Start Off with a Cushion

Warren and Poe wasted no time laying the groundwork for their new venture. They continued to hold on to their jobs at CNBC, and launched their public relations firm as a part-time endeavor. Setting up shop in Warren's 88th Street studio apartment, the two began to ready themselves for their first client.

> *We thought that we could not work with Sherman Hemsley and not be a real company. We didn't want to misrepresent ourselves, so Renée and I automatically started thinking about what we would call our business. We played around with the idea of using our first names together and then our last names. But we decided that it wouldn't have been a good idea to use either, because we were still working at CNBC. We thought that somebody might recognize our names and consider our business to be a conflict of interest with our regular jobs. So we decided to use our middle names, Noelle and Elaine, instead. Then we drew up our partnership papers and everything just flowed from that point.*

Warren and Poe officially launched their company on October 1, 1993. But, like most new business owners, they had little start-up capital so they donned their creative caps to come up with ways to get all the things they needed without spending a lot of money. They didn't need much, but their modest list cost a little more than their CNBC paychecks could buy. Unable to spend extra cash on two sets of business cards, the partners placed both of their names and home telephone numbers on one card. They couldn't afford to have an automated voice mail service either, so they created their own. In their best speaking voices, the partners recorded the following:

POE: "The person you are calling . . ."
WARREN: "Renée Warren."
Poe: "Is unavailable. Please leave a message after the tone."

They used this recording for several months but no one ever knew that it was originally homemade. Because Warren was freelancing, they did have a computer and a printer at their disposal. And the Kinko's copy center around the corner from their company headquarters could handle all of their xeroxing, collating, and faxing, so the partners were ready to get rolling. The account with Sherman Hemsley didn't pan out, but it didn't take Warren and Poe long to find another client. A stockbroker for Dean Witter Reynolds Inc. (now Morgan Stanley Dean Witter), whom Renée had met at an art show, was putting together a conference in Hawaii, and he asked the two women to coordinate the publicity for it. So, from 9:00 A.M. to 5:00 P.M., they worked at CNBC. From 7:00 P.M. until midnight, they worked on Noelle–Elaine. The duo secured press coverage for the event in various media outlets throughout Hawaii. The affair was such a huge success that the local Dean Witter office sent the stockbroker flowers for helping to bring so much attention to the company.

On the heels of the Hawaii project, the partners obtained several other small clients through referrals, which is how they generate more than 85 percent of their business today. They handled an opening celebration and press conference for Caribbean Major League Football; a press conference and luncheon touting American business in Venezuela; a restaurant's grand opening in Harlem; and many other bantam accounts. Several clients were coming through the doors, but Warren and Poe soon found out that much of the promised cash was failing to follow.

Initially, when we launched NEMC, we started off working with several small clients. Because they worked with a small budget, some of them were not able to pay us, and . . . those who could pay us rarely did it on time. We needed the work, so we continued to fulfill the contract just to build up our name. But that created financial havoc for us because we were incurring all of the expenses and the clients could not pay us back. We gave them a line of credit in the hopes that they would get on solid ground, but we just wound up in debt. In retrospect, we should have built up a cushion that we could have fallen back on, so that when payment was delayed we could still have paid our rent and other essentials, but we had a false illusion of what it meant to start a business. We knew our craft but we were naïve [about] running a business, so we didn't know that we should have started with some operating capital. We had only whatever paychecks we had coming in from our regular jobs, so we suffered financially.

Like many new business owners who are faced with the proverbial cash crunch, Warren and Poe robbed Peter to pay Paul while drumming up new business for their company. They also continued to work at their day jobs, but, by May 1994, the two had become overwhelmed. Having to pull double duty as CNBC employees and as CEOs for NEMC was wearing them down, so they left the network to operate NEMC full time. Two months later, they moved Noelle–Elaine into a small office space just a few floors below where the headquarters are currently located. It was a risky move, given their somewhat shaky start, but Warren and Poe were ready to put everything they had—and even what they didn't have—into NEMC.

Rule 3: Learn from Your Mistakes

It didn't take long for Warren and Poe to earn a reputation for getting results. They were quickly becoming New York's African-American publicists of choice. So when members of the Negro Baseball League started planning their First Annual Negro Baseball League Awards Celebration Dinner, they contacted NEMC. Forget the fact that the two had never coordinated an event before. They still took the job, in September 1994. The dinner was to be held in November, which meant that Warren and Poe had less than three months to pull it off. Putting the affair together would not be a walk in the park, even for the highly professional and extremely well connected duo. The other two firms that the organization had hired before taking on NEMC failed to get anything done, so Warren and Poe started from ground zero. No talent had been confirmed. No money had been raised. No locations had been scouted. And no menu had been selected. Every aspect of putting together the event fell on their shoulders. It was sink or swim. But relying on the production and public relations expertise they had gained while at CNBC, Warren and Poe dived right into the project and used every resource at their disposal (including a friend and former coworker who worked as a talent booker) to help round up celebrities for the dinner.

Poe coordinated the press for the event and reworked the organization's press kit. Warren handled the logistical rundown of the function, pinpointing how many volunteers would be needed to help out and where those people would go, as well as developing the guest list and defining the format for the evening. Together, the twosome took care of such particulars as travel and hotel arrangements, writing the script, booking the venue, and choosing the menu. They recruited friends to help work the event. Nearly everything that they needed to produce a gala affair was coming together. But there was still the issue of money. Warren and Poe needed money—lots of it. The hotel costs alone were $100,000. They had yet to expand their company's services to include fund-raising and sponsorship development, so they had no clue about how to collect the necessary capital. To remedy the situation, Warren and Poe decided to use a professional fund-raiser and paid him $1,000 a month as a retainer, to help them with sponsorship. But the so-called expert turned out to be a scam artist, and he never came through with the money.

> *We didn't check his credentials. We knew of people who had worked with him, and we actually knew one person from his office, so we felt he was credible. And as is customary for us, we had weekly meetings to discuss his progress. But after a while, it became pretty evident that he had more excuses than results. So, from this experience, we learned to always check references no matter who the person may be, to trust our gut feelings, and always be prepared to take care of the task ourselves just in case something goes wrong.*

Warren and Poe were now stuck for an idea of how to meet all of the costs of producing the celebration. They were particularly concerned about how they would bring more than 50 former Negro Baseball League players to New York City to be honored, when they had no money for transportation, one of their biggest expenses. It may have been less than apropos to ask the honorees to pay their own way, but they did, and the players begrudgingly agreed. Meanwhile, Warren and Poe twisted and wrung every cent they could out of their long list of contacts.

We had to raise money or the event would have been a bust, so Kirsten and I went to friends and, literally, everybody we had ever worked with and everybody we ever interviewed, and begged them for money.

Plan B worked.

When all was said and done, about 500 guests converged on the Marriott hotel in Manhattan. The R & B (rhythm and blues) group Sounds of Blackness performed. Comedian George Wallace emceed. And a slew of celebrities and dignitaries, including Ossie Davis and Ruby Dee, Willie Randolph, Bertice Berry, and Steve Garvey gathered to pay tribute to the courageous players of the Negro League.

Renée and I got cursed out initially by the baseball players in trying to pull this thing together. But when they finally got to the dinner, there was nothing but smiles and kind words. The players were so happy. They said, "We have never been honored in this way in our life." It was just nothing but praise.

By the end of their first year in business, Warren and Poe had earned a modest $250,000 in revenue and had expanded their services to include event planning and video production, which consisted of developing commercials, corporate videos, infomercials, documentaries, and video news releases. Over the next three years, they attracted more diverse clients.

In 1995, NEMC began what would become a long-lasting working relationship with BET Holdings, Inc., the parent company of Black Entertainment Television, when the budding business planned the publicity for the BET/Michael Jackson Walk of Fame celebration. BET was their first corporate client. That year, Warren and Poe also began working with several celebrities, including rapper/actor LL Cool J on a media tour to promote a film in which the entertainer appeared. They developed a documentary, "Africa: An Emerging Market for the 90s," for the U.S. Africa Chamber of Commerce, and won a Telly Award, the highest honor given to a production company. The following year, the partners planned, among others, 1,000- to 3,000-person dinners for The National Association of Black Owned Broadcasters, The Walter Kaitz Foundation, The Minority Corporate Counsel Association, and The New York Association of Black Journalists.

Business was coming mainly through word of mouth, and it only seemed to be getting better and better as time passed. But money was still tight, and the partners were beginning to feel the ripple effects of a few accounts gone bad. There was one in particular, which the two prefer to keep nameless even though the company is no longer in business. The account was 70 percent of their monthly retainer.

That was their first mistake.

Their second was continuing to wait for payment from this and other clients when it was clearly not going to come.

There is this book called Confessions of an Advertising Executive, *but it also relates to PR. The book says that you should never have one client that's more than 50 percent of your billing because (a) they basically own you and (b) if they go down, you go down. But with this particular client, a large part of our revenue hinged on him paying us, but he couldn't, and that put us in a very precarious situation. Renée and I used our own Federal Express account to send materials for the client. We had traveled to Jamaica, Grenada, and Trinidad to work on events, but when it came time for reimbursement, not only did the client not have the money to pay us our monthly fee, the client couldn't pay us back what they owed us for shipping things through Federal Express. We had a $5,000 Federal Express bill and thousands of dollars racked up in making phone calls to the Caribbean, Venezuela, and other parts of South America that we had to pay, but the client couldn't pay us. It wasn't that he refused to pay us. He could not because he was going through a financial crisis of his own. He even tried to move the expenses over to his business bank account, but because his company was unstable, the banks wouldn't even allow* *it. Still, the bills had to be paid. Our credit was out the window. We needed supplies for the office. We needed new computers. By this time, we had a small staff so we needed to make payroll and keep a straight face so that our employees would not panic and think that the business was going under. So, in dealing with this client, it changed our view of how we began to look at and solicit new clients. We wanted stable people, people that had money, and people who had a history of paying and paying on time.*

To relieve some of the financial pressure, Warren and Poe borrowed money from their parents. Poe's parents paid their daughter's rent for the entire year, to free up cash that could be used to operate the business.

Everybody in our families really chipped in to make sure that Noelle–Elaine survived, because they believed in us and knew that we could make the business work.

But the partners never used their folks' financial safety net as an excuse for poor planning and strategizing. Since starting the company, Warren and Poe had pitched the same people at the same time, which basically cut their client potential in half. After trudging through this turbulent year, the two decided to make their presentations separately. And no longer did they wait and wait and wait for a client to cough up the cash.

I think at the end of 1996 Renée and I looked at each other and asked ourselves, "Are we going to keep asking these clients who are not paying us for the money and hope that they eventually come through? Or, are we going to go out and get new clients to make up the difference?" We knew that we couldn't continue to rely on those who clearly were not going to pay, so we chalked it up as a learning experience and became more selective of which companies we decided to do business with. We are in a position now where we can actually turn business down.

Warren and Poe didn't totally abandon the smaller, less visible firms. However, they did start to create a more balanced mix of modest concerns with larger blue-chip companies. They also never let an account go 15 days past due without stopping work on the project. The partners learned their lesson. From it, they became that much stronger.

With the downturn, we simply learned what we were made of.

Rule 4: When Managing Employees, Set Quantitative Goals

By early 1998, the financial storm clouds had cleared. Clients continued to roll in like clockwork.

They added the Black Enterprise/NationsBank Entrepreneurs Conference (for the second year in a row), the BET/Soundstage Grand Opening, the Ruby Dee and Ossie Davis 50th Wedding Anniversary and Community Theatre Benefit Dinner, and the Disney Channel to their client catalogue. NEMC had also moved into new and larger offices in the same building. And, for the first time in five years, Warren and Poe had been added to the payroll. Gone were the days of sharing peanut butter and jelly sandwiches, renting gowns and jewelry to wear to events, and wearing their one good suit to solicit new business. Warren and Poe also no longer had to bear the brunt of wearing all the entrepreneurial hats. The staff had grown considerably, and the partners formed teams for each of their service areas. But delegating authority and managing their employees proved to be as big a challenge as any that they had ever encountered.

When we first started Noelle–Elaine, it was just Renée and I, so we were responsible for getting everything done. We had no one else to rely on, so not only were we the heads of the company, we were working the event, working the press conference, writing the press releases, calling the reporters on the phone, and everything else that was required to operate the business. In a way, it was good because it enabled us to learn every facet of our company. But at the same time, it was bad because it took up so much of our time that we were unable to solicit a lot of new business. We knew that we had to increase the expectations and the performance level of our employees so that we could focus on securing more clients, but it was hard to let go and trust others to do what we used to do. The hardest thing to me, out of everything that we've ever done, has been trying to learn how to manage people.

At first, Warren and Poe managed their staff with kid gloves. They didn't set specific goals for each employee. But they found that their management style only created havoc within the company because the amount and level of work that they expected was not getting done.

We've learned with employees that you've got to be quantitative if you expect good performance. For example, Renée and I found that we couldn't just say to a member of the public relations team, "Go develop a relationship with a reporter and get hits," meaning press coverage for a client. We had to set specific goals and guidelines that said, "You should have x amount of hits per client per week. And if you do not have these hits, this means that you have not done your job so you are now falling below our expectations. We therefore have the right not to give you a raise, not to promote you, and not to employ you."

Warren and Poe also had a problem getting all departments to work together. For a while, the public relations team was only concerned with coordinating the press; event planning was only interested in the logistics of producing an affair; video production only cared about splicing and editing corporate videos or commercials; and sponsorship only worried about raising money. None of the departments tried to relate to or help the other. But when the partners enforced team goals that affected everyone at NEMC, attitudes changed.

We basically started saying that all of you either sink together or swim together. We let them know that there were no individual victories or defeats. If PR messed up, then event planning had to stay to help fix the problem; and if event planning messed up, PR had to stay. By creating these team goals, it forced everyone to start talking to each other more, knowing what was going on in the other person's department, and taking the initiative to help each other out when needed and without having to be asked. It took us five years to learn these types of managerial tactics, but they work.

Today, you can't walk into the offices of Noelle–Elaine without hearing the click of computer keys or the sounds of an assertive employee pitching a client to the press over the phone. If it's the week of an event, the entire staff rallies together and stays in the office until the last detail is done. But Warren and Poe are hardly dictators who crack the whip every second of the day. They want their employees to be productive, but they also want them to be happy. So, if PR can complete their projects by four o'clock, PR can go home at four o'clock. If the working moms can knock out their assignments within deadline, they can bring their kids into the office while they work. And when it comes to the company picnic, mom, dad, sis, and baby brother are invited.

We want our employees to have happy marriages, happy kids, and a happy family life because we believe in family so we try to create a familylike atmosphere within our company.

Rule 5: Always Be Willing to Go That Extra Mile

Over the years, NEMC has obtained press coverage for its clients in such notable publications as *USA Today, The Washington Post, The Wall Street Journal, Newsweek,* and *Fortune.* TV and radio spots have included *Oprah, The Rosie O'Donnell Show, The Today Show,* and *The Tom Joyner Morning Show.* Warren and Poe have raised hundreds of thousands of dollars for organizations, worked with million-dollar corporations, and coordinated historic events overseas. With credits like these, it would be easy to simply get by on a good name. But Warren and Poe continue to go that extra mile for every client.

*I think if somebody was to pay Renée and myself $1 million
to work on an event, we would give the client $1.5 million in
terms of our efforts. It's just the way we are. And our employees have picked up that philosophy too.*

In May 1998, Warren and Poe proved that putting forth a
valiant effort, no matter what the circumstances, could lead to
obtaining business. While working in the press room at the
Black Enterprise/NationsBank Entrepreneurs Conference, the
partners got wind that Charles Watkins, president of Wittnauer
International Inc., then a $42-million watch and fine jewelry
manufacturing company, had misplaced his cellular phone.
Warren and Poe wanted very much to add Wittnauer, one of the
nation's largest black-owned firms, to their client roster. So,
hoping to make a unique and lasting first impression, they re-
trieved the phone and ensured that it was promptly returned to
Watkins.

*Kirsten left a message in his hotel room, but she also con-
tacted the front desk and informed them of the loss, just in
case he did not have a chance to check his messages. Once
Charles called back, Kirsten told him that she would leave it
for him at the front desk. Then, later on, she called the front
desk again and called Charles back to follow up and make
sure that he had the phone in his possession.*

With that, the bait was set.

In the weeks following the conference, Warren and Poe reeled
Watkins in by sending him a detailed and comprehensive proposal requesting work for their company. But their hunt for the
phone ended up being the key to their inking the deal to promote
the Wittnauer-Optmist International Junior Golf Championship,
an event that attracts 659 kids from 21 countries.

*Charles said, "If you go out of your way like you did at the
conference for a phone, you must really go out of your way for
your clients." Kirsten and I always tell our employees that
it's not the big things that people remember. It's the little*

things. It's knowing they can call you at home or on the weekends, knowing that you'll go that extra step even if it's not necessarily in the fine points of the contract, and knowing that you'll stay until the job is done and provide a helping hand at a moment's notice. It makes the clients feel that you care about their success—and we do—and that you are committed to helping them achieve their goals. It also helps make them feel you are a part of their team.

Warren and Poe had only a week to prepare and launch the campaign, but, as usual, they came through. The July tournament was covered on ESPN, the Golf Channel, CNN, the major networks, and their affiliates. Pleased with their performance, Wittnauer signed them to another contract to coordinate publicity for the Texaco Grand Prix, an event for which Wittnauer serves as the official timekeeper. The event was held in October 1998 and, thanks to Warren and Poe's public relations savvy, it was televised worldwide on ABC Sports.

Whether Warren and Poe are coordinating a quaint restaurant opening uptown or a 5,000-person dinner filled with distinguished delegates overseas, everything this dynamic duo touches seems to turn into media gold. Yet some mainstream corporations continue to stay clear of their company when it comes to handling their nonminority events. In its seven years of operation, NEMC has landed a few universal accounts (Disney and *Money* magazine), but a lot of their contracts have been to produce and plan minority affairs.

And most companies still will look at us to do their minority functions. Bob Johnson is a billionaire because of his focus on the African-American community, so I'm not saying there is anything wrong with it. I'm saying that Renée and I can definitely make money and be independently wealthy with the same focus, and we will definitely not turn down money if a corporation wants us to work on their minority campaigns. But we at least want a shot at doing more nonminority events. When we worked at CNBC, they didn't say, "OK, let's put them on the black shows" because we are black. We were expected to do our job no matter what it entailed. So if we could represent CNBC, why can't we—as two highly professional, black female business owners—represent more than just minority events? After all, the media encompass all colors.

Judging from their track record, expertise, and win–win attitude, Warren and Poe, who plan to open a West Coast office in the next couple of years, are bound to cross over completely. They simply work too hard and know too much not to.

10

ALBERT AND ODETTA MURRAY
HILLSIDE INN

Mr. and Mrs. Hospitality

When someone says that there is something that I can't do,
even though I may feel that they are wrong, I will go and test
to see whether they were right.

In the Pocono Mountains of eastern Pennsylvania, resorts come a
dime a dozen. As visitors maneuver their cars around the twists
and turns of the routes and interstates that lead to the popular
vacation area, huge billboards announce one spectacular attraction after another—everything from candle making to canoeing.
But there is but one that offers two full-course meals the way
grandma used to make, an owner who carries fresh towels to
your room, and a warm smile from "Mama" as she greets you at
the door.

However, unlike the other hotels that are advertised every five
miles along the otherwise hypnotizing stretch of highway, little
fanfare introduces this unique resort. There are no festive signs
displaying images of guests splashing about in the pool, chip-
ping out of a bunker onto the seventeenth green, or kayaking
down cascading waters. Only two signs point the way to Hillside
Inn. They are positioned beneath ads ten times their size, and by
the time drivers' eyes notice the simple wording, the entrance is
only a quarter mile away.

But don't mistake the absence of neon lights, bold lettering,
and sky banners for a carbon copy of the Bates Motel. Hillside
Inn is quietly tucked beneath a canopy of trees off a main road

203

running through the heart of the Blue Mountains, but it is a beautifully landscaped 36-room hotel situated on 15 acres of a 109-acre estate.

Hillside Inn, the first and only black-owned resort in the Poconos, is what the owners, Albert and Odetta Murray, simply call their "house by the side of the road." When the couple opened the hotel 45 years ago, it was just that. Hillside Inn, then christened Hillside House, was surrounded by hundreds of acres of farmland. One road carried visitors to and from the eight-room house. Back then, Hillside House had wooden floors, a screened-in porch, and hanging lights. There was no heat, air conditioning, or insulation, no individual bathrooms for guests to use, and no diversions except a pond six miles away. But it was a start. From these humble beginnings, the Murrays managed to build a solid business that today attracts 1,000 vacationers, conference attendees, church groups, and other guests each year, and grosses $900,000 in annual revenue.

A serene and picturesque vacation spot, Hillside Inn is loaded with activity, fine food, and feelings of family. Indoors, there is an Olympic-size swimming pool and a Jacuzzi, year-round entertainment with live jazz and gospel performers, a game room, an exercise room, full conference facilities, and a gift shop. Outdoors, visitors will find a basketball court, tennis court, softball field, volleyball court, shuffleboard, horseshoes, a lake for fishing, trails for walking and jogging, and a three-hole, all-season Canadian golf course used for round-robin play. At some resorts, patrons must fend for themselves when touring the surrounding area. Hillside Inn provides vans that take visitors into town for shopping, bingo, and other activities. But guests head back to the inn for their meals. The resort's sumptuous and mouth-watering menu includes Southern, Caribbean, and traditional American cuisine. Among the delights are: fried chicken, barbecued spare ribs, catfish, pork chops, collard greens, cornbread, yams, and potato salad. Attention is also paid to calorie-conscious diners and guests who are on special diets.

The Murrays go to great lengths to ensure that their guests feel at home. Visitors who want to make their stay a bit more permanent can be accommodated. Surrounding the inn is a small but growing community of uniquely designed homes owned by black doctors, lawyers, judges, artists, and teachers. The widow of the late Sammy Davis Jr. has taken up residence here. It is no accident that this neighborhood has taken shape so close to Hillside Inn. Over the years, the Murrays have subdivided tens of acres of their 109-acre lot and sold one-acre plots to prospective homeowners. The Murrays say their goal in starting this project is the same as when they started the hotel: to show the public that African Americans can produce as well as consume.

And there is more to come. Another 40 acres will be subdivided and sold for more residential development. A planned $700,000 expansion will add 16 additional rooms (each with its own Jacuzzi) to the $2.5-million two-story hotel, a 600-seat auditorium, and a new fitness center. Not bad for two Georgia natives who used to sell plastic aprons and liniment door-to-door. And they did it without a trust fund from "Daddy," a start-up loan, or set-asides.

Starting Hillside Inn was no easy task. The Murrays experienced the challenges that are familiar to nearly every new entrepreneur: securing start-up capital, finding good employees, and attracting and retaining customers. But their difficulties in overcoming these obstacles were exacerbated by the times. The year was 1955. Nearly 100 years had passed since the Thirteenth Amendment to the U.S. Constitution abolished slavery, but segregation was still the operative law of the land. Schoolrooms were segregated. In some states, blacks could ride only in the rear area of buses, had to sip water from "Colored Only" water fountains, and use separate public lavatories. Violent protests, sparked by forced integration, ripped through the southern states in which de jure segregation was most extreme. To start a business, especially a hotel, in the Poconos, where resorts traditionally barred blacks, was seen almost as suicidal. Yet, the Murrays didn't scare easily. Driven partly by ego—mainly Albert's—but mostly by the desire to be successful and respected African-American entrepreneurs, the couple weathered neighborhood petitions urging them to go, and gun-toting officials who broke down their doors late at night and searched for any reason to shut their hotel down.

The Murrays have been married for 56 years. Anyone who watches them bounce from one room of the hotel to another can see that their courage was not the only trait that has sustained their business for nearly a half-century. Courage is a critical trait for any fledging entrepreneur. But those who succeed have a strategic and well-thought-out plan for successfully operating a business. *Personalized attention* is just one of the sources for the Murrays' staying power. It is not unusual to find Albert helping guests with their bags or carting towels to the rooms.

At 79, the Murrays are still very spry. They take a hands-on approach to running their business. After almost going bankrupt at the hands of careless managers several years ago, they won't have it any other way. A staff of 17 full-time and part-time employees helps to run the resort, but no day passes in which the Murrays are absent from the premises. They both work virtually around the clock.

Odetta Murray is a soft-spoken and endearing woman whom the guests and Albert affectionately call "Mama" because of her ability to calm any situation with just one look. On this particular day, she stands behind the front desk and is answering the phones. In a sweet and gentle voice that has no trace of timidity, she takes reservations. Afterward, she glides quietly to the kitchen to check on preparations for dinner. Then she's off to the lobby to greet passersby who have stopped in to take a peek at the Hillside Inn because they've heard so much about it. Heading down to the ground floor to make sure the area is prepared for visitors who have reserved the conference facility, she stops to greet two guests who've just come out of the pool. Forget the fact that they have been staying at the hotel for several days and she has seen them at least 25 times since they checked in. Mama always has something warm and inviting to say.

"Oh, you out so soon."

"I've been out there since two o'clock this afternoon and it was just absolutely beautiful," says one of the ladies as she wraps a beach towel around her shoulders.

With a huge smile, the other guest adds, "I'm going again after dinner and I'm going to go every day that I'm here. It's so great, I don't want to go home."

In a zealous tone, Mama quips, "You know you don't have to go home. We hurry you in here, but not out."

The ladies fall into one another as they erupt in laughter.

After checking the conference room's readiness, Mama makes her way back upstairs. Albert is just returning with a group of tourists. As he winds up his description of how the hotel began, his deep, commanding voice can be heard in the lobby. Seconds later, the rangy retired New York City judge enters the room. Years ago, Albert, referred to by employees and guests as "The Judge," exchanged his black robe for a golf shirt, khakis, and a pair of easy walking shoes. However, he is no less frank than when he was presiding over cases in New York City's criminal courts. People who know Albert say that he has never been one to beat around the bush, especially when the topic is ownership among blacks. Whether he is being interviewed by CNN, speaking before the local Rotary Club, or just chatting with guests, he talks candidly about the challenges of building his business. A few challenges still continue. Customer retention is at the top of the list.

The travel industry has topped $400 billion. African Americans spend more than $20 billion a year in their travel plans. Still, Hillside Inn's customers, of whom more than half are black, are dropping off. Ask where they are going and Albert, in an unapologetic tenor, will say, "To the white man's place."

We have a lot of black people coming up here year-round, but there are still many of us who won't stay at Hillside. Even when I reopened Hillside Inn in 1989, after tearing down the old hotel to build a new one, I felt very strongly that if 100 of us would come to the Poconos to vacation, 70 of those people would go to the white place even if my place was better. If I had gold and the white man had silver, they would still go down the road because, for some reason, we seem to want to use what the white man already has. I ask: "Why not take a look at what Hillside has and what it needs? Support us, so that we can give you what you want and what you feel the other places have that we don't have. But don't come and say, "Ah, forget Hillside Inn. We can still go to Shawnee, Fernwood, or some of the other white-owned resorts in the area," because that does nothing for the stability and growth of black businesses or the black community.

Rule 1: Remember to Listen to Dear Old Dad

Reflecting on his road from the farmlands of Harlem, Georgia, where his family owned only one mule, to the mountainous slopes of East Stroudsburg, Pennsylvania, Albert is quick to begin with the story of his late father. A sharecropper in the Jim Crow South during the 1920s, Roland was unable to give Albert what he wanted. Still, he always gave him what he *needed*, and that wasn't easy. The misguided "separate but equal" rule spread like wildfire through public schools, housing, transportation, recreational facilities, eateries, and telephone booths. Albert, like every other "colored" child at the time, was limited in his social and educational activities. In the area in which he lived, he could only attend school for three months out of the year, up to the sixth grade. The rest of the time, he toiled in the scorching heat in the furrows, alongside his father. But Albert was not going to be anybody's field hand in the future. He was going places. His father was going to make sure that he did.

My goal in life was to own things, and I knew that I would some day because my father helped me to look up, over, and beyond what was right in front of me. He always encouraged me to do and to be more. I can remember being in the fields with him and watching him bow down to the white man and hating it, but I always respected his humility and learned from his strength, both of which are extremely important in running your own business. I remember Mr. Daniel, the white man who owned the land that my father and I farmed. He offered us a second mule and when he did he also offered me an old car. Now I wanted that car because I would have been a big shot among the other boys that didn't have one, but my father said "No, boy." He didn't want Mr. Daniel to give me anything. He wanted me to work for the things I wanted. My father said, "Mr. Daniel owns that car, he owns the land, and he owns the money that we count on him to pay us so that we can eat, because his family gave him an education. You go get a job, work your way through school, and then you can be like Mr. Daniel and have what Mr. Daniel has. But always remember to finish what you start." Perhaps one of the greatest lessons my father taught me, and one that I reflected on throughout the hard times of starting and running Hillside Inn, is about following through. *I learned the importance of execution every day I sat out in that hot sun plowing the fields. You see, when you plow out a row of crops, you can always end up leaving about two feet or so at the end of the row unfinished because there may be a ditch, tree, or some other obstacle at the end of the row that keeps the mule from going all the way. Because of the obstacles, the mule gets used to turning before the row is completely plowed. I can remember my father always checking to see whether or not I finished plowing each part of every row. He insisted that I go all the way out to the end and not leave anything unfinished, despite what lay ahead. I came to understand that he wanted me to have that attitude not only in that field, but also in life.*

With these wisdom-filled words etched in his memory, Albert, at the instruction of his father, went to live with an aunt in Augusta, Georgia, soon after leaving the sixth grade. He needed to finish what he started, and that meant school. Educational facilities had not changed for blacks. They were still segregated and inferior. Because there was no high school for black students closer to his home, he made the 30-mile trip to Augusta to finish his studies. Albert planned to attend college after getting his diploma, but he knew that he would not get there unless he worked, so the 16-year-old began pounding the pavement. His first thought was to get a job delivering groceries, but because he did not know the streets in the area, he opted for more familiar terrain: a vegetable farm. Albert also worked on the lawns and in the kitchens of rich white families. Never one to let pride cloud the bigger picture, he worked a 4:00 P.M.-to-midnight shift pushing wheelbarrows of burnt clay at a local asbestos factory for $14 a week. All the while, he attended classes at A.R. Johnson High School and then Paine College High School. During his third year in high school, Albert met Odetta Sanders, then a junior at Paine College.

Unlike Albert, Odetta was privileged. The daughter of a southern minister, she lived on top of a hill, rode to church in a black limousine, and attended a private black high school. There was every indication that this poor farm boy from the Deep South would have no chance at winning her heart, especially since her mother did not approve of his social upbringing. But this was the girl Albert wanted and was determined to get, no matter what.

Albert finished high school in 1942 and, that same year, enrolled at Paine College. World War II had already begun, and the government was calling all college men to enlist. Those that did could continue in the classroom until needed for the war, so Albert signed up. By his twenty-first birthday, he had been drafted. Meanwhile, Odetta finished her undergraduate studies in natural sciences, home economics, and French. She graduated in 1943, joined the Army, and served in the medical corps as a nurse. Albert and Odetta had been courting for a couple of years by this time, and they kept in touch whenever possible. In October 1944, they were married.

Six months later, Albert, while riding on a tank destroyer outside of Munich, Germany, was hit in the back with shrapnel from an enemy bomb.

Rule 2: Take Advantage of Opportunities as They Come; You Never Know Where They Might Lead

In April 1946, Albert, still recovering from his injuries, was discharged from the Army. Eager to pick up his studies, he applied to several colleges and was accepted at Columbia University in New York City. That summer, he hopped a bus and headed for the Big Apple, where he lived in Brooklyn with a cousin. Odetta stayed behind to teach school in Jasper, Georgia, for a spell, but soon joined her husband in New York. They lived in a one-room house filled with furniture from the Salvation Army. To make a living, they began selling Watkin's face creams and other toiletries door-to-door. Odetta also worked as a nurse at a nearby hospital and attended the New York School of Interior Design. Albert, who was late accepting the offer to attend Columbia, enrolled at Long Island University that fall.

After graduating in just two and a half years with a degree in accounting, he attended Brooklyn Law School—all paid for by Uncle Sam. In June 1952, four months after earning his law degree, he passed the New York State bar examination. Albert's long-term plan was to form the first black law partnership in Brooklyn (with three other black students who had also passed the bar), and to ultimately work his way up to becoming a judge. But a chance meeting with Abraham Kaufman, a Jewish attorney and investment maverick, altered his career plans. Kaufman, then a well-known business mogul in Kings County, New York, operated a real estate and law firm. He bought, renovated, and sold houses for a living, and was very good at his craft. But after a while, trouble brewed between Kaufman and the Internal Revenue Service, and he needed a sharp accountant and attorney to represent him. At the recommendation of one of Kaufman's real estate agents, to whom the Murrays sold Watkin's products, Albert was brought in to assist. The two became fast friends. Before long, they formed a 50–50 partnership in Kaufman's two operations and began working Wall Street for investment deals. Kaufman handled the negotiating, and Murray managed the legal aspects of the deals. One deal involved foreclosing on 109 acres of prime Poconos real estate.

> *A German man who owned an eight-room house, and all the land surrounding it, needed some money to bring his family to the United States, so we loaned him $40,000. But he got into trouble with immigration and couldn't bring his family back. Nor could he come back, so we lost the $40,000. We had to foreclose on the property.*

This created an unexpected opportunity for Albert. He could envision the property's growing into a successful business in the future, so he jumped at the chance. He and Kaufman talked about transforming the tiny rooming house, which sat on 15 acres of the 109-acre lot, into a full-fledged resort. In May 1955, they took over all of the land, added cosmetic touches to the eight rooms of the house, and installed baths. These changes were required so that the two could obtain a liquor license. Three months later, with the proper paperwork and permits in hand, they started to make more detailed plans to expand. Unfortunately, Kaufman, who became ill soon after the foreclosure, was still recovering from a hospital stay of nearly seven weeks. He went back and forth to New York to check on the businesses he ran with Albert, but his condition grew worse. In December, Kaufman, then only 49 years old, suffered a massive heart attack and died. Albert now shared a partnership in the upcoming hotel with Kaufman's wife. But not for long. Not really interested in running a resort, she soon handed her interest in the business over to Albert and Odetta.

In the blink of an eye, Albert had become like Mr. Daniel, just as his father said he could. The times, however, were scarcely conducive to integration in public hotel accommodations, let alone black entrepreneurship, so the Murrays braced themselves for resistance. It didn't take long for word to spread about the new neighbors and their intended venture. Before the Murrays could settle in, the Poconos Vacation Bureau rushed to the property and offered to reimburse them for whatever amount they had spent to acquire the property. Bureau officials claimed that opening the hotel would attract a bad element.

That was just the beginning.

Rule 3: Build Your Business One Step at a Time

Today, looking at Hillside Inn's neatly manicured lawns, polished aluminum siding, and majestic, yet comfortable, interior, it's hard to believe that it all began as just a drafty, clapboard rooming house with a handful of antique mahogany bentwood chairs, red dining-room tables, few amenities, and no private baths. But seeing is believing, and a photo album that the Murrays keep tucked inside a wicker basket in the hotel lobby illustrates the tremendous transformation of the inn during the past four decades.

Hillside Inn was quite gaunt in the early years. But it didn't stay that way for long. The Murrays knew that, to attract and keep customers, they would have to not only refurbish the place inside and outside, but also expand to accommodate more black vacationers. Having worked with Kaufman for many years, Albert had experience buying and renovating houses and knew what would make the hotel shine. But he questioned how he would get the money for development. In the 1950s, banks were no friendlier to black business owners who needed start-up and working capital than southern lunch counters were to black customers who asked for a simple cup of coffee. Still, Albert readied himself for step one of his venture: securing capital.

The rejection and animosity the Murrays faced when trying to secure a $10,000 mortgage for the hotel are easy to describe. The answer was simply "No." And the response they received had far less to do with their being new and precarious entrepreneurs, than it did with the color of their skin. They knew that, but they persevered. They had not come through years of plowing fields, walking nine miles to school every day, and serving in a major world war to throw in the towel.

Quit because a bank said "No"? We had come too far and gone through too much to give in.

They needed money for everything that was required to renovate their meek structure. But they could not get any credit—not even for the littlest things.

For the first five years of business, Mama had to pay the milkman up front when he delivered the milk. He would stand right at the back door and wait until she got him the money. Also, back then, Sears & Roebuck was in charge of stocking the hotel supplies. I had to pay cash there as well. Later, I asked them if I could sign a credit slip and they said yes, so I filled it out. But I was never approved.

Times were rough for the new entrepreneurs, and some local residents tried their best to discourage them. Still, the Murrays were determined to take their rightful place in the growing and very competitive hospitality industry. They continued to search for seed money; in Albert's connection to Kaufman, they found it.

While Abe was alive, we ran four real estate and law offices, plus the headquarters. We had 125 houses under contract, so, when Abe died, I became in charge of all of that. His son, also an attorney, didn't want the businesses in New York, but his wife did want to be a part of the operation, so she stayed on as a partner, but she gave me total control over running all of it. Since the banks would not help finance starting Hillside Inn, I used the profit we made from making investment deals to open the doors.

With some cash now in their coffers, the Murrays were able to get started in 1956. Working his contacts in the architectural industry, Albert hired a construction company to build the 26-room extension onto the original building. An outdoor swimming pool was added, as were many of the amenities of a "real vacation," such as tennis, basketball, shuffleboard, and boating. The Murrays dug out a lake and put in catfish and speckled bass. They also put in a nine-hole golf course, which, in later years, was changed to Canadian greens. The expansion cost about $100,000 and took almost eighteen months to complete. During the hotel's development, the persistent couple eventually managed to squeeze a $40,000 loan out of one bank to cover some of the expenses, but the difference came from their own pockets.

With a larger and more upscale resort now in place, the Murrays moved to step two: hiring employees to help operate it. At first, they recruited professional waiters and attendants from New York to assist the guests. But they found them to be too impersonal, so they restructured their staff after just one year in operation.

Mama and I wanted Hillside Inn to be more than just a place to listen to some music, eat, and play shuffleboard. We wanted to foster communication among black professionals, and we always wanted our guests to feel as though they were right at home. The first staff we hired was not able to help us carry out this vision because they didn't care about communicating with the guests that stayed with us. They were only interested in how much money in tips they could get by serving and helping with the bags.

Odetta came up with another idea. She decided to bring in students from black universities. In addition to hiring them as waiters/waitresses and housekeeping attendants, she could give them an opportunity to work, live, and network with black professionals who were staying at the hotel.

I made contact with many universities, both in the North and the South, about employing their students for the summer season. I told them about Hillside, the opportunity I wanted to extend to their students to come and work, and before I knew it they were coming. Since I had studied home economics in college, I trained the students how to serve, make beds, cook, and all the other tasks required to run a hotel. Those that came initially would stay for years, and then they would tell others and they would come and stay a while. I had students from all types of colleges, including Tuskegee, Columbia University, Benedict College, Howard University, Johnson C. Smith, Paine College, Wilberforce, Morgan State, and the list goes on and on. I think from 1957 until 1982 I saw about 800 students come through Hillside. At this point, I still hear from quite a few of them who come back to show their appreciation.

Once its doors opened, Hillside Inn operated on a seasonal basis from June through September. Mama took command of the hotel, managed the young college students, and oversaw the entire operation while Albert continued to fulfill his law career in New York. Using a creative mix of motherly love and military-style discipline, she had few problems supervising the hotel and her cadre of student-employees. She took care of virtually everything, from assisting the chef to creating copy for advertisements—another important step for building and branding Hillside Inn.

Like many new entrepreneurs, the Murrays used word of mouth as their initial and primary method of marketing. To help spread the word about their new venture, they also promoted their business in *Ebony*, then a relatively new magazine that chronicled black life economically, politically, and socially. *The Amsterdam News*, a New York newspaper, also featured the hotel in a weekly column by listing prominent people who stayed there. Segregation persisted, so few mainstream newspapers, especially those in the Poconos, would advertise black-owned businesses. Mama pieced together her own announcements and sent them to the black press to encourage black vacationers to stay at the inn.

By the hotel's tenth anniversary, Albert's law career had really taken off, so he sold the businesses he once owned with Kaufman and focused on being a hotel owner and an attorney.

Since acquiring Hillside Inn, Albert had advanced from law partner to Assistant U.S. District Attorney in Kings County, New York, and then to judge. He was the first black appointed to the criminal court bench in Brooklyn. But he maintained a presence at the hotel. He arrived on Fridays, handled the brunt of the hard labor, and headed back to Brooklyn on Sundays.

The Murrays seemed to be living beyond their wildest dreams. Albert was a prominent judge. Odetta was a judge's wife. And they co-owned a new hotel, had a staff full of eager, young students ready to work, and had earned sufficient capital to stay afloat. But some observers questioned how they would compete with Peg Leg Bates, Paradise Farms, Johnson Lake, Kings Lodge, and the other popular and more luxurious resorts in the area.

> *I had no problem competing because blacks couldn't go to the white-owned resorts at that time. It wasn't a question of competing with them because if [blacks] showed up at one of the white lodges, they would call us, and before Mama could put the receiver on the hook, they would be in the door with them.*

The inn was consistently packed with black politicians, judges, doctors, teachers, and other vacationers in search of a little R & R. In time, Hillside Inn was not the only black-owned resort in the area. Three other black-owned inns—Orchard Cottage, Beach Lodge, and Swift Water Inn—followed Hillside's lead. But Hillside Inn still reigned supreme—until integration. As a result of the civil rights movement, de jure segregation began to diminish in the late 1960s. Albert says that while blacks experienced greater gains than ever before, black businesses, including his own, also suffered some losses.

> *Once the white places opened up to blacks, minorities barely supported us anymore.*

Unable to weather the storm, the three other black-owned lodges in the Poconos closed their doors. Hillside Inn may have followed, had it not been for the Murrays' determination. Drawing on what his father told him so many years before about following through and executing "'til the end," Albert could not, and would not, let go of the business. They watched once-loyal customers drift away, but the Murrays adjusted by turning the resort, which had operated on a daily basis during the season, into a weekends-only getaway. They continued to employ college students. Mama continued to meet and greet. And the judge continued to sit on the bench.

By 1976, the Murrays had moved from their residence in New York to the Poconos. On a hilltop, overlooking the hotel and the plush acres surrounding it, they built a modest two-story home. Always a builder and a forward thinker, around that same time, Albert subdivided a portion of the property opposite the hotel, carved out twelve one-acre lots, and sold them to prospective homeowners for residential development. Besides bringing additional money into the business, it was the start of what would become a lifelong project of the Murrays: to construct a neighborhood of black professionals. Each lot sold for $15,000. Soon, single-family homes began to sprout. Hillside Inn was becoming more than just a hotel. It was turning into a community. But the inn, after surviving years of operation during desegregation, continued to take a beating in customer losses. Also, Mama was feeling overworked and stressed.

Albert decided to close the inn's doors.

Rule 4: Know When to Evaluate Your Progress and Regroup Anew

Hillside Inn closed its doors in 1982. Albert felt as though he had failed his father, Mama, and her pupils. The couple had many acres of land, but what would they do with it now that the hotel no longer existed? After evaluating their financial and emotional status, Albert made plans to tear down the hotel, build town houses in its place, sell the property for a hefty profit, and keep his private house on the hill. However, prospective buyers had a different agenda in mind.

They wanted me out completely. When we were closing title on the property, the lawyer came over to me and said that his client, who was white, was a little reluctant to buy the rest of the place and have me still live on it. That infuriated me, and that's when I decided in my own mind that I would never sell the place.

Albert pulled out of the deal to sell the property, continued with his plans to build the town houses, and developed eight units directly across from the inn. The hotel was now dormant. Albert was still on the bench when the hotel was shut down. It would be another four years before he would retire. But Mama, with little left to do, was like a fish out of water and felt very fatigued. Most of it was brought on by her managing the hotel almost singlehandedly for 25 years. But some of it was related to the stress of supporting her husband's budding law career.

In 1955, the year he foreclosed on the Poconos property, Albert was to be appointed to the criminal court bench in Kings County. Instead, he was temporarily appointed Special Prosecutor to the District Attorney's office. Albert didn't expect to stay there long; there was a judgeship in his near future—or so he thought. But he stayed in the D.A.'s office for nearly six years, and his appointment started to look grim. Albert grew concerned. So did Odetta.

As one year rolled over into the next, Albert heard no word about his expected judgeship. The Mayor of New York, Robert Wagner, traveled to the White House for the inauguration of President Lyndon B. Johnson in January 1965. While he was there, Mayor Wagner was confronted by the media and his selection of judges was described as a political ploy of some sort. With such an exposé, Albert thought he would surely get his gavel. But nothing happened for several months, and rumors started to fly that something was wrong with the Special Prosecutor. Whether through divine intervention or some coaxing from the President, Mayor Wagner finally made the appointment in May 1965, and Albert donned his black robe. By that time, Mama, who had worked every day in the hotel while coordinating the festivities for his swearing-in ceremony, was beginning to feel feeble. Under strict orders from her doctor, she relinquished her duties at the inn. Albert then formed a corporation with a five-person management group and transferred control of the resort, which continued to operate under the name Hillside Inn, to the group. Albert stepped out of the picture for nearly two years to let them run things freely. But when he got word that the new managers were not paying bills and the hotel was up for foreclosure, he immediately stepped back in.

They just didn't know how to run a business and they didn't devote themselves to it. They just played the big shot, so I had to step back in and pay off whatever debts they racked up. I gave them back whatever money they invested in the hotel and Mrs. Murray took over once again.

For the next 15 years, Hillside Inn operated under Mama's watchful eye. But, as time passed, her fatigue deepened. Competing resorts with sleeker interiors and a roster of amenities continued to pull customers away. Hillside Inn was struggling to survive. The Murrays felt as though they had no choice but to surrender. But in the years that followed the closing, they never forgot about Hillside Inn or the whole point of becoming entrepreneurs in the first place. During the period when Hillside Inn was closed, Albert continued to subdivide and sell more land. One single-family home after another began to dot the landscape that surrounded the hotel. The community that they had dreamed about creating was coming to life. Still, the wooden structure that had jump-started it all just stood there, empty. The resort stayed vacant for six years. In 1988, two years after Albert retired from the bench, the Murrays decided to regroup and rebuild.

At first, I surveyed the area where the hotel is to build 24 town houses. But after seeing the other black places close . . . one next to Mount Airy Lodge had just closed around that time, I felt that it was a shame that we couldn't have at least one minority-owned hotel to come to in the Poconos. Also, I felt that the community was not complete. Even though I had 35 lots by then, the hotel is really what started it all, so I felt we needed it to make our Hillside community whole. I didn't want people to think that we, as minorities, could not develop a complete community, so I decided that I would do away with the plan to build the town houses, even though that would have meant profit for me, and rebuild the hotel so that I could give the public a complete community. In other words, if you as a visitor wanted to live here permanently, I could offer you the opportunity to purchase land and build your own home. Or, if you just wanted to come to the Poconos to vacation, we could offer accommodations for you to do that as well. So those are the reasons why we decided to reopen.

By then, developers were throwing up one eye-popping resort after another in the Pocono Mountains. Each project had a laundry list of amenities that vacationers, white *and* black, were willing to pay top dollar to enjoy. To compete with the mainstream resorts, Albert began looking for funding to rebuild from the ground up. But even years after segregation became illegal, getting working capital proved to be tough.

Four banks turned me down. They said, "Well, judge, you were successful with the old hotel, but now you want to move up into competition with Mount Airy Lodge and the others because you want it first class. We don't think you're going to make it."

Always the optimist, Albert was determined to prove them wrong.

When someone says that there is something that I can't do, even though I may feel that they are wrong. I will go and test to see whether they were right.

The Murrays envisioned creating a modern hotel with new rooms and full resort facilities that would include an indoor heated swimming pool and Jacuzzi, a large dining room, conference room, recreation room, entertainment area, and gym. Ironically, the bank that granted them a $1.8 million loan to rebuild was the same bank that had denied them a $10,000 mortgage to start Hillside Inn. The entire project cost $2.5 million, so the Murrays put together the difference from their personal savings and by selling shares of stock to 24 shareholders. Then they hired an architect to start construction.

After the old hotel was demolished in 1988, architects broke ground for the new structure. The Murrays meticulously watched the rebirth of their hotel. After the exterior was complete, Mama, using her interior design skills, worked her magic inside by adding warm and homey touches to every corner of the inn. This time around, they hired a professional staff of managers, cooks, waiters, housekeepers, and other attendants.

By August 1989, Hillside Inn was back in business.

Rule 5: Stay on Course

Frutchey Drive starts high, dips downward, curves to the left, then offers another peak and a final valley before leveling off at the bottom. Travelers on this road wonder what esoteric entity awaits behind the trees. An ostentatious estate belonging to some well-known dignitary? A stuffy country club where golf has become the unofficial favorite pastime?

Neither.

Follow the twists of Frutchey Drive downward and you will find The New Hillside Inn. Gone are the shuttered windows, screened-in porch, and outdoors in-ground pool of the old hotel. Hillside Inn, drenched in polished ivory aluminum siding and trimmed in white, now boasts a tennis court where the pool used to be and a basketball court just 500 feet from that. Look to the right or the left and you will find cozy benches and picnic tables scattered about the plush grounds. In the distance, golf bags are perched along the links.

Guests who visited the hotel in the 1950s and 1960s may remember a simple wooden structure with few frills. Hillside Inn is very different these days. And although no crystal chandeliers are dangling from the ceiling and no Italian marble floors stretch tens of feet from the door, there is comfort in every corner, and it can be felt from the first step into the lobby.

Decorated in brown, blue, and hints of pink, the lobby offers cushioned chairs and sofas. African artwork hangs above the fireplace. The aroma of fried chicken and catfish filters from the kitchen. There are still traces of the old hotel, however. In the break-out room on the lower level are several pieces of the hotel's original furniture, including a bar, red dining-room tables (the tops have been laminated), and a cluster of antique chairs, now painted beige.

Hillside Inn has become a respected vacation destination in the Poconos. But, in many ways, going to Hillside Inn is like going home. In the Maple Room, which is just a few paces from the foyer, guests gather around oval tables for family-style dining. Soup's on twice daily, and visitors can enjoy generous helpings of some tasty down-home vittles. After dinner, it's off to the Walnut Room for cocktails and live entertainment. Guests who feel a bit spry can get their 15 minutes of fame during a round of karaoke or take a dip in the indoor heated pool or Jacuzzi before retiring for bed. Most people who step onto the grounds of Hillside Inn are there to vacation. But many use the hotel's conference facilities to hold retreats, meetings, and religious services.

Since its inception, Hillside Inn has operated under the motto "Old Fashioned Warmth, Good Food, and Personal Service." When Hillside Inn reopened, customers expected and received nothing less. Staying on course, the Murrays continued to cater to their guests as if they were family. Once again, the hotel became the talk of the town. *Emerge* and *Essence* magazines, publications targeted toward African Americans, printed articles about the new edifice. And "The Judge" and "Mama" appeared on local radio stations in New York, and on *Good Morning America, The Today Show,* and CNN. Word-of-mouth advertising plus a push from the local and national press put Hillside Inn back on the map.

With such widespread coverage, customers came back to the hotel in droves. Shirley Chisholm, the first black woman ever elected to the U.S. Congress, was the first guest to stay at The New Hillside Inn. Soon after, other well-known political leaders, entertainers, and businesspeople began to travel to its doors: former Philadelphia Mayor Wilson Goode, the Reverend Al Sharpton, singer Dionne Warwick, *Essence* Editor-in-Chief Susan Taylor, and businesswoman Terrie Williams, president of the Terrie Williams Agency. "Everyday folk" came too; church groups form New Jersey, Delaware, and New York traveled nearly 100 miles to enjoy fellowship and to relax. African-American organizations and other nonminority groups such as the National Association of Black Journalists, the United Nations Development Fund for Women, the New York National Bar Association, the National Association of Black Accountants, Merrill Lynch, and the American

Association of Retired Persons also used the facilities. But, in recent years, the dwindling numbers have cut the hotel's customer base in half.

It's a struggle because we are losing more and more customers and I don't really understand why. Our rates are lower than the other places and we have the same activities as the other resorts. We have forms in the rooms asking the guests to put down whether or not the accommodations and the staff were satisfactory. We get back at least 99 percent of those who say that everything was beautiful. Still, organizations like the Urban League cancel and everyday vacationers refuse to book rooms here.

Searching for a logical explanation, Albert points to the offers of "dollar-down time-shares" and discounted bus trips that neighboring resorts are increasingly promoting to African-American vacationers. But, he contends, that's not the only reason.

I believe that many of us want to go to the big-name places up here, such as Caesar's Palace and Mount Airy Lodge, and they do. Then there are those people I've talked to who say that they have been coming up to the Poconos for the past ten years and that they didn't know that Hillside Inn existed. That's almost impossible because it's listed in all the tour books and hotel guides. Plus, we send our literature to thousands of travel agents nationwide, so people know about us. So it's puzzling to me as to what else I can do to convince a larger portion of blacks to stay at Hillside. It's frustrating, but Mama and I just continue to keep pushing on in the manner in which we've always operated Hillside Inn. I just wish that were enough to get the kinds of numbers . . . my competition does. Sometimes people will come down here to make reservations to eat because our food is very different than what you can get up the street, but then they'll say that they are staying at Fernwood or at some other site. I know that a majority of us still want to go to the white man's house for some reason. But it is my feeling that we've been able to go there for the last 20 years, so why in the world are we still going there, giving him our money, and not having some pride in developing whatever we want in Hillside Inn?

The lobby is quiet on this particular Thursday afternoon. Mama walks the floor putting her hands into anything she can. Suddenly a guest who visited the hotel 15 years ago comes through the doors.

"Do you remember me?" asks the lady.

"Sure I do," responds Mama with a loving smile and warm hug. The two embrace as if they are old friends reuniting.

"I just stopped by to see how you are doing."

"Why don't you stay with us?"

"Oh, we have a time-share at Shawnee's."

Mama drops her head slightly. Her excitement tapering, she mutters, "Oh. . . ."

Rule 6: Prepare for the Future Now

Commanding the wheel of his silver, four-door Jaguar, Albert exits the hotel parking lot and begins to cruise the grounds. Turning into the private roads that lead to the growing black community, he points out one house after another. Then he dips the car into a beautiful area opposite the lake and points out another Hillside gem: the Rustic Inn. The Murrays built the structure around 1960 to accommodate the children of guests. Today, it is used for picnics, barbecues, and special events.

Passing Murray Hill Road and Sanders Court (Mama's maiden name was Sanders), he peers through the windshield toward a hill where 40 additional acres will be subdivided for another 25 families to build homes. The project, which is scheduled to begin soon, will not be just another cluster of condominiums. Each home will be uniquely designed and each lot will sell for $20,000 per acre.

Making a sharp turn up yet another private entryway, Albert proceeds toward his own home. Perched atop a huge hill that overlooks the hotel and the entire Hillside community, the Murrays' house is not a showplace. There are no Tiffany lamps or Stickley armchairs. Like the hotel, it is comfortable and functional. The Murrays don't get an opportunity to spend much time there. Typically, their day starts at 8:00 A.M. and does not end until one or two o'clock the next morning. After this quick tour of the grounds, they head back to the valley to check on the shop.

For more than four decades, operating Hillside Inn has been a labor of love for the Murrays. But, always true to themselves, both realize that they can't stand at the helm forever.

I'm not getting any younger, and contrary to what Mama thinks, I get tired. She feels that she can continue, but . . . I know that I am not what I was five years ago and there are no two ways about it. I know what Hillside Inn still needs. It needs an energetic person and it needs one now. You don't wait until this fails. For me to wait until I am paralyzed or can't get up the steps doesn't make sense, so I have to find someone now who can carry the hotel forward.

An obvious choice would be their son Sonny. But he is a successful lawyer and an Assistant U.S. Attorney in Scranton, Pennsylvania. He does not desire to become a hotel operator. So, the Murrays are actively looking for a successor. They want to keep the name but transfer management of the hotel to someone else. Albert admits that has not been an easy decision.

I've come across many people who say, "Oh yes, I would love to take over," but when I explain to them the basic principle of what they have to do, they back off. Names alone will not run a hotel because you've got to have people who know what they're doing. It's not hard, but the people have to be committed to the future of the business. There is no shortcut to running a resort, and you've got to deal with whatever the problem is. You can't say in advance that you are only going to deal with certain issues. You have to have an open mind and be able to adjust to all sorts of situations, not just those that are comfortable for you. So I've been trying to get groups, who can handle all of the duties and perpetuate our vision, to step in and manage the place, but it has been a challenge. We had one group that was ready to come in, but the leader wanted to turn the hotel into a club. Hillside Inn was never designed for that. It is a family and Christian retreat.

Many large corporations, including Marriott and American Realty, as well as long-time competitors—Fernwood Resort and Country Club, and Shawnee Inn and Golf Resort—have offered to buy them out. Bids have come fast and furiously, each one inching a little higher than the next. One offered $3.3 million. The next, $3.5 million. Then came a proposal for $3.7 million. Whatever the figure, the Murrays say they are not going to sell. But if they do not find someone soon, they may ditch their plans to expand the hotel, even though an area bank has already approved a $5 million loan for its construction.

Expansion could be a way to attract more customers and increase revenue. But Albert says growing the business is not about money. Starting and maintaining Hillside Inn has always been about one thing: showing that African Americans can produce. And without enough people to support the expansion and an energetic person to see it through, the Murrays will have missed their mark.

Hillside Inn can still exist as it is. We're not bankrupt and we don't have to sell it to anybody. Basically, if I lived 100 years, I wouldn't need a dime. My pension is $60,000 a year and it ain't nobody but Mama and me. But what would I be doing now if I just sold it off or if I lost the place? How could I sit up there on the hill, in my home, and say that I, as a black person, excelled, when, given the opportunity to move forward, I just gave up? Before Martin Luther King and all the other civil rights leaders, I would have had an excuse. But now I don't. King did not die so that I could go to Fernwood or to Shawnee. He died so that I could develop Hillside Inn. I want people to understand the importance of that. It's not about putting an extra dollar in my pocket. It's about producing. So my main question to all those who have been to Hillside Inn and have not come back, to those who claim that they didn't know about the hotel, and to those who are reluctant to participate in taking Hillside to new heights, is this: Do you want to produce or are you satisfied with being just consumers?

Hillside Inn was no gift. The Murrays have earned every shingle, every floor tile, every table, and every chair. Understandably, they want to pass it on to someone who will maintain the vision that began it all, and they are determined to find just the right person to do it.

Swinging back the car door, Albert steps out and heads for the lobby. A group of people from a major corporation in Philadelphia were supposed to meet with him at 10:00 A.M. to talk about investing in the hotel's future. It's now after 1:00 P.M. They have not called, nor have they shown up. Albert prepares to find out why.

It hurts that they did not show up. But I don't give up.

Reflecting once more on the days spent working with his father, he says, "I can't. I still have plenty of plowing to do."

INDEX

229

 Kidpreneurs Club & teenpreneurs club

club benefits:

- Club newsletter:
  KidpreneursNews for 8 to 12 year olds or *Black Enterprise for Teens* for 13 to 18 year olds. Each edition features youth that are business owners, money-making ideas, money management tips and historical African American entrepreneurs.
- Club membership card
- Birthday card
- Premium gift items

Club membership is $20 annually. To register your child in the club or for additional information, please call...

1-877-KID-PREN (877-543-7736) or visit our website at www.blackenterprise.com and click on Kidpreneurs.

Receive a coupon for 10% off of the registration rate at the next Black Enterprise Event

☐ Please send my discount coupon today and as a special bonus, I'll receive a FREE copy of the Unlimited Options newsletter from Black Enterprise.

☐ Please tell me more about Black Enterprise Unlimited's events.

Name _____

Address _____

City State Zip _____

e-mail _____

Phone _____

BLACK ENTERPRISE Bank of America
Entrepreneurs CONFERENCE

☐ Entrepreneurs Conference

☐ Ski Challenge   ☐ Golf & Tennis Challenge

Send to **Black Enterprise Unlimited** * 130 Fifth Avenue, New York, NY, 10011

For more information, call 800-543-6786 for the Entrepreneurs Conference and 800-209-7229 for the B.E. Challenges or visit our website www.blackenterprise.com.
Limit one coupon per person. Offer valid through June 2002.